Strategy Instruction
for **Middle** and **Secondary** **Students** with **Mild Disabilities**

Creating Independent Learners

Greg Conderman | Laura Hedin | Val Bresnahan

CORWIN
A SAGE Company

FOR INFORMATION:

Corwin

A SAGE Company

2455 Teller Road

Thousand Oaks, California 91320

(800) 233-9936

www.corwin.com

SAGE Publications Ltd.

1 Oliver's Yard

55 City Road

London EC1Y 1SP

United Kingdom

SAGE Publications India Pvt. Ltd.

B 1/I 1 Mohan Cooperative Industrial Area

Mathura Road, New Delhi 110 044

India

SAGE Publications Asia-Pacific Pte. Ltd.

3 Church Street

#10-04 Samsung Hub

Singapore 049483

Acquisitions Editor: Jessica Allan

Editorial Assistant: Lisa Whitney

Production Editor: Amy Schroller

Copy Editor: Cate Huisman

Typesetter: C&M Digitals (P) Ltd.

Proofreader: Susan Schon

Indexer: Diggs Publishing Service

Cover Designer: Edgar Abarca

Permissions Editor: Karen Ehrmann

Copyright © 2013 by Corwin

Printed in the United States of America

A catalog record of this book is available from the Library of Congress

ISBN 9781412996327

This book is printed on acid-free paper.

MIX
Paper from
responsible sources
FSC® C014174

13 14 15 16 17 10 9 8 7 6 5 4 3 2 1

Contents

Appendices

Preface

Y ou have probably heard of the Chinese proverb: Give me a fish, and I eat for a day; teach me to fish, and I eat for a lifetime. This statement reflects the learning strategies philosophy. The strategies approach teaches students *how to learn and be independent learners* rather than isolated skills or facts.

RATIONALE FOR THE BOOK

Special and general educators from all grades and subjects are searching for ways to be more effective and efficient in their teaching. They are looking for ways to help students eat for a lifetime. School administrators and teachers must demonstrate that students are making academic and social-behavioral gains. For various reasons, some students are more challenging to teach, and they require more powerful instructional tools in order to make significant gains. The good news is that years of research—as well as our experiences teaching adolescents with mild disabilities—support the strategies approach.

Middle and high school students with disabilities are especially well suited for strategy instruction, because they are expected to meet rigorous general education curriculum standards and pass state and district tests. To accomplish these tasks, students need more than exposure to skills, which is an approach that helps them only to eat for a day. Rather, they need powerful and effective methods to help them understand, retain, and apply difficult skills and concepts. Because the strategy approach teaches students a new way of thinking, it requires more deliberate and explicit instruction (especially teacher modeling) and therefore takes more time than other approaches, but the results, we believe, are well worth it.

Secondary students are also unique because they have only a few more years remaining of their K–12 education. Unless secondary general and special education teachers use powerful instructional approaches, students may not make sufficient growth to meet goals on their individualized education program (IEP) or meet annual yearly progress goals under the Elementary and Secondary Education Act (ESEA) / No Child Left Behind Act of 2001 (NCLB). Further, without an approach that emphasizes independent learning, students are at a higher risk for dropping out of school and accepting and maintaining entry-level jobs over the course of their lifetime.

In addition to identifying a need for powerful instructional strategies, researchers have questioned existing instructional practices at the secondary level. One concern is that resource rooms often function as modified study halls, where students primarily complete homework for their general education classes. This often leaves little time for strategy instruction. Admittedly, students need support to maintain satisfactory progress in their general education classes. The challenge (and not an easy one) is for special educators to find the balance between helping students with their class work and teaching them strategies that help them become more independent in those classes and with future tasks.

Researchers have also noted confusion about the secondary special education teacher's role in co-taught classrooms. Many secondary special education co-teachers function as assistants in general education classrooms because they have not mastered the content to assume instructional parity with their general education co-teaching partner. The one-teach one-assist model is the most frequently used yet least effective co-teaching approach. This model often does not expose students to powerful instructional strategies. In contrast, special educators in co-taught general education classes can establish themselves as strategy experts by teaching efficient and effective learning, organizational, study, or behavioral strategies to all students in the class.

HOW TO USE THIS BOOK

With these thoughts in mind, we present this practical book on instructional strategies for secondary (middle and high school) students with mild disabilities. The first two chapters provide the context and background for teaching secondary special education. Chapter 1 introduces the array of instructional approaches used by secondary special educators. Of the approaches discussed in Chapter 1, the strategies approach is the focus of Chapter 2 because many experts in the field recommend this approach for initial skill instruction. Strategy instruction is the focus of this book.

The remaining chapters are of two kinds: assessment chapters and methods/strategies chapters. Using case studies and the strategies approach, each assessment chapter connects student informal assessment results to IEPs, and in the subsequent corresponding methods/strategies chapter, evidence-based strategies are connected to IEPs. The assessment chapters provide background information about the skill or content, informal assessments, and the student's IEP. Methods/strategies chapters describe strategies teachers taught to meet the student's IEP goals in each case. Therefore, "matching" chapters (e.g., chapters 3 and 4 on vocabulary) make more sense if read together. Many chapters provide ready-to-use forms as well as teacher think-alouds for modeling the featured strategy. Subheadings direct readers to a specific strategy, and end-of-the chapter questions provide application activities. This book is also unique in that rather than providing short descriptions of numerous strategies, chapters provide a more intense look at specific evidence-based vocabulary, reading, writing, study, textbook, self-regulation, math, and science strategies.

INTENDED AUDIENCE

Strategy instruction can occur in general, special, and Response to Intervention (RTI) settings and is appropriate for all learners (students with and without disabilities) who are learning common core state standards. Therefore, the informal assessments, suggested IEP goals and objectives, and think-alouds provide templates for you, whether you are teaching in inclusive, resource, or self-contained settings; consulting or co-teaching with general educators; designing RTI approaches; studying special or general education as a preservice teacher; or providing district-level leadership as an administrator, teacher-mentor, curriculum coordinator, or staff development planner. Therefore, regardless of your current position, we trust that you will find the ideas in this book informative as you teach your students to eat for a lifetime.

Acknowledgments

C orwin gratefully acknowledges the contributions of the following reviewers:

Sally Jeanne Coghlan
Special Education Teacher
Rio Linda Preparatory Academy, Twin Rivers USD
Rio Linda, CA

Debi Gartland
Professor of Special Education
Towson University
Towson, MD

Cheryl Moss
Special Education Teacher
Gilbert Middle School
Gilbert, IA

Catherine Orlando
Teacher, Administrator, Adjunct Professor, Consultant
Miami-Dade County Public Schools
Miami, FL

Karen L. Tichy
Associate Superintendent for Instruction and Special Education
Archdiocese of St. Louis
St. Louis, MO

About the Authors

Greg Conderman is full professor of special education at Northern Illinois University in DeKalb, Illinois, where he teaches methods and collaboration courses for elementary education, secondary education, and special education majors. He was a middle and high school special education teacher and special education consultant for 10 years before entering higher education. He has authored over 70 articles on instructional methods and collaboration, which have been published in special education and general education journals. He is a frequent presenter at local, state, and national conferences. He has also received numerous teaching awards for excellence in instruction at the college level.

Laura Hedin is an assistant professor in the Department of Special and Early Education at Northern Illinois University. She teaches instructional methods courses, including reading methods, in both the graduate and undergraduate special education certification programs. Her research interests include reading in the content areas for intermediate and secondary students with disabilities as well as teacher preparation, science instruction for students with disabilities, and co-teaching.

Val Bresnahan, EdD, is currently a middle school language arts teacher in a Chicago suburb. She has been a speech-language pathologist, special education teacher, general education teacher, and adjunct university instructor. She has authored books on vocabulary instruction and co-teaching as well as articles on study skills. She also has made numerous presentations on vocabulary instruction, co-teaching, and differentiation.

PART I

Introduction to Secondary Special Education

Instructional Approaches at the Secondary Level

1

Secondary special education teachers fulfill many roles and have diversified responsibilities.

(Conderman & Katsiyannis, 2002)

MEET MRS. GREEN

First year high school special education teacher Mrs. Green is reviewing student files before school starts, so she can begin instructional planning. As she reads files, individualized transition plans (ITPs) and individualized education programs (IEPs), she records each student's present level of performance, goals, objectives, and other pertinent information on an Excel spreadsheet, so she can plan each student's program. Having each student's information on one document helps her view all critical student information at a glance. As she enters student information, Mrs. Green quickly realizes that her students have numerous varied needs. She wonders how she can help all of her students experience success.

CHAPTER OVERVIEW

The purpose of this chapter is to describe the realities of teaching secondary special education. Understanding these realities—such as unique curricular, student, and instructional issues—will help teachers like Mrs. Green prepare for her new position. The chapter describes and provides examples of the seven instructional approaches used by secondary special educators and acknowledges that teachers work from more than one approach—often even within a single lesson.

THE REALITIES OF SECONDARY TEACHING

Welcome to the world of teaching middle or high school (or secondary) special education. Mrs. Green will soon discover that she will assume numerous roles and responsibilities. Secondary special education teachers teach content, skills, and strategies; modify curriculum; assess students; coordinate work experiences; write IEPs; collaborate with parents and community members; serve on committees; consult with general education teachers; collect and analyze behavioral and academic data; plan for paraprofessionals; and help students meet common core state standards. Clearly, the roles and responsibilities of the secondary special educator are varied and challenging.

Researchers have discovered some reasons for these challenges. Many special education teacher preparation programs do not offer methods, collaboration, or transition courses specifically for the secondary special educator (McKenzie, 2009; Morningstar, Kim, & Clark, 2008) or provide adequate clinical or student teaching experiences in exemplar placements, so special education majors lack opportunities to observe and experience best practices. Secondary special educators also feel pressure to help students pass classes, and these teachers experience challenges collaborating with some general educators who appear reluctant to implement individualized interventions (Conderman & Pedersen, 2007).

UNIQUE ISSUES AT THE SECONDARY LEVEL

For many reasons, the roles and responsibilities of secondary special educators are unique and much different from those of elementary general and special education teachers. First, the *students* themselves are different, as they are experiencing physical, emotional, and intellectual changes. Some secondary students are able to think more abstractly, debate moral and ethical issues, and hypothesize more than elementary students. They are seeking to understand themselves, their future, and their belief systems. Adolescents are also trying out new behaviors and seeking approval from peers. Peer pressure may lead to unhealthy behaviors or poor choices. Some students struggle with self-esteem issues, while others experience depression and isolation that lead to suicidal thoughts or actions.

Second, *curricular expectations* at the secondary level are different from those at the elementary level. Secondary students with and without disabilities are expected to meet rigorous academic and social-behavioral standards. However, many secondary students with mild disabilities function academically well below grade level, have short attention spans, experience difficulty processing information, test authority figures, display poor organization skills, and rely on adults for assistance. Similarly, they often have an external locus of control, as they attribute success or failure to outside factors rather than assume personal responsibility. They also use strategies ineffectively and have a limited awareness of the usefulness of specific strategies for given tasks.

Secondary schools are also *organized differently* than elementary schools. Most secondary schools are organized by departments or subjects rather than grade levels. This structure often adds more bureaucracy, and teachers from each area may have different behavior, grading, and assignment expectations. Students move from teacher to teacher and therefore must adjust to varied teaching styles and expectations, which is often difficult. The number of teachers also makes collaboration and co-teaching more challenging for special educators who must also adjust to multiple instructional approaches, expectations, and personalities. These differences in organizational structure require more flexibility on the part of students and special educators.

Finally, general education secondary teachers are *prepared differently* than elementary teachers. Elementary education majors typically do not specialize in a content area, but middle and high school general education teachers are experts in their specialty area due to their concentrated preparation in a particular subject. Elementary education majors typically take many methods courses, while secondary general education majors typically take fewer methods courses, so they may be less familiar with instructional adaptations and strategies for students with disabilities within their content area. Co-teaching in these specialized subjects is more challenging for special educators who do not possess content knowledge to contribute meaningfully. Based on this discussion, we offer the following dos and don'ts to guide your instruction.

Do

- Determine, from each general educator, requirements for being successful in the general education class, and explain these explicitly to students. Emphasize that each class and each teacher may have different expectations, grading scales, and rules.
- Provide general educators with a list of accommodations—and their rationale—as listed on each student's IEP. Indicate your sincere interest in collaborating with them.
- Role-play with students appropriate ways to approach teachers to remind them of or request accommodations.
- Ensure that students know why they receive special services and understand the content in their IEP. Encourage them to be active

members of their IEP meeting. If they did not attend their IEP meeting, share their IEP with them, and request their signature showing their understanding of their goals and objectives.

- Proactively communicate a clear vision for your special education program; otherwise students, teachers, administrators, and parents may assume your primary role is to help students with homework. Post your mission statement on your website and refer to it often.
- Plan opportunities for students to research various career options by having them interview community members; make college campus visits; complete transition, interest, and aptitude inventories; and research military requirements.
- Get to know each student, and note behavior or personality changes that may signal serious issues such as drug or alcohol use, depression, or thoughts of suicide. Suicide is the third leading cause of death for 15- to 24-year-olds, and one of the most serious emotional issues facing young adults is depression (American Academy of Child and Adolescent Psychiatry, 2008).

Do Not

- Use instructional materials developed for younger children, even if your students have skills considerably below grade level.
- Rely on the one-teach one-assist approach as your primary co-teaching model.
- Use the resource room as a modified study hall.
- Succumb to pressure from others to just tutor students or just help them pass their classes.
- Assume that students with mild disabilities cannot understand complex material.
- Assume that general educators fully understand the unique characteristics and needs of students with disabilities.
- Assume that you and only you can meet all of your student's needs.
- Encourage students to become overly dependent on you.

INSTRUCTIONAL APPROACHES

Researchers have identified seven instructional models or approaches used in secondary special education programs. We will discuss and provide examples of each approach, which will help teachers like Mrs. Green determine which model or combination of models to use with each student. These include the functional, tutorial, basic skills remedial, compensatory, career or transition, co-teaching or collaboration, and strategy approaches.

Functional/Life Skills Approach

The functional approach emphasizes everyday survival skills that students need to be independent in society and tends to be used more frequently with students with more moderate disabilities. Examples of functional skills include shopping, cooking, cleaning, reading and following recipes, completing job applications and other forms, using public transportation, and paying bills. Many teachers use the community as the core curriculum by taking students shopping, practicing using transportation systems, and gathering application forms from local businesses for student practice. The functional approach may also include social skills instruction in such areas as getting along with employers and coworkers.

Some limitations or concerns include (a) outcomes, activities, and standards are much different from those in the general education curriculum, which is an issue if students take state and district tests; (b) teachers can incur extra expenses associated with taking students into the community; (c) teachers may be unsure which skills to emphasize with each student; and (d) developing authentic assessments that indicate student growth may be more challenging.

This approach prepares students for some of their adult responsibilities. The special education teacher carefully selects and teaches functional skills. As Mrs. Green reviews student files, she notices that David has a functional math goal associated with determining the best value when given two shopping items, and Rael has a functional writing goal of independently and accurately completing job application forms.

Tutorial Approach

The tutorial approach emphasizes helping students complete assignments from their general education classes and is frequently used in high school resource rooms. Using this approach, teachers remind students of upcoming assignments, provide time for assignment completion, assist students with assignments, and prepare students for tests. They might also break down complex assignments into smaller parts, provide student feedback on each part before advancing to the next part, and preteach or reteach skills from the general education class that confused or might confuse students. The general education curriculum is used with this approach.

Some advantages of this approach are that students complete homework, pass classes, and earn their high school diploma. Some disadvantages are that special education classrooms often become study halls, teachers devote little time to teaching new skills or strategies, and students often become dependent on the special education teacher. As Mrs. Green reviews her students' schedules, she realizes that Lonnie, JoAnn, and Brianna are taking chemistry. Due to the difficulty of this course, she realizes she will need to provide some tutorial support.

Basic Skills Remedial Approach

Used more often in the elementary grades, the basic skills remedial approach focuses on teaching students basic reading, writing, spelling, or math skills. The goal is to remediate skill weaknesses through explicit, sequential, or direct instruction. Examples of the remedial approach include teaching students math facts, sight words, or spelling words. Instructionally, this approach typically includes teacher modeling (teacher demonstrates the new skill and talks through each step), guided practice (teacher and students complete problems or tasks together), and independent practice (students complete a task on their own).

The remedial approach addresses the issues that led to the students' qualification for special services, provides systematic and individualized instruction, and uses assessment results to inform instruction. Teachers misuse this approach when they use elementary-looking materials that insult older learners or when they use this approach (e.g., spending a considerable amount of time teaching high school seniors multiplication facts) when a different approach (e.g., teaching students calculator use) would be more beneficial. The teacher's roles are to diagnose and remediate student errors and provide explicit instruction to remediate skill weaknesses. As Mrs. Green inventories her curriculum, she notices scripted curricula such as *Corrective Reading* (Science Research Associates, SRA), *Spelling Through Morphographs* (SRA), and others that introduce skills in small steps and provide explicit teacher modeling of each step. She will administer placement tests to determine which students will benefit from a remedial approach using these materials.

Compensatory Approach

The compensatory approach accommodates for student weaknesses by providing support or technology to help students access the curriculum or assessment. In other words, this method bypasses a student's weakness. For example, students may use spell or grammar checkers, cue cards, calculators, multiplication cards, audio tapes, and assistive technologies that provide access to the general education curriculum or an assessment. Consequently, this approach allows students to be included in general education classes and meet general education standards. Students also learn how to become proficient with various technologies.

Disadvantages are that students do not learn new skills, some compensatory tools are expensive, students often need training, and students might be embarrassed using their tools in front of others.

Using this approach, the teacher's role is to develop compensatory tools for students or advocate for the purchase of them. Some assistive technologies appropriate especially for secondary learners include (a) Thinking Reader (Tom Snyder Productions), (b) Kurzweil 3000 (Kurzweil Educational Systems), (c) Start-to-Finish books (Don Johnston), (d) Read: Outloud (Don Johnston), (e) Draft:Builder (Don Johnston), and (f) Inspiration (Inspiration, Inc.).

Most students who benefit from the use of compensatory tools also have necessary accommodations (or modifications) noted on their IEP. *Accommodations* are techniques that provide student access to the curriculum or assessment without changing the standard. They do not give the student an advantage, but rather they even the playing field. Accommodations generally fall in one of the following four categories:

- *Presentation accommodations* allow students to access information in a mode or modality that bests suits their learning preference. For example, rather than reading print materials, the student with a reading disability who has good comprehension skills accesses the text through taped materials, such as text-to-speech presentations. Some textbook publishers now include websites featuring the text in different presentation formats.
- *Response accommodations* allow students to display their learning in a different mode or modality. For example, rather than writing an essay, the student who has difficulty writing but has good expressive language is allowed to speak the essay response. The essay question has not changed, and unless writing skills are being evaluated, the assessment tool has not changed, either.
- *Setting accommodations* refer to the time, location, and conditions of an assignment or assessment. For example, due to distractibility or other processing issues, some students prefer study carrels, while others need a quiet location outside of the classroom to complete an assignment or assessment.

- *Timing and schedule accommodations* adjust the amount of time the student is allowed to complete a task. Students who work or read slowly often need time-and-a-half to complete assignments or assessments. Similarly, some students need to have large assignments or tests divided into smaller sections.

Modifications, on the other hand, are *significant changes* in the assignment or assessment. Students might have a simplified test, they may have a different assignment (but on the same topic) that corresponds with an adjusted learning standard, or they may be working at a different skill level.

Just like IEP goals and objectives, accommodations and modifications are individualized and listed on the IEP, and they should be communicated to all IEP team members, including the student. Team members should also periodically review the accommodations or modifications to determine if they are appropriate and if the student still needs them. Team members need to be sensitive to changes in the student as well as to changes in curricular demands and adjust accommodations and modifications accordingly, as necessary.

As Mrs. Green reviews her students' IEPs, she reads that Michael, Elizabeth, and Steven are allowed to use the accommodation of cue cards for math. Cue cards are portable, low-tech devices (such as a note card) that include steps, prompts, processes, abbreviations, or a mnemonic for completing a task or solving a problem. Cue cards may contain the steps, a checklist for students to check off as they complete each step, visuals, and/or examples (Conderman & Hedin, 2011). Cue cards are helpful for learners who, due to processing or other issues, need a memory support system. Figure 1.1 provides an example of Michael's math cue card for remembering the steps of dividing fractions.

Figure 1.1 Michael's Cue Card for Dividing Fractions

Step	Example	Check When Completed
Copy the problem	$\frac{1}{2} \div \frac{1}{4}$	
Flip the second fraction	$\frac{1}{2} \div \frac{4}{1}$	
Change the division sign to multiplication	$\frac{1}{2} \times \frac{4}{1}$	
Multiply numerator by numerator and denominator by denominator	$\frac{1}{2} \times \frac{4}{1} = \frac{4}{2}$	
Check your answer; simplify if possible	$\frac{4}{2} = 2$	

Career/Transition/Vocational Approach

An important outcome of secondary special education is to prepare students for the world beyond high school. Teachers using the career approach achieve this goal by having students complete career assessments, reflect on their strengths and weaker skills, explore jobs, consider future goals, and research jobs, careers, postsecondary settings, and military options. During this process, students and team members collaborate to gather information from various sources to develop an accurate picture of the student's strengths, preferences, interests, and needs (SPIN) (Conderman, Hartman, & Johnston-Rodriguez, 2009). This information helps team members craft the ITP.

Challenges with the career approach are that many special education teachers are inadequately prepared in this model, teachers must reserve time for completing career assessments, the student's team members must find common time to collaborate, some students and their family members may have inaccurate or unrealistic future goals, and some students are placed repetitively in the same types of service jobs.

Teachers using this approach update career assessments and coordinate transition planning activities. As Mrs. Green reviews students' transition plans, she discovers that her students lead their ITP meeting by discussing their goals through a multimedia presentation that they develop. Some career or transition assessments and curricula that Mrs. Green may use with her students include (a) Transition Planning Inventory (TPI) (PRO-ED), (b) Choicemaker Self-Determination Series (Sopris Learning), (c) Reading-Free Vocational Interest Inventory (PRO-ED), (d) Your Employment Selections (YES) (Trisped), and (e) The Arc's Self-Determination Scale (The Arc), available free from

www.ou.edu/content/dam/Education/documents/miscellaneous/the-arc-self-determination-scale.pdf.

Co-teaching/Collaboration Approach

As students with disabilities increasingly receive more of their education in inclusive settings, general and special educators collaborate to ensure students have access to a rigorous general education curriculum and receive individualized accommodations. One method of collaborating is co-teaching.

Co-teaching involves co-planning, co-instructing, and co-assessing. Generally, researchers describe five co-teaching models, which include (a) one teach, one observe; (b) one teach, one assist; (c) station teaching; (d) parallel teaching; (e) alternative teaching; and (f) team teaching. In some secondary co-taught classrooms, the special educator is considered the strategy expert who introduces strategies to all students.

Secondary co-teaching can be especially challenging, because special educators typically are not highly qualified in academic subjects. They need time and support to learn or relearn the general education content, so they can contribute meaningfully to the co-taught classroom. When special education teachers lack content knowledge, they often assume a passive role in the co-taught classroom, and in such cases, co-teaching does not realize its purpose or potential.

Other times, special educators serve as consultants to general education teachers by providing ideas and materials that the general educator can use with students in inclusive environments. When the general educator expresses a need for support regarding a student, the special and general educator often engage in a problem-solving process to clearly identify the issue, determine an intervention, and evaluate the effectiveness of the intervention. Sometimes the consultation supports requirements of a school's RTI (Response to Intervention) approach. The consultation may take the form of a mentoring or coaching relationship. Regardless of the purpose or approach, the goal of consultation is to provide support to students as they receive instruction in the general education setting.

The special educator's roles in the collaborative model are to advocate for students with disabilities, ensure student accommodations or modifications are in place, contribute meaningfully by consulting or co-teaching, and maintain open lines of communication with parents, teachers, and students.

Although Mrs. Green is not co-teaching this year, as she reviews her students' schedules, she identifies all the general educators with whom she will collaborate. Her first task is to develop a student summary sheet with pertinent student IEP goals, accommodations, and other special notations for each general educator. She wants to be proactive in collaborating with her general education colleagues.

Strategy Approach

The final approach, and the one emphasized in this book, is the strategies approach. This approach focuses on *teaching students how to learn*, not what to learn, and therefore fostering student independence. Many strategies have a metacognitive component, requiring students to stop, think, reflect, and evaluate their progress using the strategy, thus promoting self-regulation. Perhaps the most well-known, researched set of learning strategies for adolescents with learning disabilities has been developed and published through the University of Kansas Center for Research on Learning (KU-CRL) and is referred to as the Strategic Intervention Model (SIM).

We will describe some of these strategies in subsequent chapters. Teachers can learn more about the SIM approach at http://kucrl.org/sim/index.shtml. These strategies are quite specific, and to implement these with fidelity, teachers must receive training and materials from certified strategy trainers. Teachers should e-mail simpd@ku.edu to request information about SIM trainers in their state or geographical area.

The teacher's role in the strategies approach is to choose or develop a few applicable strategies to teach students. Introducing too many strategies can confuse and overwhelm students. Therefore, we do not support the "teach a strategy a week" approach. Teaching robust strategies, such as many of those described in this book, usually takes several weeks of instruction. As Mrs. Green reviews student files, she believes several students will benefit from strategy instruction, but she knows she will be selective regarding which ones she will introduce.

The Combination Approach

For illustration purposes, we described each instructional approach separately, but in reality, teachers use them in combination with individual students and groups of students. For example, as Mrs. Green helps Sarah complete an English homework assignment (tutorial approach) requiring a written composition comparing and contrasting two main characters in a novel, Mrs. Green reviews capitalization, spelling, and grammar rules (remedial approach) and teaches Sarah the steps of writing a comparison essay (strategies approach). This approach helps Sarah independently complete a similar future task.

Several factors—such as the student's IEP, ITP, number and type of general education classes, and input from the student and the student's family members—guide which instructional approach or combination of approaches teachers should emphasize with each student. The instructional emphasis for each student is fluid and may—and in fact should—change from year to year based on new and revised goals and the student's vision for the future. Figure 1.2 provides additional recommendations about these various instructional approaches.

Figure 1.2 Instructional Approaches

Approach	Cautions or Reminders	Suggestions or Uses
Functional	Outcomes are typically not aligned to common core state standards.	Use occasionally for skills not tested on high-stakes assessments.
Tutorial	May not address student's original purpose for receiving special education services.	Combine with basic skills or strategy approaches to increase instructional power.
Basic Skills Remedial	Analyze age-appropriateness of materials and methods.	Combine with student goal-setting and frequent monitoring to increase student motivation.
Compensatory	Does not teach the student new skills.	Use occasionally but not as sole instructional approach.
Career/ Transition	Begin early and be flexible with changing student needs.	Involve the student, family, and community agencies.
Co-teaching/ Collaboration	Build relationships with colleagues, and if possible, begin with co-teaching volunteers.	Be proactive in establishing yourself as an equal in the co-taught classroom.
Strategy	Appropriate sufficient time to teach strategy to mastery.	Collaborate with colleagues to promote strategy generalization.

SUMMARY

This chapter overviewed secondary special education and described seven approaches special educators use at this level. Secondary special educators assume numerous and varied roles and responsibilities. The "job description" of secondary special educators is much different from that of their elementary counterparts due to the characteristics of adolescents, curricular expectations, the organization and structure of secondary schools, and the way secondary general education teachers are prepared. Researchers have identified seven main instructional approaches used in secondary special education programs. Each has its own purpose, advantages, and concerns. Teachers may feel pressure by parents, administrators, and students to emphasize the tutorial model, which provides only short-term student gains. Rather than rely on one approach, most teachers use a combination of approaches with each student, based on the student's vision for the future as noted in the IEP and ITP.

CHAPTER APPLICATION ACTIVITIES

Apply your knowledge from the chapter by discussing or completing the following application questions or activities. Suggested answers are provided below.

1. As noted in Chapter 1, teachers often operate from more than one instructional model simultaneously within a single lesson. Which combination (of at least three different instructional models) is Mrs. Yates using when, while working with ninth grader Diane in the resource room on math story problems from Diane's general education math class, she allows Diane to use a calculator and asks her to read the problem, paraphrase what the problem is asking, think of which operation(s) to use, complete the problem, and check her answer?

2. You also work with Diane, and you decide to develop a basic two-column cue card for Diane containing the steps of solving the math story problem noted in Question 1. What might that cue card look like?

3. Diane's IEP meeting is soon approaching, and you are on Diane's IEP team. The team will be discussing Diane's accommodations. Diane has short- and long-term memory issues that make memorization difficult and language processing issues that affect comprehension in both written and spoken form. What accommodations would you recommend for Diane?

Suggested Responses

Responses will vary, but here are some suggested ideas:

1. Mrs. Yates is providing tutorial support by helping Diane with work from her general education classes, she is using a compensatory method (allowing Diane to use a calculator), and she is teaching Diane a learning strategy.

2. Here is a cue card for solving math story problems:

Step	Check (✓) when that step is completed
Read the problem.	
Paraphrase what the problem is asking.	
Think of which operations to use.	
Complete the problem.	
Check my work.	

3. Diane may benefit from various accommodations. The IEP team may consider these: cue cards, calculators, spell checkers, allowing the use of some "fact notes" or graphic organizers during tests, having questions on study guides or tests reworded or simplified, allowing test questions to be reworded or paraphrased, etc. These kinds of accommodations are directly related to her memory and language processing issues.

SUPPLEMENTAL RESOURCES FOR CHAPTER 1

Dieker, L., & Murawski, W. (2003). Co-teaching at the secondary level: Unique issues, current trends, and suggestions for success. *The High School Journal,* *86*(4), 1–13.

Friend, M., & Cook, L. (2012). *Interactions: Collaboration skills for school professionals* (7th ed.). Upper Saddle River, NJ: Pearson.

Sabornie, E., & deBettencourt, L. (2009). *Teaching students with mild and high incidence disabilities at the secondary level.* Upper Saddle River, NJ: Pearson.

The Strategies Approach

2

Strategies are potentially powerful, but unless they are taught correctly, strategies are unlikely to result in improved academic performance.

(Reid & Lienemann, 2006, p. 33)

MEET MENTOR TEACHER EVELYN KOUREY

Evelyn Kourey is a mentor teacher at Rosenquist Middle School, a large school that includes fifth through eighth grades in a suburban midwestern city. She provides support for several beginning teachers in her building. At the conclusion of last year, these teachers indicated that they wanted to learn more about strategy instruction after several colleagues shared promising results from their master's-level research projects, which emphasized evidence-based strategy instruction. Ms. Kourey was excited about her teachers' interest, as she knows that few educators receive professional development on strategy instruction or have more than a brief exposure to teaching strategies (Reid & Lienemann, 2006).

She also knows that some of her teachers will be reluctant to embrace "another new approach." However, her teachers want to be effective, and they desire to instill independent learning skills in all their students. Knowing that the strategy approach can accomplish these goals, Ms. Kourey gathers some information about the strategies approach. As a starting point, she believes her teachers need a definition of strategies, reasons for teaching strategies, an overview of the types of strategies, and the evidence-based instructional sequence for teaching strategies.

CHAPTER OVERVIEW

This chapter serves as a foundation for subsequent chapters, as it summarizes information that Ms. Kourey discovered as she researched strategy instruction. Of all the instructional approaches described in Chapter 1, many special education researchers recommend strategy instruction as a preferred method for introducing initial skills to students with mild disabilities. Further, as noted in the chapter quote, teachers need to teach strategies *correctly* in order for students to learn the most. Therefore, the chapter also presents the six stages of instruction that produce maximum student gain.

WHAT ARE LEARNING STRATEGIES?

Teachers often use the term *strategies* to refer to any number of methods, but in this book, we refer to strategies as a *specific instructional approach*. Specifically, learning strategies are principles, procedures, or rules for solving problems and independently completing tasks (Friend & Bursuck, 2012). Therefore, when teachers teach that the three branches of our government have a system of checks and balances (principle), the steps of solving an algebra problem (procedures), or that a negative number plus a negative number always equals a negative number (rule), they are teaching a learning strategy. Additionally, strategies are *efficient* ways of approaching or completing tasks. A student learning to multiply two-digit by one-digit numbers, such as 48×5, could add $48 + 48 + 48 + 48 + 48$ to solve the problem, but that approach is inefficient in terms of time, steps, and the likelihood of making errors. In contrast, using the multiplication algorithm would be much more efficient. Strategies should be efficient in terms of the number of steps, time, and effort required by students.

Many strategies themselves are strategies in the form of an acronym or mnemonic which helps students remember the steps. When students want to edit their paper, for example, they can remember the mnemonic COPS, which represents capitalization, overall appearance, punctuation, and spelling.

WHY SHOULD WE TEACH STRATEGIES?

First, teachers should consider teaching strategies because by their very nature, strategies *help students compensate* for some of their learning challenges. Students with disabilities tend to be inefficient in their approach to learning tasks. They also experience memory issues that interfere with academic success. In many strategies, a set of steps composes a mnemonic that supports a weak learning or memory system. Some students have attention issues and do not focus on the important qualities or characteristics of a task or problem. Strategies help students focus on what is important by making steps explicit and purposeful.

Similarly, some students have difficulty with *self-regulation*. Self-regulation includes the processes of goal setting, self-instruction, self-monitoring, and self-reinforcement. Often, students with disabilities begin a task without a goal (or the right goal) in mind, forget what process to use with a problem or task, forget which step they have completed, and forget where they are in their process. Further, they may not detect when they are experiencing a problem, have the skills to correct the situation, or "reward" themselves when they successfully complete a task. Many strategies include supports (such as cue cards—see Chapter 1) that help students improve their self-regulation skills.

Next, strategies are *flexible and versatile*. They can be taught at any grade level and in any subject area by general or special educators. With some creativity, strategies can be differentiated for a student or group by adjusting the number of steps, simplifying language, including more review and practice activities, and providing additional scaffolds such as cue cards, examples, reminders, visuals, or support from peers, technology, or teachers. Some students need only a quick review of a strategy. Teachers should not view strategies as an extra or add-on to the curriculum; rather, strategies support what teachers already teach.

Finally, perhaps more other approaches, strategies *teach students to be independent*. Strategies do not tell students answers; rather they provide a system for helping students arrive at answers themselves. The metacognitive process in learning strategies helps students assume ownership of their work and their learning process.

WHAT IS THE RESEARCH ON STRATEGIES?

Teachers should also consider using strategies due to their solid research base. Numerous researchers and teachers have conducted studies on strategy instruction and have concluded that strategy instruction can be very effective.

Some researchers have investigated the effectiveness of specific strategies. For example, over the last 30 years, researchers have thoroughly studied strategies developed at the KU Center for Research on Learning at the University of Kansas (KU-CRL). Before dissemination, these strategies met rigorous standards. They had to include instructional procedures that were (a) suitable for teachers, (b) powerful enough to result in significant gains for students who struggle, and (c) useful to students in various settings and situations.

Others have validated the self-regulated strategy development (SRSD) model with over 20 years of research. This approach includes six specific instructional steps (described later in this chapter) for teaching strategies that help students become active participants in the learning process, which promotes self-regulation.

Finally, some researchers have focused on strategy instruction in general. For example, Swanson and Sachs-Lee (2000) used meta-analysis to determine the effectiveness of various instructional approaches used in special education with students with learning disabilities. The most effective methods included step-by-step prompts or instructions as well as cues or reminders to use strategies or procedures. Compared to students taught with other methods, students taught through strategy instruction showed the most improvement.

Strategy instruction, therefore, is highly effective. However, researchers have also determined that for maximum gain, students need daily and sustained instruction, multiple opportunities to practice the strategy in a variety of situations, individualized feedback, and teachers who hold them accountable for mastering the strategy and who present the strategy using validated instructional steps.

WHAT ARE REASONS TEACHERS DO NOT USE STRATEGIES?

If strategy instruction has a solid research base, why don't all teachers embrace it? Several factors probably prevent teachers from using strategies as much as they could or would like. Ms. Kourey needs to be mindful of the day-to-day issues that may prevent her new teachers from considering strategy instruction.

First, teachers acknowledge feeling pressure to cover more learning standards and more material. Teaching strategies, at least initially, takes a fair amount of instructional time, and naturally teachers may feel uneasy about the trade-offs. Because many strategies contain steps that students must memorize, practice, and practice some more, teachers must prioritize which few strategies will produce the greatest student gains. For example, students enrolled in several courses that include tests as a major component of the course grade would benefit from learning a test-taking strategy. Some teachers have strategy instruction as part of their curriculum, so it is built in to what they do. Others teach strategies a couple days a week for part of the instructional period, either in a co-taught or pull-out setting. Finding time to teach a strategy to mastery is admittedly difficult, so we will provide some time savers in some of the chapters.

Second, teachers may unaware of strategies for their specific class. Researchers have developed few evidence-based strategies specifically for content areas, such as science and social studies, as well as math skills such as algebra or geometry. Therefore, teachers teaching these subjects will need to develop and field-test their own strategies with the help of their students. We have discovered that students enjoy developing and sharing their own strategies, especially if the teacher models enthusiasm for this.

Training also is an issue. Most teacher preparation programs do not infuse strategy instruction in their courses, so teacher candidates are unaware of their potential and use. Other strategies, such as those published at KU-CRL require training from a certified trainer before implementation. Those responsible for staff development may be unaware of the strategies approach and certified trainers in their geographical area, or they may lack funds for such training. Also, because most teachers are not trained in strategies, they may not automatically identify strategy instruction as an evidence-base practice that can be used with other educational initiatives or mandates such as Response to Intervention (RTI). Finally, teachers may be aware of strategies but unfamiliar with the preferred instructional sequences for them, so they have been disappointed with their efforts to teach them.

WHAT INSTRUCTIONAL STEPS ARE RECOMMENDED WHEN TEACHING STRATEGIES?

Several researchers (e.g., Graham, Harris, & Mason, 2005) have validated the SRSD model mentioned previously with over 20 years of research. This model includes the following six instructional steps. For maximum student learning, teachers should use these steps while teaching learning strategies.

- *Develop and activate background knowledge.* The first step includes conducting some informal assessment *and* ensuring students have the necessary background knowledge or skills *or* compensatory tools to engage in the strategy. Consider, based on your knowledge of the student and available assessment data, if the student has the necessary preskills, if you need to teach those preskills before teaching the strategy, or if you will provide accommodations or compensatory methods for the student in the absence of necessary preskills. When developing an informal assessment, consider a pretest with two parts: (1) having students list strategy steps in order and (2) requiring students to apply *all* the strategy steps. Students who perform well on the pretest may not need any strategy instruction, or they may just need a refresher of some steps. Depending on the strategy, administering a short pretest may take only 20–30 minutes, but teachers also need to analyze pretest results and consider instructional groupings based on the results.

- *Discuss the strategy.* Next, teachers introduce the strategy, provide a rationale for learning the strategy, indicate how the strategy will benefit students, indicate how other students who have learned the strategy have benefitted, note environments where students can use the strategy, and introduce steps. Teachers present the strategy in a positive light, motivate students to want to learn the strategy, and emphasize that with hard work, they, too, can be successful with the strategy. Typically, this step takes one instructional period.

- *Model the strategy.* This is the meat of instruction and the step that some teachers short circuit. Some teachers present strategy steps and model them, but they miss critical elements associated with effective modeling. In modeling, teachers use a think-aloud process to share how to successfully complete the strategy. Teachers model their metacognitive processes, so students know what the step involves, what questions they should be asking themselves, what to do if they get stuck, and how to maintain effort and persistence using positive affirmation statements. In other words, teachers explain *why* they are doing each step, *how* to do each step, and *how* to use positive self-talk. During modeling, teachers *model every step and possible variations* which often requires multiple class periods.

- *Have students memorize the strategy steps.* Students memorize the steps in order, so they develop automaticity. Some teachers have students individually complete a checkout in which they say the steps in order *and* tell a little about each step before they advance to learning the strategy. To support students, teachers can provide a mnemonic, develop a rhyme, use repeated verbal rehearsal, allow students to quiz each other, or make flashcards or other supporting material. Most students can memorize steps fairly quickly, especially if the steps create a mnemonic or have an associated visual.

- *Support the strategy.* In this step, the students *and* teacher practice the strategy several times together with new, additional examples.

Teachers gradually involve students in the instructional dialogue by asking questions such as, What is the first step? and What do we ask ourselves in the first step? With each step, students practice the strategy, and teachers provide specific feedback. Teachers typically distribute this activity over several instructional periods and continue periodic review until students can perform the task independently.

- *Provide independent practice.* After sufficient practice with many examples and many variations with gradually reduced support, students complete the strategy independently. Teachers readminister the pretest or develop additional examples for students to complete independently. Readministering the pretest, now as a posttest, allows teachers to show students how much they have learned, which is motivating for many students.

Although these six steps reflect the research-based recommended SRSD instructional sequence, students often need a refresher from time to time or reminders or prompts to use the strategy. Therefore, to promote generalization, teachers monitor students' use of the strategy and discuss or remind them of times, places, or occasions where they can use the strategy.

WHAT ARE SOME DIFFERENT KINDS OF STRATEGIES?

Researchers categorize strategies in several ways. We differentiate strategies by who uses them, their structure, and their skill area. Knowing these categories helps teachers identify appropriate strategies for their class. In this section, we include a few brief examples of the different types of strategies to illustrate the wide array of strategies available to teachers and students.

Teacher Routines and Strategies

These help teachers improve their efficiency and effectiveness in instructional planning and delivery. Some examples include the following:

- *Content enhancement routines* (KU-CRL) help teachers think about, adapt, and present critical content in an efficient and effective manner by making concepts explicit. Specific examples include the *unit organizer routine, the lesson organizer routine,* and *concept anchoring.* Mr. Hanson's unit organizer helped him link his current unit with previous and future areas of study, identify "big ideas," schedule learning activities, and develop self-test questions for students.

- *SCREAM,* which stands for structure, clarity, redundancy, enthusiasm, appropriate pace, and maximized engagement (Mastropieri & Scruggs, 2010), prompts teachers to remember these components as they develop and deliver lessons. This strategy reminded Ms. Youngstown to have a predictable routine for her "unpredictable" last hour math class.
- *Other routines* help teachers assess students' understanding and set a purpose for learning. Examples include beginning class with a bell-ringer, attention grabber, anticipatory set, or sponge activity; concluding class with a review or closure activity; sharing the agenda; stating why the information or skill is important; informing students how they will be held accountable for their learning; using unison responses; calling on volunteers and nonvolunteers; using random ordered turns; maintaining a brisk pace; and ensuring all students have equal opportunities to learn (Ellis, 2011). Calling on all students provided Mrs. Wachal with information about how each student was processing her science lecture.

Student Strategies

These are used by students. They are categorized as structured or unstructured, general or specific, behavioral-social, or self-regulatory, but most can be placed into more than one category.

Structured Strategies

Structured strategies contain steps that must be completed in a specific order. Teachers must model the steps in order, model what to do if some steps do not apply (e.g., what if the math problem has no exponents?), help students remember those ordered steps, and insist that students follow that sequence. Some examples include the following:

- *Please excuse my dear Aunt Sally* (parenthesis, exponents, multiplication, division, addition, subtraction) for the order of operations
- *RAP* (*read* a paragraph, *ask* yourself the main ideas and details, *put* the main ideas and details into your own words) for monitoring comprehension and summarizing text
- *SQRRR* (*survey* the chapter, turn subheadings into *questions, read* section by section looking for the answer to your question, cover up the text and *recite* what you remember; at the end of your study session, *review* all the material) for studying text from a chapter

Unstructured Strategies

These strategies contain steps that can be completed in any order. Some study and behavioral strategies are unstructured, such as the following:

- *The 4 Ds.* Richard considers these questions as he organizes himself each morning before school: (1) *Did* I put my completed homework in my backpack? (2) *Do* I have my lunch money? (3) *Do* I have any special items such as permission slips or gym clothes? and (4) *Do* I have all my books and materials? Regardless of the order, as long as Richard completes each step, he will be ready for school.

General Strategies

These can be used in multiple settings. Some students tend to compartmentalize learning, but prompting students about strategies they have learned in other classes promotes generalization. Therefore, teachers need to know what strategies colleagues are teaching and ask students what strategies they could use when completing an assignment or approaching a task. Some general strategies include these:

- *Mnemonics, graphic organizers, test-taking skills, note-taking skills, and most study skills.* For his social studies quiz, Eduardo remembered the mnemonic ADMIT (accommodate, dominate, move, invent, and tolerate) as the five types of solutions that humans have used to react to problems.
- *RCRC* (*read* a little bit of information; read it more than once; *cover* the material; *recite* what you have read; *check*) for memorizing information, spelling words, and formulas. Madeline used this strategy to memorize formulas and abbreviations for her chemistry class.

Specific Strategies

These are task specific and are used to accomplish a specific type of problem or task. Here is an example:

- *STAR* (*search* the word problem, *translate* the problem into an equation, *answer* the problem, *review* the solution) for solving word problems

Behavioral or Social Skill Strategies

These support appropriate student behavior. When teaching these, thoroughly model the desired behavior; don't just explain it. For example, explaining the rule "raise your hand and wait to be called upon before you speak" will be more powerful if you explicitly model what that behavior looks like (with examples of the appropriate behavior) and does not look like (with nonexamples of the inappropriate behavior), so students see the full range of possibilities. This helps students understand exactly what the rule entails and helps teachers consistently follow through. Teachers can also use video modeling to show examples and nonexamples. Finally, posting the strategy or rule with its steps or components in a visible area prompts students and reminds teachers of the strategy. Here is an example of a behavioral strategy:

- *TASSEL* (*try* not to doodle, *arrive* at class prepared, *sit* near the front, *sit* away from friends, *end* daydreaming, *look* at the teacher) for meeting class expectations. Sometimes these strategies are called *teacher pleasing behaviors*, because they focus on behaviors that please teachers and keep students out of trouble.

Self- Regulatory Strategies

Many strategies promote metacognitive skills such as goal setting, self-monitoring, self-instruction, and self-reinforcement. Students begin by setting goals to learn and use all strategy steps. During self-instruction, students ask themselves questions such as, What can I do next? or Will rereading help me in this situation? in order to fix problems. Students make self-monitoring statements such as, How well did I understand what I read? or Is this a reasonable answer to the math problem? Finally, students use self-reinforcement when they tell themselves that their success occurred because they applied a strategy and remained engaged. An example of a self-regulatory strategy is the following:

- *Am I paying attention?* When Leonard hears a beep from a tape, he immediately asks himself if he was paying attention. He then marks on a tally sheet whether or not at that moment he was paying attention. The beep signals him to monitor his behavior. Leonard has set a goal of being on task during 18 out of 20 beeps. If he reaches his goal on four of five days, he will earn a reward.

HOW CAN TEACHERS DESIGN THEIR OWN STRATEGIES?

In addition to using research-validated strategies, teachers and students can develop their own strategies. This is important, because researchers have not developed strategies for every content area, skill, or situation, strategies can and should be individualized, and students and teachers together can develop strategies based on their curriculum or standards.

Probably the best way to develop a strategy is to complete the task yourself. Think of the most efficient way of completing the task and be cognizant of what you are thinking and doing as you complete each step. As you develop the steps, consider critical preskills associated with each step and include the following requirements for a good strategy, as noted by Sabornie and deBettencourt (2009):

1. The strategy should contain a series of steps leading to a successful outcome.

2. The steps should be sequenced, so they provide the most efficient way to complete the task.

3. The steps should cue the student to use cognitive and/or metacognitive strategies (e.g., What is my first step? Why do I do this? Does this answer seem reasonable?).

4. The steps should cue the student to take some type of overt physical action.

5. Each step should begin with a verb to cue action for the student.

6. The strategy should contain no more than seven steps to avoid processing or memory overload.

Math teacher Mr. Marcus applied these steps and developed the look, square, multiply, check, and label strategy for his seventh graders to remember the steps of determining the area of a circle, which corresponds to one of the common core state standards. Students *look* for the radius labeled in the diagram, *square* the radius, *multiply* the radius by pi (3.14), double *check* their answer by completing the multiplication step once more and asking themselves if the answer makes sense, and finally, *label* their answer.

SUMMARY

For various reasons, new general and special education teachers often have limited knowledge or experience teaching learning strategies. Therefore, their mentors or administrators can encourage them to identify strategy instruction as a goal for their personalized growth plan.

Learning strategies are principles, procedures, or rules associated with a task or behavior that promote student independence and efficiency.

Strategies are unique, as they include steps to *efficiently* complete a task, but because they also include a metacognitive component, they promote self-regulation, an important skill lacking in many students with disabilities. Strategy instruction is a research-based intervention that teachers can use in any setting and for tiered interventions. Because many strategies are available, teachers need to select those they believe will have the greatest impact on student achievement, utility, and generalization. Researchers recommend a six-step instructional sequence that emphasizes explicit teacher modeling using a think-aloud with many different examples of the strategy. In addition to validated strategies available through the professional literature, teachers can develop their own strategies with students to individualize or differentiate instruction.

CHAPTER APPLICATION ACTIVITIES

Apply your knowledge from the chapter by discussing or completing the following application questions or activities. Suggested answers are provided below.

As noted in this chapter, teachers often have to develop their own strategy for a student or a class. For example, Mr. Marcus developed the look, square, multiply, check, and label strategy for his seventh graders to remember the steps of determining the area of a circle. With this in mind, assume you are co-teaching with Mr. Marcus, and you are going to describe the strategy to the class.

1. What would your introductory description sound like?

2. What would be an interesting way to help students memorize the steps of this strategy?

3. What type(s) of strategy is the look, square, multiply, check, and label strategy (i.e., teacher, student, structured, unstructured, general, specific, behavioral or social, or self-regulatory)?

Suggested Responses

Responses will vary, but here are some suggested ideas:

1. Class, today we are going to learn a strategy that will help us determine the area of a circle. I know that for some of you remembering the steps has been frustrating. I am going to describe a strategy that will help you remember the steps and solve these kinds of problems

quickly and accurately. Students in the past who have used this strategy said it helped them perform well on homework assignments and quizzes. The strategy has five steps and is called the look, square, multiply, check, and label strategy. To determine the area of a circle, you follow these steps in this order: First, you *look* for the radius labeled in the diagram, then you *square* the radius, then you *multiply* the radius by pi (3.14), then you double *check* your answer by completing the multiplication step once more and asking yourself if the answer makes sense, and finally, you *label* your answer. Next, I will model the strategy for you . . .

2. Teachers could develop a mnemonic such as *lucky students might cheer loudly* to help students remember the strategy steps. They might develop a poster with a visual, have students develop cue cards and quiz each other, develop a little song, or use repeated verbal rehearsal.

3. This is a student, structured, specific strategy, because the strategy is performed by students, they must follow the strategy in the ordered steps, and it is used only to determine the area of a circle.

SUPPLEMENTAL RESOURCES FOR CHAPTER 2

Cognitive strategy instruction. (2006). Lincoln: University of Nebraska. Retrieved from http://www.unl.edu/csi/teachingstrategy.shtml

Deshler, D., & Schumaker, J. (2006). *Teaching adolescents with disabilities: Accessing the general education curriculum.* Thousand Oaks, CA: Corwin.

Minskoff, E., & Allsopp, D. (2003). *Academic success strategies for adolescents with learning disabilities and AD/HD.* Baltimore, MD: Paul H. Brookes.

Schloss, P., Schloss, M., & Schloss, C. (2007). *Instructional methods for secondary students with learning and behavior problems.* Boston, MA: Pearson/Allyn & Bacon.

The Learning Toolbox Special Education Program of James Madison University. http://coe.jmu.edu/LearningToolbox/index.html

PART II

Informal Assessments, IEPs, and Strategies

Vocabulary: Informal Assessments

3

There is nothing simple about knowing a word. . . .Words themselves are just plain interesting, and our ultimate goal is to create lifelong word lovers.

(Rasinski, Padak, Newton, & Newton, 2008, pp. 14, 22)

MEET TANIYSHA

Taniysha is a sixth grader who performed poorly on recent state reading assessments, especially in reading comprehension and vocabulary. In addition to resource support, she receives co-taught language arts instruction as a Tier 1 intervention. After reviewing assessment results from all students, co-teachers Mr. Kiburz and Ms. Monroe decided to emphasize reading comprehension and vocabulary development with their class.

To address student needs, the co-teachers conducted several informal vocabulary assessments with Taniysha's class. They wanted to have as much data as possible to prepare for Taniysha's upcoming IEP meeting and plan an intensive, integrated vocabulary instruction program for all students in their co-taught class.

CHAPTER OVERVIEW

This chapter provides background knowledge regarding the importance of vocabulary. This information shows why Mr. Kiburz and Ms. Monroe want to emphasize vocabulary instruction in their co-taught class. The chapter then includes examples of informal assessments these teachers used in their class and how they linked Taniysha's assessment results to her IEP.

IMPORTANCE OF VOCABULARY

Vocabulary, or word knowledge, is critical for school success for many reasons. First, as suggested in Taniysha's case, vocabulary and reading comprehension are closely connected. The National Reading Panel (2000) identified vocabulary as one of five essential skills connected with reading. If, after third grade, students can decode accurately at an acceptable rate but still experience comprehension difficulties, the issue may be a vocabulary deficit. These students often struggle with the less common, more academic words in content-area texts. If students do not know the meaning of 90–95% of the words in their text, they will experience great difficulty with comprehension and reading fluency.

Second, vocabulary is highly correlated with content-area success. Poor vocabulary knowledge negatively affects a student's ability to participate fully in classroom routines and conversations. Students who have poor vocabularies have difficulty understanding much of the oral and written language around them. They have difficulty processing new words within the rapid flow of classroom conversation.

Third, vocabulary impacts knowledge acquisition and thought development. Students who know more words have more abstract language to categorize new concepts. Without labels provided by words, students often lose ideas, because they have no systematic labels under which to file newly learned concepts. This is especially true in content areas such as science, social studies, and math. Vocabulary is essential to knowledge acquisition.

VOCABULARY DEFINED

Truly knowing a word encompasses the entire spectrum of language: listening, speaking, reading, and writing. By carefully analyzing the various features of word knowledge, teachers determine how best to provide vocabulary enhancing experiences for students.

First, vocabulary development is *incremental*, that is, it takes place in small steps over time. Students gain additional information about a word with each meaningful contextualized encounter. Experts maintain that students need 10–15 encounters with a word in meaningful contexts to truly "own" the word.

Word knowledge is *multidimensional*. To know a word means knowing the phonological form (sounds, syllables), morphological form (prefix, root, suffix), spelling, meaning, the role the word can play in sentences, and the linguistic history or etymology. To promote student vocabulary growth, teachers must consider all these dimensions through explicit vocabulary instruction.

Words are *polysemous*; that is, they have multiple meanings. The more common the word, the more meanings it is likely to have. For example, *check* can mean *to examine, inspect,* or *hold back* as a verb, or as a noun it can mean *a mark* or *a note for money.* Students must learn that a word's meaning can change depending upon its use. This is often difficult for students with disabilities, as they tend to be convergent in their vocabulary application.

Words are not isolated units but are connected in categories and sub-categories, and each is associated with related words. Students remember and retrieve new words more easily if the words are connected in a meaningful network to background knowledge. Activating background knowledge and developing associations are critical to the successful development of word knowledge.

INFORMAL ASSESSMENTS

Few classroom friendly vocabulary assessments are available that inform instruction and measure vocabulary growth (Stahl & Bravo, 2010). Even so, teachers can use various informal assessments to assess student vocabulary knowledge and growth.

Assess Vocabulary Through Writing

One method is to tally the number of *mature words* (words containing eight or more letters) a student used in a timed writing sample (even if the word was misspelled) in response to a specific prompt. In this approach, the teacher (a) provides a uniform writing prompt, (b) instructs students to think about the prompt for one minute, and (c) provides three minutes for students to write. However, giving students a specified writing prompt might not assess the full depth of their writing skills. An alternative is to read a short story, ask students to write brief phrases about any connections that came to mind as they listened to that story, have them talk about their connections with a classmate, and after several minutes of sharing, tell students to select one connection to write extensively about. Set the timer for five minutes.

When using either method, collect samples and tally results. Use the chart in Figure 3.1 to document results. Do this several times throughout the school year, noting changes in the student's use of mature words. You may want to involve students in scoring or return the scored passage to be rewritten with more sophisticated vocabulary.

Figure 3.1 Mature Word Use Chart

Date	Total Words Written	Total Mature Words Used Correctly	Percentage Of Mature Words Used

Assess Knowledge of Specific Words

One assessment that uses specific vocabulary words, which is sensitive to incremental vocabulary growth and uses self-reporting, is the vocabulary knowledge scale (VKS) (Stahl & Bravo, 2010). Figure 3.2 provides an example of a VKS that Mr. Kiburz and Ms. Monroe developed for Taniysha's class.

Figure 3.2 Stages of Word Knowledge Assessment

1. Read the word in column one.

2. After you read the word, think about your knowledge of that word.

3. Select the column that matches your knowledge of the word.

   a. If you have never seen that word before, check column 1.

   b. If you have seen the word before, but you do not know what it means, check column 2.

   c. If you think you know what the word means, write the meaning in column 3.

   d. If you have seen this word before and are sure you know what it means, write the meaning in column 4.

   e. If you wrote the definition in column 4, go to column 5 and write the word in a complete sentence.

(Continued)

Figure 3.2 (Continued)

Points Awarded > Section ∨	1	2	3	4	5
Word	I've never seen this word before.	I've seen this word, but I do not know what it means.	I think it means . . .	I know this word. It means . . .	I can use this word in a sentence. My sentence is . . . (You must also fill in Column 4.)

The co-teachers administered and scored the assessment using this guide:

For filling in Column 1, earn 1 point as indicated in the top row.

For filling in Column 2, earn 2 points as indicated in the top row.

For filling in Column 3, earn 3 points if the definition provided is correct, 2 points if it is incorrect, even if the student has attempted to fill out columns 4 and 5.

For filling in Column 4, earn 4 points as indicated in the top row if the definition provided is correct.

For filling in Column 5, earn 5 points as indicated in the top row if the sentence is both grammatically and semantically correct. If the sentence is not grammatically correct, 4 points are earned. If the word is not used appropriately in the sentence, 3 points are awarded.

In this assessment, students must prove what they know rather than merely indicating they have knowledge. The VKS can be used as a pre- and posttest to indicate growth. Using numeric scores, teachers can develop a class rank order. A student's score can be compared to the class average to include on an IEP or for RTI data collection.

Assess Knowledge of Word Parts

Mr. Kiburz and Ms. Monroe can also assess student knowledge of word parts, which are prefixes, root words or base words, and suffixes. All multisyllable words have at least one base word or root word. A base is a complete word that can stand by itself, such as *believe*. A root also provides meaning, but it is not a complete word; an example is *struct* in the word *construction* (Bursuck & Damer, 2007). For brevity, we will use only the term *root* in this chapter.

One informal assessment of student knowledge of word parts is part of the University of Kansas's word mapping program (Harris, Schumaker, & Deshler, 2008). Teachers develop an assessment of five words containing common prefixes, roots, and suffixes that will be covered that year or semester, or an assessment of words using common affixes. (See Appendix A for common prefixes and suffixes). Students subdivide each word into its meaningful parts, write the meaning for each part, and write the meaning of the entire word, as they have determined it based on their understanding of the parts.

Teachers calculate the score based on the number of correctly completed sections. For example, the word *construction* can be divided into three parts (*con* = with, *struct* = to build, *tion* = act or process) and would be worth seven points: one point for dividing each syllable correctly, one point for each correct syllable definition, and one point for the correct overall definition, which is "the act of building with something." Because this assessment yields a numeric score, teachers can determine the class average and rank order scores.

Mr. Kiburz and Ms. Monroe developed and administered this assessment and also included a question that asked students to list the steps of the EDGE strategy, a strategy they developed for teaching affixes that includes these steps, using the word *biology* as an example:

E—*Examine* the word for morphemes.

D—*Divide* the word according to morphemes (*bi* and *ology*).

G—*Gain* meaning for each morpheme (*bi* = life, *ology* = study of).

E—*Enter* the meaning of the whole word (biology is the study of life).

Assess Vocabulary Through Speaking

Teachers can also informally assess vocabulary in oral language. Mr. Kiburz and Ms. Monroe decided to assess Taniysha's use of oral language in class. They agreed on a discussion topic that would elicit the most verbal responses. Mr. Kiburz led the discussion and called on Taniysha while Ms. Monroe recorded and tallied Taniysha's words. Teachers can use these data to assess oral vocabulary use and growth over time. Teachers teaching by themselves can request assistance from a colleague or use a tape recorder.

TANIYSHA'S INDIVIDUALIZED EDUCATION PROGRAM

Mr. Kiburz and Ms. Monroe summarized these informal assessment data to develop Taniysha's present level of functioning for her IEP meeting. They will share these data with the team, develop goals and objectives, and plan ways to support Taniysha's vocabulary development.

Figure 3.3 Taniysha's IEP

Individualized Education Program

Name: Taniysha   Grade: 6   Skill Area: Vocabulary

Present Level of Performance: Informal assessments reveal that Taniysha (1) wrote 20 words with two mature words (10%) during a 3-minute writing activity; (2) earned 11/50 points on the *VKS* assessment, in which she was unable to correctly define any vocabulary terms from the sixth-grade language arts curriculum; and (3) earned 8/35 points on the *word mapping* assessment, in which she identified five prefixes and the correct meaning of three of those five prefixes from words from the sixth-grade language arts curriculum. These scores placed Taniysha in the lowest 10th percentile of her class. During class discussion, Taniysha provided two- to three-word responses to direct questions. She also indicated that she did not know how to study vocabulary words except to "try to memorize them."

Annual Goal: Taniysha will correctly write vocabulary words (from the sixth-grade language arts curriculum) in original sentences through classroom activities, homework assignments, and on vocabulary quizzes with at least 80% accuracy.

Objective 1: Each quarter, when provided with a written list of 20 new multisyllabic vocabulary words from the 6th grade language arts curriculum containing common morphemes, Taniysha will independently separate each word into its morphemes, write the meaning of each morpheme, and write the meaning of the whole word with at least 80% accuracy.

Objective 2: By the end of 36 weeks, when verbally given a story starter followed by 1 minute to think and 3 minutes to write, Taniysha will write at least 40 words (with at least six mature words) that complete the story starter.

Objective 3: Each week, upon teacher verbal request, Taniysha will correctly write the key word and definition for four of five new vocabulary words presented that week.

SUMMARY

For various reasons, many students do not possess the extensive vocabulary knowledge that is critical for school success. For these students, especially, we cannot leave our vocabulary instruction to chance; instead we must use careful and purposeful planning. This planning begins with using assessment data to pinpoint student needs. Teachers can assess students' vocabulary through their writing or speaking, using a variety of informal assessments.

CHAPTER APPLICATION ACTIVITIES

Apply your knowledge from the chapter by discussing or completing the following application questions or activities. Suggested answers are provided below.

1. Mrs. Sloan had students write about what they did over July 4th. How many mature words (eight letters or more if the word was spelled correctly) are contained in Vicki's response, shown below?

   Over july 4th, we had a lot of fun. We went to the Dow City celabrasun and it was magniffacent. They had good food and rides for everyone. I liked the sky esposives the best.

2. You decide to use the VKS to assess your students' vocabulary knowledge. How many points would you award to Candice, who wrote the following?

Points Awarded > Section ∨	1	2	3	4	5
Word	I've never seen this word before.	I've seen this word, but I do not know what it means.	I think it means . . .	I know this word. It means . . .	I can use this word in a sentence. My sentence is . . . (you must also do Section 4)
imprinting			X to write something neatly		

3. You also decide to assess Malachi's knowledge of selected words from the curriculum using the word mapping procedure. The first word on the assessment was *reformable.* Malachi completed the assessment as follows:

   re- form- able re means to do again The word means to form something again

How many points (out of 7) would you provide Malachi on his response?

Suggested Responses

Based on the directions from the chapter, here are the correct responses:

1. (4): celebration, magnificent, everyone, explosives

2. (2) the response is incorrect; award credit that Candice acknowledges seeing the word

3. (5) Malachi divided the word correctly, so he earns 1 point for each syllable (3 points total), he correctly indicated the meaning of "re" for 1 point, and he provided a correct definition of the whole word for 1 point.

SUPPLEMENTAL RESOURCES FOR CHAPTER 3

Beck, I., McKeown, M., & Kucan, L. (2002). *Bringing words to life: Robust vocabulary instruction.* New York, NY: Guilford Press.

Foil, C., & Alber, S. (2002). Fun and effective ways to build your students' vocabulary. *Intervention in School and Clinic, 37*(3), 131–139.

Mountain, L. (2002). Flip-a-chip to build vocabulary. *Journal of Adolescent and Adult Literacy, 46*(1), 62–68.

Vocabulary: Methods and Strategies

4

There is little emphasis on the acquisition of vocabulary in school curricula.

(Biemiller, 2001)

CHAPTER OVERVIEW

Now that Mr. Kiburz and Ms. Monroe have collected some informal vocabulary assessment data from Taniysha and her peers, what do they do? They realize that their language arts class is a fertile setting for discussing words, their origins, and their uses. They also realize that vocabulary instruction can be boring and ineffective for teachers and students. They want to avoid having students look up words in the dictionary and memorize definitions for a quiz. With some research, this team discovered several evidence-based vocabulary methods and strategies to implement in Taniysha's class.

This chapter presents a variety of vocabulary strategies that general and special educators like Mr. Kiburz and Ms. Monroe can use. After providing information regarding which vocabulary words to teach, the chapter features the following strategies and methods.

FEATURED METHODS AND STRATEGIES

Chapter Strategies	Corresponding Common Core State Standards
Kid-Friendly Definitions EDGE Concept Diagrams Semantic Mapping Vocabulary Maps Semantic Feature Analysis Keyword Strategy	Determine or clarify the meaning of unknown and multiple-meaning words, choosing flexibly from a range of strategies. Demonstrate understanding of figurative language, word relationships, and nuances in word meanings. Acquire and use accurately grade-appropriate general academic and domain specific words and phrases; gather vocabulary knowledge when considering a word or phrase important to comprehension or expression.

Source for standards: Common Core State Standards Initiative, 2012

VOCABULARY METHODS AND STRATEGIES

The National Reading Panel (2000) concluded that because there is no single research-based method for effectively teaching vocabulary, teachers like Mr. Kiburz and Ms. Monroe should use a variety of vocabulary methods. After doing some research, and based on Taniysha's assessment results, (and those of her peers) these co-teachers decided to incorporate a variety of vocabulary methods in the class to engage all students. First, though, this co-teaching pair wondered how to select which words to teach.

SELECTING WORDS TO TEACH

Planning vocabulary instruction thoroughly, which includes deliberately selecting certain words, is critical because teachers can teach only a small percentage of unfamiliar words. Experts recommend selecting 5 to 10 words per chapter or unit for explicit vocabulary building instruction. These words should be unknown to the student, critical for understanding the text, and likely to be encountered again by the student because they relate to the chapter or unit's "big ideas." Students may also need clarification of many other words within a chapter or unit to understand the material; teachers can accomplish this by providing a quick definition when students encounter these words.

Before their instruction, Mr. Kiburz and Ms. Monroe first considered these various word categories:

1. *Important words:* Words important to understanding the text. These may be found directly in the text, or they may not be in the text but are important for understanding big ideas.

2. *Useful words:* Words with general utility likely to be encountered in the future, such as Tier II words, explained below.

3. *Confusing words:* Words or expressions that may need interpretation, such as multiple-meaning words, abstract nuances, idioms, and metaphoric expressions.

One method to help determine which words to target for explicit vocabulary instruction is the utility check. Teachers can analyze words according to these utility levels:

Tier I

These basic words commonly appear in spoken language (e.g., said, come, go, etc). Because Tier I words are heard frequently and in numerous contexts, most students already understand these words, or they have the synonym in their vocabulary. These words may need to be directly taught to English language learners.

Tier II

These words characterize the vocabulary of mature readers and writers and are encountered predominantly through written texts. They are uncommon labels for common concepts: *scowled* in place of *frowned*; *plethora* in place of *many*. Because Tier II words are not used often in oral language, they are difficult for students when they read content-area texts. These must be taught deeply.

Tier III

Tier III words are low-frequency, rare words, specific to content domains that do not generalize well, such as history, biology, and mathematics terms. They are important to building knowledge and conceptual understanding within a specific academic content area, but they rarely appear in general vocabulary usage. Unfortunately, most teachers' guides for novel study and content-area text books focus solely on Tier III words. Although these words may be important for developing content knowledge, they will not improve general vocabulary for written texts, because they do not transfer out of the content area.

KID-FRIENDLY DEFINITIONS

After teachers have selected words for explicit vocabulary instruction, they can begin by creating a *Kid-Friendly Definition* (KFD) that (a) uses words students already know, (b) includes words that are easy to understand, (c) is succinct, and (d) demonstrates how the word is typically used. The steps for creating a KFD include

1. *Locate* the most common dictionary definition.

2. *Underline* difficult, multisyllabic, multimeaning, and repetitive words.

3. *Replace* those difficult words with words students already know.

4. *Rewrite* the definition using easily understood words and sentence structure.

5. *Double-check* your KFD by asking, Would this definition be understood by a younger student? If it would, then you have created a definition that students will understand. Here are three examples:

Word	Dictionary Definition	KFD
rebel	One who rebels or participates in a rebellion	A person who goes against the law
disagree	To differ in opinion	When you say or think an idea that is not the same as someone else's idea
scornful	Full of scorn, contemptuous	When you really do not like something or someone and you show it with your face, words, or body in a very disrespectful way

Next, as shown in Figure 4.1, provide three examples that illustrate the use of the word. The examples should be related to students' experiences and include various situations that exemplify nuances of the word.

Similarly, provide three nonexamples that are relevant to students and illustrate possible confusions with the word. Next, ask students for examples and nonexamples to assess their understanding of the word and help them discriminate further, as needed. Finally, ask several yes/no questions to briefly assess students' understanding of the word and extend meaning to the text. These steps provide numerous opportunities for students to gain exposure to the new word.

TEACHING PREFIXES, SUFFIXES, AND ROOTS

An effective way to infer the meaning of words is through the study of morphology. The smallest part of a word that has meaning is a morpheme,

Figure 4.1 Examples and Nonexamples for *Scornful*

KFD	*Scornful* means when you really do not like something or someone and you show it with your face, your words, or your body in a very disrespectful way.
Examples	If there is broccoli on your plate for dinner and you really do not like broccoli, you might make a scornful face. It might look like this (show them).
	If want to go out with your friends, but your mom makes you sweep the porch first and hands you a broom, if you take it in a scornful manner, it would look like this (show them).
	If a penalty is called in a soccer game, and you want to show your disapproval in a scornful manner, what might you do?
Nonexamples	Scornful is not the same as being sad. If you get a bad grade on a test, and you feel sad or cry, you are **not** being scornful.
	Scornful is not the same as being loud. If you cheer for a play made in soccer, you are **not** being scornful.
	If you do not like broccoli and politely ask your mom for something else, you are **not** being scornful.

such as a prefix, root, or suffix. Directly teaching these parts and modeling how to locate them in words facilitates vocabulary growth, supports reading decoding, and improves spelling. Mr. Kiburz and Ms. Monroe knew that Taniysha and her peers would be encountering more multisyllabic words in the content areas as the year progressed and that these students did not have a systematic way of approaching these words. They also recognized that students in their class responded well to visuals and color coding, so they decided to use a class chart to teach and display morphemes.

CHART PREPARATION

On the front of a 5 × 8 card, they wrote the word part (e.g., a particular prefix, root, or suffix) in large black letters. On the back of the card, they wrote the meaning and about ten words containing this word part. The co-teachers found examples of words in M. K. Henry's book, *Unlocking Literacy: Effective Decoding and Spelling Instruction.*

Color coding provides additional student cues, so Mr. Kiburz and Ms. Monroe used different colored cards for each word part (e.g., prefixes on green cards). They created a large poster (see Figure 4.2) to display word parts as they introduced them. They titled the poster and included three columns (one each for prefixes, roots, and suffixes). They recorded each introduced morpheme in the appropriate column. They also created a smaller version for students to keep in their binders.

Figure 4.2 Poster With Morphemes

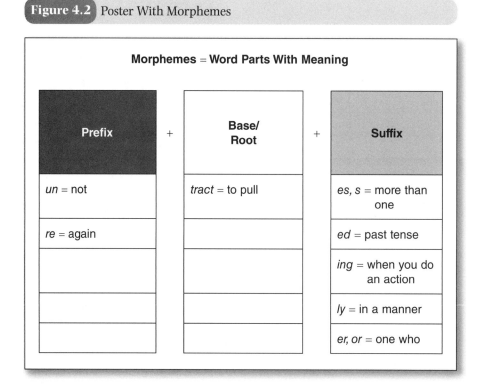

As the co-teachers introduced a new morpheme on the class chart, students wrote it on their chart. This created a permanent record to use during instruction. The color coding and the action of writing helped Taniysha understand different word parts and their meanings. Twice a week, one of the co-teachers led this activity for about 15 minutes, following the instructional sequence outlined below.

CONTENT AND SEQUENCE OF MORPHEME INSTRUCTION

1. Present no more than five new morphemes at a time, starting with the most common. At the start of each lesson, review previously learned morphemes.

2. Present the most common suffixes added to words that involve no spelling change (teaching, teacher, walked, hits, foxes, sadly, etc.).

3. Present common suffixes that involve a spelling change in this sequence:

   a. Double final consonant (jogger, skipped, running)

   b. Drop final *e* (baker, tamed, writing)

   c. Change *y* to *i* (cried, silliness)

4. Present common prefixes added to familiar base words (e.g., unhappy, distrust, rethink, pretest, misspell).

5. Present common roots (in the sequence listed on the Common Latin Roots chart in Appendix A).

THE EDGE STRATEGY

In addition to these five steps, Mr. Kiburz and Ms. Monroe felt that they needed a consistent format for students to follow that would help them determine the meaning of words containing morphemes. They wanted a strategy that students could apply across courses and disciplines. Therefore, the co-teachers developed the *EDGE* strategy, which includes these steps:

E—*Examine* the word for morphemes.

D—*Divide* the word according to morphemes (bi ology).

G—*Gain* meaning for each morpheme (bi = life; ology = study of)

E—*Enter* the meaning of the whole word (biology is the study of life).

Appendix A includes common prefixes and suffixes as well as Greek and Latin roots.

Modeling the EDGE Strategy

Mr. Kiburz and Ms. Monroe knew that modeling the EDGE strategy using a *think-aloud* was critical in order for students to begin to approach words in an organized manner. Here's the co-teacher's model step in action:

> I see a long word that I do not know, so I will use the *EDGE* strategy. It might help me figure out the word and its meaning. What do I do first?
>
> The first step is E, which stands for *examine the word for morphemes.* I know that some words do not have morphemes and others do. I am going to look carefully for any prefixes, roots, or suffixes that we have studied. The word has these letters: u-n-b-e-l-i-e-v-e-a-b-l-e. First, I look for prefixes. I need to remember that some words have none, some have one, and some have more than one. OK, I can do this—I start at the beginning of the word. I see u, u-n; oh—I see u-n is a prefix from our chart. Are there other prefixes? I'll keep looking. I recognize the next two letters b-e, but I do not see b-e or b-e-l as a prefix on my chart, so I will look for a root. Let's see b-e, b-e-l, oh, I see b-e-l-i-e-v-e on my chart. That whole group of letters is the root. Could there be another root? The next part is a, a-b, a-b-l, a-b-l-e—I do not see any roots, but I see able as a suffix.
>
> OK—I have examined the word for a prefix, root, and suffix, so I am ready for step two—D for *divide the word.* What do I do in this step? I separate the word by the parts I found in the *E* step like this: un believe able. That helps me study each part separately. I'm doing a good job, but I will double check these once more by looking at the chart—yes, un believe able matches the chart. I know I divided the parts correctly because I double checked them.
>
> The next step is G for *gain meaning.* I will look at my chart for the meaning of each part. OK—I'm on track—un means not, believe means credible, and able means can be done. Those meanings help, but I don't know what credible means, so I need to ask someone or look it up. My online thesaurus says that credible means likely. I know that likely means probably, so I am ready for the last step.
>
> The last step, another E, reminds me to *enter the meaning* of the whole word. So far, I have the meanings not, credible or likely or probably, and can be done. Putting those parts together, I think the word means that something is not likely to be done.

The teacher continues to model with additional words such as those with more than one prefix, ones without a suffix, etc.

CONCEPT DIAGRAMS

Because students in Mr. Kiburz and Ms. Monroe's class often have a surface understanding of terms, when these teachers want to teach a concept or vocabulary term thoroughly, they use a concept diagram (see Figure 4.3)—a graphic organizer that students and the teacher discuss and complete together (Bulgren, Deshler, & Schumaker, 1993). Each student is provided with a blank concept diagram sheet, and the teacher models how to complete the diagram as students do the same on their copy.

To clarify the new concept, the co-teachers follow an ordered set of steps, as indicated by the numbering system on the concept diagram. Following those steps, the teacher

1. Introduces the concept by writing it in the concept box as students follow along and do likewise on their paper copy.

2. Presents the overall concept (the broad category to which the concept belongs).

3. Asks students for keywords associated with the concept and writes those in the keyword section along the left side. In this same space, the teacher may also underline keywords associated with the concept, circle examples of the concept that they will discuss, and use a broken circle to illustrate nonexamples, which they will also discuss.

4. Presents qualities or characteristics that are always, sometimes, and never present with the concept.

5. Provides examples and nonexamples of the concept.

6. Assesses students' understanding of the concept by presenting additional examples (e.g., newspaper feature article) to assess whether students can identify each as an example or nonexample.

7. Summarizes by sharing an overall definition.

Although this process takes some time (the majority of a class period), students fully understand a concept after teachers use this method. Figure 4.3 shows a completed concept diagram that Mr. Kiburz and Ms. Monroe used in Taniysha's class to teach the concept *persuasive writing* in preparation for their next unit.

Figure 4.3 Concept Diagram

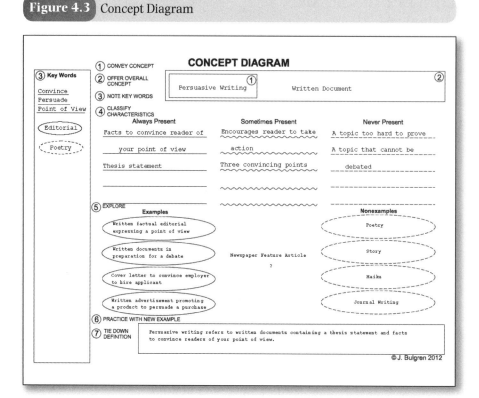

© J. Bulgren 2012

SEMANTIC MAPPING

Semantic mapping provides students with a visual map for organizing ideas, making connections between new vocabulary and prior knowledge, and seeing relationships among ideas and subideas. They are helpful for students like Taniysha who have difficulty organizing information or understanding how parts fit together to make a whole. In language arts, mapping can be used as a prewriting strategy, a prereading discussion generator, and a postreading review activity.

When using mapping for these or other purposes, Mr. Kiburz and Ms. Monroe and their students (1) write the topic in the middle of the map, (2) share background knowledge of words associated with the topic, (3) discuss how to group those responses into broad categories and discuss meanings of words generated, (4) determine labels for categories/subcategories, (5) generate words for categories/subcategories, and (6) discuss vocabulary and relationships of all categories. Figure 4.4 presents the completed class map for the concept *literary terms*, which Taniysha's class developed to synthesize terms prior to a test. Sometimes these co-teachers use semantic mapping computer programs, such as *Inspiration*, to help students create their own maps for planning a paper, making a presentation, or reviewing for a test.

A modification to semantic mapping is to select just a few critical categories or questions to focus class discussion. For example, because Mr. Kiburz and Ms. Monroe wanted to highlight only a few aspects of haiku, they developed, with their class, the modified map shown in Figure 4.5, following the same instructional principles noted earlier. This focused map provides reminders about the essential haiku features; students can use it as a cue card when writing their own haikus.

Figure 4.4 Semantic Map

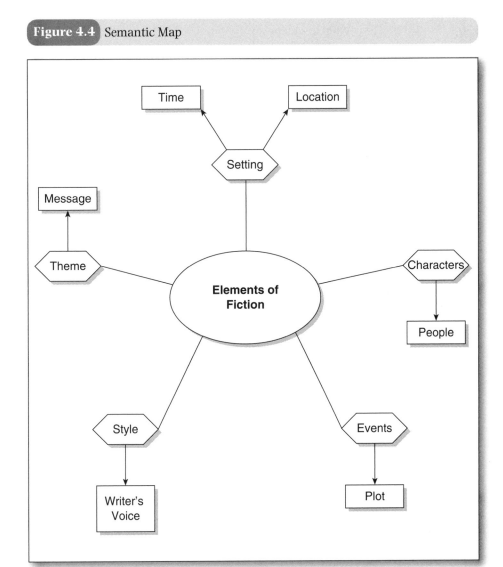

Figure 4.5 Modified Semantic Map

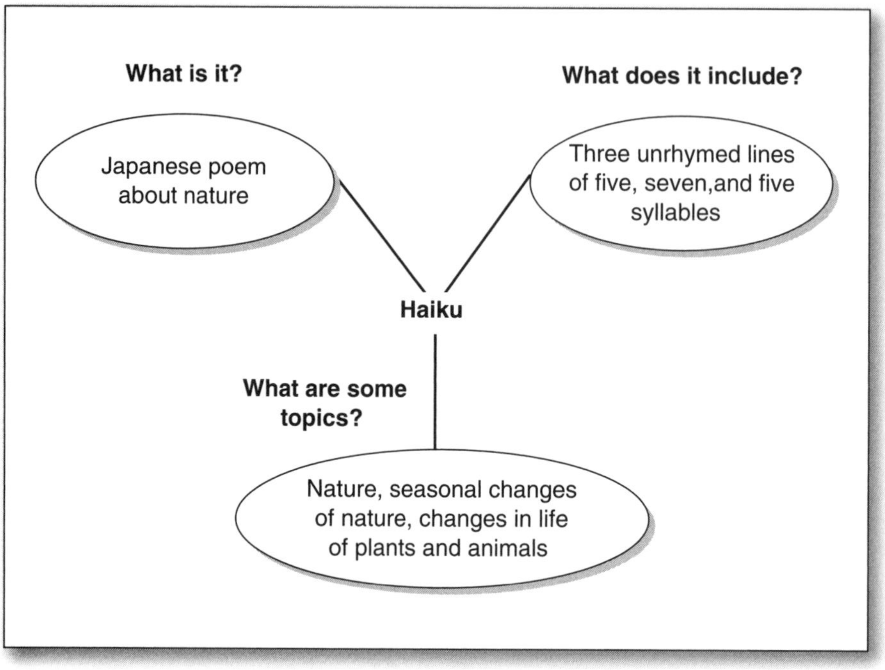

What is it?

What does it include?

Japanese poem about nature

Three unrhymed lines of five, seven, and five syllables

Haiku

What are some topics?

Nature, seasonal changes of nature, changes in life of plants and animals

VOCABULARY MAPS

Vocabulary maps are visuals that allow students to elaborate on a word or concept by recording definitions, sentences, synonyms, pictures, or other word features. Therefore, vocabulary maps accommodate various learning preferences. The Internet has numerous examples of vocabulary maps for teacher use. As Figure 4.6 shows with two examples, vocabulary maps can be basic or complex. Using the first, basic map, students write the vocabulary word, its definition, an original sentence, and a visual that will help them remember the meaning. The second map includes other word features such as antonyms, synonyms, and the student's connection to the word. Teachers can change map components depending on the words being studied or the students completing the maps, thus differentiating instruction. Mr. Kiburz and Ms. Monroe's students were more successful with vocabulary maps when these teachers first modeled them during large group instruction, provided opportunities for partner work, and eventually had students work independently. Completed maps serve as a cumulative vocabulary study guide for the unit.

Figure 4.6 Vocabulary Maps

Basic Vocabulary Map:

1. Vocabulary Term: _____

2. Definition:

3. Sentence:

4. Visual

1. Vocabulary Term: _____

2. Definition:

3. Sentence:

4. Visual

1. Vocabulary Term: _____

2. Definition:

3. Sentence:

4. Visual

(Continued)

Figure 4.6 (Continued)

Complex Vocabulary Map:

My connections to the word:

Word:

Meanings:

Synonyms:

Visual

Antonyms:

My sentence using the word:

SEMANTIC FEATURE ANALYSIS

To help students integrate new information with prior knowledge and show relationships among word meanings, Mr. Kiburz and Ms. Monroe sometimes use a semantic feature analysis. This method supports vocabulary acquisition and comprehension and fosters precise word knowledge and use. It involves developing a chart or grid that includes features that distinguish words within a particular category. Generally, the grid presents new vocabulary words in columns and semantic features (words or phrases that refer to characteristics that may or may not be shared among the vocabulary terms) along the top row. Teachers follow these steps: (1) choose the terms and qualities to be studied, (2) develop a grid, (3) with students, discuss the meaning of each word and the relationship of words to the features, and (4) place a + or – sign indicating whether or not the word contains that feature. As a culminating activity, Taniysha's class developed the semantic feature analysis in Figure 4.7 after they had written compare/contrast, descriptive, narrative, and persuasive compositions.

Figure 4.7 Semantic Feature Analysis

Qualities / Essays	Compare/Contrast	Descriptive	Narrative	Persuasive
Includes thesis statement				
Presents different points of view				
Contains intro, body, and conclusion				
Creates impression or mood				

THE KEYWORD STRATEGY

The keyword strategy is best used when students need to learn or memorize unfamiliar words or concepts, such as technical Tier III terms (Mastropieri & Scruggs, 2010). The method uses mnemonics, visuals, and acoustic associations to help students retrieve the word's meaning. This strategy is intended to facilitate initial learning and support delayed recall of factual information. A keyword is a word or phrase, familiar to the student, which sounds like the vocabulary word and can be easily drawn. Mastropieri and Scruggs (2010) discovered that students learned and remembered vocabulary better when they used familiar and concrete associations. The strategy works by strengthening initial encoding of information into the student's learning system, providing a direct link or association, and encouraging later retrieval of information through this association.

Steps for teaching vocabulary using keywords include the following:

(a) Reconstruct the term to be learned into a similar-sounding, familiar, and easily drawn keyword.

(b) Draw the vocabulary word and keyword interacting together; this is referred to as an *interactive image.*

(c) Model how to remember the definition by

(1) thinking of the keyword,

(2) remembering the drawing, and

(3) retrieving the definition.

Figure 4.8 provides examples of keywords Taniysha's class developed to remember new and difficult words from their book *The Pigman.* Mr. Kiburz modeled how to remember the word *patron* by saying, Let's think—the word is *patron.* How can I remember its meaning? Oh, yes, let's think of our keyword. It sounded like patron. I remember now; it was "paid a ton." How did we put both of those in an interactive image, or in other words, how did we draw both of these items interacting with each other in a picture? We drew a person "paying a ton" at a store because she was a *patron.* That helps me remember the definition—a patron is someone who pays for things, like a customer at a store. Mr. Kiburz's modeling shows students how to retrieve information using the association connected to the keyword.

These are just a few vocabulary methods or strategies that secondary teachers and students can use to learn new words, understand complex concepts, and differentiate among similar concepts or terms. After teacher modeling and sufficient large group practice, students can complete small group or partner activities using these methods, which will prepare them for independent use.

TIME SAVERS

Many of these methods are typically completed via large group instruction, thus eliminating the need for individualized interventions, which

Figure 4.8 Keywords

1. Vocabulary Word: *patron*—someone who pays for services or goods, a customer

   Keyword: "paid a ton"

   Interactive Image: customer paying a ton for goods

   McGregor's Store

2. Vocabulary Word: *proficiency*—being very good at something, skilled

   Keyword: "pro"

   Interactive Image: pro golf player

3. Vocabulary Word: *predicament*—being in a dangerous situation

   Keyword: "she's in a tent"

   Interactive Image: girl in a tent during bad weather

would be more time intensive for teachers. Being organized with student folders and charts is essential for teaching and modeling word parts and will save instructional time. Having examples prepared well ahead of time is also essential for all of these methods. Teachers can save time using the concept diagrams by having some or most of the responses typed on student sheets, which eliminates the need for students to copy the teacher's responses from a whiteboard or projected image. When students are ready to make their own maps, having an example of a completed map as a visual reference saves teachers from reteaching the format.

SUMMARY

This chapter presented various strategies to expand students' vocabulary. Teachers can develop their own strategy, such as the EDGE strategy developed by Mr. Kiburz and Ms. Monroe, and use existing research-supported methods, such as concept diagrams, semantic maps, semantic feature analysis, vocabulary maps, and the keyword strategy. These approaches support student learning while adding interest, novelty, and variety to vocabulary instruction. Teachers need to carefully choose the method or methods best suited to their instructional objectives.

CHAPTER APPLICATION ACTIVITIES

Apply your knowledge from the chapter by discussing or completing the following application questions or activities. Suggested answers are provided below.

1. Provide kid-friendly definitions for the following words: (a) addiction, (b) clone, (c) extinct.

2. In your co-taught science class, you are teaching the concept *mammals*. Provide several "always" characteristics of mammals for the concept diagram.

3. Develop keywords for the following vocabulary terms: (a) generate, (b) legislature, (c) ancestor.

Suggested Responses

Responses will vary, but here are some suggested ideas:

1. *addiction*—when you feel like you really need a certain chemical like a drug, *clone*—an exact copy of something, *extinct*—when there are no more left of a certain animal.

2. Mammals are warm-blooded; they have a backbone, a four-chambered heart, and skin covered with fur or hair; young mammals can be fed with mother's milk; and they have teeth.

3. *generate*—"dinner at 8" with an interactive image of someone generating (making) dinner with a clock showing 8:00; *legislature*—"ledge is slate, sir" with an interactive picture of male members of the legislature making laws while on top of a ledge made of slate; *ancestor*—"Ann's dress tore" with an interactive image of Ann standing in her torn dress with older relatives (ancestors) all around her.

SUPPLEMENTAL RESOURCES FOR CHAPTER 4

Baumann, J., Ware, D., & Edwards, E. (2007). Bumping into spicy, tasty words that catch your tongue: A formative experiment on vocabulary instruction. *The Reading Teacher, 61*(2), 108–122.

Bulgren, J. A., Schumaker, J. B., & Deshler, D. D. (1988). Effectiveness of a concept teaching routine in enhancing the performance of LD students in secondary-level mainstream classes. *Learning Disabilities Quarterly, 11*(1), 3–17.

Bulgren, J. A., Schumaker, J. B., & Deshler, D. D. (2004). *The professional development program for the concept mastery routine.* Lawrence, KS: Edge Enterprises.

Inspiration Software. (2012). *Inspiration 9.* Available from http://www.inspiration .com/Inspiration

Jitendra, A., Edwards, L., Sacks, G., & Jacobson, L. (2004). What research says about vocabulary instruction for students with learning disabilities. *Exceptional Children, 70*(3), 299–322.

Santa, C., Havens, L., & Valdes, B. *Project Crisis.* Dubuque, IA: Kendall/Hunt. (Chapter 9 is on vocabulary.)

Winters, R. (2009). Interactive frames for vocabulary growth and word consciousness. *The Reading Teacher, 62*(8), 685–690.

Yoshimoto, R. (1997). Phonemes, phonetics, and phonograms: Advanced language structures for students with learning disabilities. *TEACHING Exceptional Children, 29*(3), 43–48.

Vocabulary Curriculum and Teaching Resources

Ebbers, S. M. (2004). *Vocabulary through morphemes: Suffixes, prefixes and roots for intermediate grades.* Longmont, CO: Sopris West.

Flanigan, K., Hayes, L., Templeton, S., Bear, D., Invernizzi, M., & Johnston, F. (2011). *Words their way with struggling readers: Word study for reading, vocabulary, and spelling instruction, Grades 4–12.* Boston, MA: Pearson.

Harris, M., Schumaker, J., & Deshler, D. (2008). *The word mapping strategy.* Lawrence, KS: Edge Enterprises.

Henry, M. K. (2003). *Unlocking literacy: Effective decoding and spelling instruction.* Baltimore, MD: Paul H. Brookes.

Henry, M. K. (2010). *Words: Integrated decoding and spelling instruction based on word origin and word structure* (2nd ed.). Austin, TX: Pro-Ed.

Moats, L. (2003). *Speech to print: Language exercises for teachers.* Baltimore, MD: Paul H. Brookes.

Rasinski, T., Padak, N., Newton, R., & Newton, E. (2008). *Greek and Latin roots: Keys to building vocabulary.* Huntington Beach, CA: Shell Educational Publishing.

Readwritethink. http://www.readwritethink.org/

Zike, D. (2009). *Foldables, notebook foldables, and VKVs for spelling and vocabulary.* San Antonio, TX: Dinah-Might Adventures.

Reading Decoding: **5** Informal Assessments

Gathering and using pertinent reading assessment information to guide instruction to enhance student success in school is particularly important in middle and high school grades for students with mild disabilities.

(Bear, Kortering, & Braziel, 2006)

MEET MARSHALL

Marshall is a ninth grader who has been receiving special education services since second grade. He has IEP goals and objectives in reading (decoding), written language, and study skills. Each year, Marshall makes growth in these areas, but he continues to struggle with decoding multisyllable words. He is included in general education courses (i.e., science, social studies, math, electives) and receives two hours of resource support daily (one for language arts and one for resource/study skills support). Marshall receives accommodations in all classes such as extended time for assignments and tests, text to speech assistive technologies, and oral testing, which help him access the general education curriculum, but they do not teach him ways to improve his reading skills. Resource teacher Mr. Sabin wants to teach Marshall reading strategies that will improve his decoding skills, especially with words from the content areas.

CHAPTER OVERVIEW

What informal reading assessments are available for teachers like Mr. Sabin who teach secondary students? Do these tools respect the age and grade level of secondary students? This chapter answers those questions. First, the chapter provides background information about reading decoding for secondary students. Then, the chapter presents informal assessments that teachers can use as a basis for writing IEPs for students who need reading decoding intervention.

IMPORTANCE OF ORAL READING

Teachers, parents, the public, and policy makers are interested in the reading growth of our nation's youth. Consequently, teachers probably read more books, research more articles, and attend more conferences on reading than any other subject. The majority of students receive special services for reading, many students receive tiered reading interventions, and some teachers have doubled their efforts on reading instruction. Reading is a central focus of schools because reading skills are associated with success in school and life.

Reading is the complex process of gaining meaning from print, which requires that students simultaneously use many skills and subskills. Proficient readers consider their background knowledge; apply sound–symbol relationships; recognize word parts such as prefixes, roots, and suffixes; remember what they have read; consider the text structure; continually monitor their comprehension and adjust accordingly; use context clues; and immediately recognize words and word parts. Less proficient readers are less successful with many or all of these critical reading skills.

Being able to quickly and accurately decode becomes increasingly important as students progress through school. Students encounter more words and longer words with each grade level in content-area classes. Therefore, students with decoding issues, like Marshall, will clearly be at a disadvantage in accessing the curriculum and being independent, because they read less in the same amount of time as their peers and therefore have less text to process, remember, or comprehend.

According to Peterson, Caverly, Nicholson, O'Neal, & Cusenbary (2000), basic decoding skill requires readers to apply sound–symbol relationships and recognize words that do not entirely follow those rules (*mischief*) and words that are linguistically unique (*colonel*). By the secondary grades, even struggling readers can recognize many words by sight, yet most of their reading words will be "exception words" unless they can manipulate the sound–symbol system to apply relationships among words in print and with spoken words they already know.

INFORMAL ASSESSMENTS

Informally assessing reading with secondary students with mild disabilities presents some unique challenges. Teachers should use assessments that respect the age and grade level of students even though students' skill level may be years below grade level. Mr. Sabin can use several informal assessments to gather data about Marshall's reading skills for his upcoming IEP meeting.

Informal Reading Inventories (IRIs)

IRIs are published or teacher-created tools that typically include several word lists of increasing difficulty and passages at various reading levels with associated comprehension questions. At the secondary level, IRI results help teachers choose appropriate leveled materials for an instructional reading program and judge the appropriate reading level of content-area reading materials (Gartland, 2007). Typically, students begin orally reading word lists, starting with the list in which they will be successful and concluding with the list in which they make numerous errors. Reading experts recommend that teachers administer word lists in timed *and* untimed procedures to gain the most diagnostic information. Then students orally read passages and answer associated comprehension questions, again beginning with the level in which they will likely be successful and concluding with the passage in which they make numerous errors. Some teachers also have students silently read passages and answer comprehension questions to determine differences between oral and silent reading effects on comprehension. As the student reads orally, teachers often use a stop watch to determine reading rate and a tape recorder to later double check their recording of student errors. Typical oral reading errors include these:

- *Mispronunciations*: The student either reads a word that is much different from the word (*gross mispronunciation*) or incorrect due to syllabication, accented syllable, or phonetic mispronunciation (*partial mispronunciation*).
- *Unknown or aided words*: The student does not attempt the word within three seconds, so the teacher provides the word.

- *Insertions or additions*: The student inserts or adds a word or phrase not in the text.
- *Omissions or deletions*: The student omits or skips a word, phrase, line, or word part.
- *Substitutions*: The student replaces the word in text with another word.
- *Repetitions*: The student repeats a word, part of a word, phrase, et cetera.
- *Hesitations:* The student takes a longer than usual amount of time before reading the word.
- *Self-corrections:* After making an error, the student corrects the error.

Self-corrections (and usually repetitions and hesitations) are not counted as word errors, but teachers should include them as anecdotal information as they indicate how the student approaches text. Some informal reading inventories for older students include the *Qualitative Reading Inventory (QRI-5)* (Leslie & Caldwell, 2010); *The Cooter, Flynt, and Cooter Comprehensive Reading Inventory: Measuring Reading Development in Regular and Special Education Classrooms* (Cooter, Flynt, & Cooter, 2007); and *The Critical Reading Inventory: Assessing Student's Reading and Thinking* (Applegate, Quinn, & Applegate, 2008). The *Classroom Reading Inventory* (Wheelock, Campbell, & Silvaroli, 2008) contains passages for older students, and the *Bader Reading and Language Inventory* (Bader & Pearce, 2009) has a form for older students.

IRIs provide information about the student's reading levels, typically referred to as *independent* (the level in which the student reads with about 98% decoding accuracy or higher and answers comprehension questions with at least 90% accuracy), *instructional* (decoding accuracy at least 95% and comprehension at least 75%), and *frustrational* (decoding accuracy below 90% and comprehension at 60% or lower).

Making Your Own Informal Reading Inventories

Mr. Sabin can also make his own IRI that reflects Marshall's textbook reading demands by (a) selecting two 200-word passages unfamiliar to Marshall (the second passage can be used as a reliability check, as needed) taken from each level of a secondary series and typing each passage on a separate piece of paper; (b) developing five comprehension questions per passage that assess vocabulary, literal (factual), inferential, sequencing, and main ideas; (c) developing a list of vocabulary words for each level by randomly selecting 20 to 25 words from the glossary from each grade level text; (d) following the same administering and scoring procedures used for a commercially purchased IRI by having the student orally read word lists and then passages. Results indicate the appropriateness of the text for the student.

Sight Words

Sight words are words that students should read within three seconds. Many sight words are irregular, which means that they cannot be sounded out. Elementary teachers typically use the *Dolch List* to assess sight vocabulary. We recommend that Mr. Sabin assess Marshall with words he will encounter in the community, such as those on *Wilson's Essential Word List* (Wilson, 1963) and representative critical vocabulary words from general education texts. Marshall can read these words from lists, or Mr. Sabin can write each word on a note card and present them to Marshall, allowing no more than three seconds for a response for each word before presenting the next word. Mr. Sabin should also ask Marshall the meaning of these words and note his responses.

Sound–Symbol Relationships

To read advanced words, students need to quickly decode clusters of letters and identify syllables in words (Bursuck & Damer, 2007). Therefore, Mr. Sabin can administer an informal assessment to assess Marshall's ability to produce clusters (Part 1) and apply syllabication rules (Part 2). Mr. Sabin can neatly print the letter combinations from Part 1 on individual note cards or provide Marshall with the letter combinations in a list format, as shown in Figure 5.1. Marshall will make the sound(s) represented

Figure 5.1 Informal Reading Assessment

Part 1: When your teacher tells you to begin, make the sound or sounds represented by these groups of letters. Go down the column. Those with an * have two (2) common sounds.

ai	igh	ow *
ar	ing	oy
au	ir	ph
aw	kn	qu
ay	le	sh

(Continued)

Figure 5.1 (Continued)

ch	ng	tch
dge	oa	th*
ea *	oi	ur
ee	oo*	wh
er	or	
ew	ou	

Teacher note: The groups with two sounds include *ea* as in beat or bread; *oo* as in look or moon; *ow* as in low or brown; *th* as in bath or then

Part 2:

1. What are the six types of syllable patterns, as noted by the mnemonic CLOVER?

C—

L—

O—

V—

E—

R—

2. When your teacher tells you to begin, orally read these nonsense words. Go down the column. With your pencil, divide the words with an * into syllables.

hapsip *	fertor *	nackle *
mo	voan	jike
zikle *	surpar *	metlop *
juke	lilu *	weam

by each cluster as Mr. Sabin records Marshall's response on his record sheet. In Part 2, Marshall will read and divide nonsense words to assess his ability to apply phonics and syllabication rules. Thinking that part of Marshall's reading issue might be related to his not knowing the six types of syllables (according to the CLOVER strategy they include closed, consonant le, open, vowel team, silent e, and r controlled), he also included a question on Marshall's quiz about these syllable types.

Interests and Motivations

Mr. Sabin also wants to know about Marshall's thoughts about reading, so he can ask Marshall these questions during an individual interview:

1. What topics do you like to read about?

2. Which of these would you like to read: newspapers, magazines, textbooks, forms, job applications, spiritual books, driver's manual, recreational books, other?

3. What are your strengths in reading?

4. What is most difficult for you in reading?

5. What do you do when you come to a word you do not know?

6. What are your reading goals?

7. What accommodations do you need in reading?

8. What is the title of your favorite book?

MARSHALL'S INDIVIDUALIZED EDUCATION PROGRAM

Mr. Sabin concluded his informal assessment with Marshall and summarized the data to share with Marshall and members of Marshall's IEP team. A draft of Marshall's IEP is in Figure 5.2.

Figure 5.2 Marshall's IEP

Individualized Education Program

Name: Marshall   Grade: 9   Skill Area: Reading

Present Level of Performance: According to results from informal reading inventories, Marshall orally reads fourth-grade materials with 97% accuracy, fifth-grade materials with 95% accuracy, and sixth-grade materials with 90% accuracy. His most frequent errors were with multisyllabic words. He orally read the *Wilson Essential Words* with 90% accuracy. Marshall provided correct sounds for 20 out of 32 selected letter combinations and correctly read 8 of 12 teacher-selected nonsense words. He was unable to list any of the syllable types, according to CLOVER. He indicated that he skips words he does not know, wants to take his driver's test without assistance, and likes to read his grandfather's woodworking magazines.

Annual Goal: Marshall will improve his reading level to orally read mid-sixth-grade materials with 95% accuracy.

(Continued)

Figure 5.2 (Continued)

> **Objective 1:** By the end of the school year, when given 25 randomly teacher selected multisyllabic words from his science or social studies text that do not contain prefix or suffixes, Marshall will underline the vowels and consonants, divide the words into syllables, say the sounds for each word part, and orally read the words with 96% accuracy.
>
> **Objective 2:** By the end of the school year, when given 25 randomly teacher selected multisyllabic words from his science or social studies text that contain prefixes and/or suffixes, Marshall will underline prefixes and suffixes, verbally state how he sounded out each root, and sound out the whole word with 96% accuracy.
>
> **Objective 3:** By the end of the school year, when given 12 flashcards each containing letter combinations missed on his pretest, Marshall will provide the letter sounds and the associated key word with 95% accuracy.

SUMMARY

Gathering student data is the first step in developing an individualized reading plan. Some students, like Marshall, experience *only* decoding difficulties. Therefore, their assessments may include IRIs, teacher-made reading inventories, sight vocabulary analysis, and phonics tests. Asking students about their reading goals and strategies invites their participation in the IEP process and provides team members with information to consider when planning instruction.

CHAPTER APPLICATION ACTIVITIES

Apply your knowledge from the chapter by discussing or completing the following application questions or activities. Suggested answers are provided below.

1. Assume Marshall orally read a 100-word passage and made these reading errors: *commune* for *communication; salmonella*—did not know, so you provided the word for him; *important* for *importance;* said *science* but then self-corrected and said *scientific;* hesitated but then said *prevent* correctly; *furniture* for *future; extras* for *experiments;* read *theory* but then self-corrected and read *theories; concave* for *concept.* How many errors would you count?

2. According to the number of words Marshall missed, is this passage at his independent, instructional, or frustrational reading level? (Typically we would also consider his comprehension scores.)

3. Based on the short section in this chapter within the heading Sight Words, write one factual/literal question and one inferential question.

Suggested Responses

Responses will vary, but here are some suggested ideas:

1. Marshall's six errors included *commune, salmonella, important, furniture, extras, concave.*

2. Marshall read the passage with 94% accuracy, which suggests this is close to his instructional reading level.

3. A factual/literal question is one in which the answer is right there. Using the section under the heading Sight Words from this chapter, some factual questions would be the following: How quickly should students read sight words? What word list do elementary teachers typically use to assess sight word development? What are two ways teachers can present sight words to students during an informal assessment? Inferential questions are those in which the answer is not so obvious such as these: Why should secondary teachers use a different list than elementary teachers in assessing sight words? Why should Marshall need to be able to quickly read certain words from his general education classes?

SUPPLEMENTAL RESOURCES FOR CHAPTER 5

Applegate, M. D., Quinn, K. B., & Applegate, A. J. (2008). *The critical reading inventory: Assessing students' reading and thinking* (2nd ed.). Upper Saddle River, NJ: Pearson Education.

Bader, L. A., & Pearce, D. (2009). *Bader reading and language inventory* (5th ed.). Upper Saddle River, NJ: Pearson.

Carnine, D., Silbert, J., Kame'enui, E., & Tarver, S. (2009). *Direct instruction reading.* Upper Saddle River, NJ: Prentice-Hall.

Cooter, R. B., Flynt, E. S., & Cooter, K. S. (2007). *Comprehensive reading inventory: Measuring reading development in regular and special education classrooms.* Upper Saddle River, NJ: Pearson.

Gunning, T. (2010). *Assessing and correcting reading and writing difficulties.* Boston, MA: Allyn & Bacon.

Leslie, L., & Caldwell, J. (2010). *Qualitative Reading Inventory-5.* Boston, MA: Pearson.

Wheelock, W., Campbell, C., & Silvaroli, N. (2008). *Classroom reading inventory.* Boston, MA: McGraw-Hill.

Reading Decoding: 6
Methods and
Strategies

Reading is the most frequently mentioned academic difficulty among adolescents.

(Gartland, 2007, p. 235)

CHAPTER OVERVIEW

After reflecting upon Marshall's assessment results and talking with Marshall and other IEP team members, Mr. Sabin decided to emphasize three methods with Marshall: (1) the CLOVER strategy, (2) the DISSECT strategy, and (3) explicit phonics instruction. Mr. Sabin believes that these three evidence-based methods collectively will help Marshall achieve his reading goals. Although Mr. Sabin is already using a well-respected reading program with Marshall in the resource language arts class, Marshall is still not automatic with his syllabication and decoding skills. Mr. Sabin believes he needs to supplement his usual reading instruction with Marshall with some targeted strategy instruction.

FEATURED METHODS AND STRATEGIES

Chapter Strategies	Corresponding Common Core State Standards
CLOVER, DISSECT, LIST	Read and comprehend complex literary and informational texts independently and proficiently.

Source for standards: Common Core State Standards Initiative, 2012

THE CLOVER STRATEGY

The CLOVER strategy teaches sound–symbol correspondences for vowels within the six major types of syllables, represented by the acronym CLOVER, as shown in Figure 6.1. Marshall is a good candidate for this strategy

Figure 6.1 Six Syllable Types (CLOVER)

C—closed	A closed syllable has only one vowel and ends in a consonant. The vowel is usually short. The number of consonants before or after the vowel does not matter.	CVC (bed), VC (in), VCC (and), CCVCC (flash), CVCC (sand), CCVC (trip), CCCVCC (strand)
L—consonant-*le*	A consonant-*le* syllable is a final syllable in which the e is silent. When the first syllable ends in *s* and is followed by *tle*, the *t* is silent.	Words ending with *ble, cle, dle, fle, gle, kle, ple, stle, tle, vle,* or *zle* such as apple, babble, table
O—open	An open syllable ends in one vowel. The vowel is usually long.	*go, solo, hi, me*
V—vowel team	A vowel team has a cluster of two or three vowels or a vowel–consonant unit with a sound or sounds unique to that unit.	Words containing *ai, ay, all, alk, alm, ald, alt, aw, wa, ax, qua, au, augh, ee, ei, ey, eigh, ey, ea, ew, eu, ie, ind, igh, oi, oy, ou, oup, ough, owl, ow, oo, oal, oe, old, olk, olt, oll, ost, ue,* or *ui*
E—silent *e*	A silent-*e* syllable has one vowel followed by a consonant followed by an e. The e is silent and makes the preceding vowel long. Special cases: Words with a single sound consonant term (usually *th*) between the first vowel and the e usually have the long sound (e.g., *bathe, tithe*). In English, we never end a word in *v*; we add an e. In those words, sometimes the vowel is short (e.g., *give, have*), but usually it is long (e.g., *dive, gave*). Exceptions to the rule: *love, give, explosive.*	*ate, ice, slope, these, -ote, -ine, -ume*
R—*r*-controlled	An *r*-controlled syllable has a vowel followed by an *r*, which modifies the vowel sound.	*car, shirt, pure, deer, course*

because he is unsure of syllabication rules and certain vowel combinations within syllables.

Introductory Instruction

First, Mr. Sabin reminds Marshall that a syllable is a word or part of a word. A syllable can contain one or more letters, but each syllable will have only one vowel sound. On the first day of instruction, Mr. Sabin teaches Marshall these two initial steps in syllabication:

1. In an unknown word, *identify the vowels* (V) *that sound* (remember that the *e* at the end of a word might be silent, so do not mark it). Students can place the letter V above each vowel or a dot above each vowel and a line connecting vowels.

trumpet

trumpet

2. *Identify consonants* (C) *between sounded vowels.*

In the example below, Mr. Sabin has marked only consonants between vowels, and he did not mark the ending *e* on these words, because they are silent.

VCCV	V C CCV
d i s p o s e	c o m p l e t e

Marshall and Mr. Sabin practice marking vowels and consonants with several words, so this step becomes automatic for Marshall.

The Visual Step of Seeing Syllabication Patterns

On the next two days, Mr. Sabin introduces Marshall to these five syllabication patterns. For each pattern, Mr. Sabin explains, models, and provides several exemplar words. He provides Marshall with a cue card as an initial scaffold.

1. VC/CV: When two or more consonants are between two vowels, divide between the consonants, keeping blends or digraphs, such as *pup-pet* and *hun-dred,* together.

2. V/CV: When a single consonant is surrounded by two vowels, usually divide before the consonant, making the vowel in the first syllable long as in *hu-man* and *lo-cate*.

3. VC/V: If the V/CV rule does not help you figure out the word, divide *after* the consonant and use the short vowel sound as in *rap-id* and *sol-id*.

4. */cle:* Divide before the consonant-le. Count back three letters from the end of the word and divide as in *star-tle* and *ea-gle*.

5. V/V: Only a few words divide between the vowels; examples are *di-et* and *qui-et*.

These five patterns help Marshall practice where to divide words into syllables—the first step is a visual step. He is not yet sounding out those syllables. For several days, Mr. Sabin and Marshall take time to practice these five syllabication division patterns with real and nonsense words until Marshall has them mastered. Using his cue card, Marshall practices dividing words for about 15 minutes for five days and is becoming quicker at seeing patterns.

The Auditory Step of Sounding Out Syllables

The next step is the *auditory step* in which Marshall will sound out each syllable. After Marshall has visually divided a word into its syllables, he applies the CLOVER acronym by identifying each sy*llable* (C, L, O, V, E, or R) and applying the vowel sound associated with that syllable (see Figure 6.1).

Instructional Sequence

In this auditory step, Mr. Sabin teaches closed syllables, then open, silent *e*, vowel team, *r*-controlled, and consonant-*le* because many multisyllabic words contain closed syllables, and most words with the remaining syllable types contain a combination of the previous types (Knight-McKenna, 2008). His instructional approach includes modeling, guided practice, and independent practice. Mr. Sabin introduces the next pattern only after Marshall has mastered the existing one. For each syllable type, Mr. Sabin and Marshall read (a) numerous single-syllable words with that syllable type; (b) two and then three syllable words of the syllable type in lists and then in connected text; (c) two-, then three-syllable words of mixed syllable types in lists and in connected text

(Knight-McKenna, 2008). Therefore, Mr. Sabin and Marshall typically spend several days on one syllable type.

Mr. Sabin teaches the closed syllable first because many long words are composed of two or more closed syllables. Marshall is ready to learn this pattern because his assessments indicated he can produce letter sounds making this pattern. Two exceptions to the closed syllable rule are *find* and *cold* (Knight-McKenna, 2008), which Mr. Sabin teaches as sight words.

Open syllables end with a single vowel that is usually long. Although not many two- and three-syllable words contain only open syllables, after learning closed syllables, Marshall practices and reads words containing a combination of closed and open syllables such as *frozen, robot,* and *pretend.* Exceptions to the open syllable rule include *do* and *to* (Knight-McKenna, 2008).

The silent *e* syllable (also called the vowel–consonant–silent *e* rule) ends in one vowel, one consonant, and a final e. Mr. Sabin can teach Marshall to cross out the final *e* and make a macron symbol over the preceding vowel indicating the long sound or draw an arrow from the silent *e* to the vowel to demonstrate the long vowel.

tāke̸

tāke̸

The vowel team syllable has two vowels in succession, or in some cases, as noted in Figure 6.1, a vowel–consonant unit that makes a unique sound. The consonants *y* and *w* can also function as vowels. Experts recommend teaching all the vowel combinations that produce the same sound within the same lesson such as au, aw, and augh; ei, eigh, ey; and oa and oe.

The *r*-controlled syllable contains an *r* after the vowel that causes the vowel to have an unexpected sound. *R*-controlled syllables can be closed such as *car, shirt,* and *her;* silent *e* such as *care, pure,* and *here;* or represent a vowel team such as *air, deer,* and *course.* Mr. Sabin teaches Marshall that ur, ir, and er make the same sound. Two exceptions to the *r*-controlled syllable rule include *fire* and *admire* (Knight-McKenna, 2008).

The final syllable type is the consonant-*le* syllable, which is spelled with a consonant and an *le.* This is the only syllable type without a sounded vowel. Mr. Sabin teaches Marshall to look for the ending consonant-*le,* divide that as a separate syllable, pronounce the previous syllable(s), and add the final syllable to make the whole word.

Mr. Sabin devotes about 20 minutes daily of the resource language arts class over the next three weeks teaching CLOVER to Marshall and other students needing the strategy. He knows this auditory step takes the longest and is the most difficult for students.

Modeling the CLOVER Strategy

Mr. Sabin models each syllable type with a think-aloud. Here's an example for closed syllables:

> I am reading along in my book, and I come to the sentence, "Minnie traveled from Germany to the United States on the *Atlantic*." I can read all the words in the sentence except the one in italics, so I will use the CLOVER strategy. I remember that the first step is a visual step. I identify vowels that make sounds. OK, I can do this—I know that *a, e, i, o, u, y,* and *w* are vowels, and I do not see any silent *e* vowels at the end of the word, so I will label the vowels:

V V V
Atlantic

> I'll double check to make sure I have them all. OK, yes, I have marked the *a,* the next *a,* and *i.* I don't see any more vowels. Next, I identify consonants between those vowels. The consonants are the rest of the letters. Now my word looks like this:

V C C V C C V
A t l a n t i c

> I'll double check this, too. Do I have a V or C label above each letter between each vowel? Yes, so I am ready to look for patterns. I look for patterns by starting with the first vowel (*a*) and reading my V and C labels until I reach the next vowel (*a*). I always read from vowel to vowel. So, I see V/C/C/V as my first pattern, and I stop.

VCCV
A t l a

> Am I done with the whole word? No, I see more letters that I have labeled. So, I start again with that second vowel (the second *a*) and continue to the next vowel—V/C/C/V.

VCCV
a n t i

Now I stop because I have not labeled any more letters. OK—that looks good. Now I divide the word based on the patterns I identified.

The first pattern (from *Atla*) is V/C/C/V. I remember Rule 1 indicates that when there are two consonants between two vowels, usually we divide between the consonants, so I divide between the *t* and *l* and get the letters *a-t* for the first syllable.

VC/CV

At/la

Hey, I can do this! I start again with the next vowel (*a*) and continue to the next vowel (*i*). I remember that I am looking for patterns from vowel to vowel. This is tricky, so I need to concentrate. The next pattern is also V/C/C/V, so again, I divide between the consonants, so I divide between the *n* and *t*.

VC/CV

an/t i

I'll put those all together, and I have

VC/CVC/CVC

At- l an-t i c

OK—that completes the visual part, and now I am ready for the sounding out step.

I'll look at the first syllable (*at*) and my chart, and I see that the syllable type V-C is a closed syllable, so the vowel *a* will probably be short. The next syllable (*lan*) has the C-V-C pattern, which is also closed, so that vowel is probably short. Finally, I see *tic*, and I see again that that pattern (C-V-C) is closed, which indicates a short vowel. I know my short vowels and consonant sounds, so I can sound out each part and then read them together for this word. The first syllable is *At*, the next *lan*, the final *tic*. The word is *Atlantic*. The sentence reads, "Minnie traveled from Germany to the United States on the *Atlantic*."

THE DISSECT STRATEGY

Mr. Sabin could also teach Marshall the DISSECT strategy (Lenz, Schumaker, Deshler, & Beals, 1984) or, to save time, perhaps just the first three steps to complement the CLOVER strategy. DISSECT is a University of Kansas

Center for Research on Learning (KU-CRL) strategy for helping students read multisyllabic words. DISSECT is different from CLOVER as it teaches students to consider context clues as well as prefixes and suffixes (see Chapter 4) and reminds students to check with someone or use the dictionary if none of the previous steps help. DISSECT steps include:

D—*Discover the context.* (Students skip the unknown word and make a good guess based on surrounding words.)

I—*Isolate the prefix.* (Students look for a prefix or prefixes.)

S—*Separate the suffix.* (Students look for a suffix or suffixes.)

S—*Say the stem.* (With prefixes and suffixes separated, students attempt to read the remaining stem/root.) If students cannot read the stem, they continue with the next step.

E—*Examine the stem.* (If students cannot read the stem, they use the rules of twos and threes.)

- If the stem or part of the stem begins with a vowel, count off two letters and divide the stem into syllables.
- If the stem or part of the stem begins with a consonant, count off three letters and divide the stem into syllables.
- If these steps do not help, cover the first letter of the stem and use the rule of twos once again.
- When two different vowels are together, make both vowel sounds.
- If that does not work, pronounce the vowel sound using just one vowel sound.

C—*Check with someone.* (Politely ask someone for help.)

T—*Try the dictionary.* (Look the word up in available reference material.)

The Isolate the prefix and Separate the suffix steps are like the steps in EDGE (Chapter 4) for locating morphemes in words as students learn common prefixes and suffixes and their meanings. The Examine the stem step is different from CLOVER, but many words are divided the same using both methods. However, some students might be confused if they learned both CLOVER and DISSECT. Because DISSECT is a specific KU-CRL strategy, teachers need training from a certified trainer to teach it with fidelity.

EXPLICIT PHONICS INSTRUCTION

The CLOVER and DISSECT strategies will help Marshall divide words into syllables, but if he is unsure of sounds of letters or letter combinations, he will still be unsuccessful with decoding whole words. Marshall missed 12 letter combinations from Part 1 on his pretest. Therefore, Mr. Sabin decided to explicitly teach these 12 combinations during the pull-out language arts class by following this explicit instructional approach.

- He showed Marshall the printed letter combination on an index card and made the sound (e.g., *oa* makes the /o/ sound)
- Marshall made the sound with him and then by himself. (Say the sound with me; say it by yourself.)
- Together, they read key words with that targeted sound (*oak, cloak, soak*), calling attention to the targeted letter combination and sound.
- Marshall chose one key word (*oak*) for remembering the sound and made a cue card.
- Marshall developed a picture or mnemonic to remember the sound.
- Marshall read longer words containing *oa* such as *bemoaned, downloadable, encroachments, inapproachable, scapegoat, freeloading, stagecoaches,* and *steamboats.*
- Marshall read words containing *oa* from his textbooks to practice reading connected text.

THE LIST STRATEGY

Not finding an age-appropriate strategy to help Marshall remember his sounds, Mr. Sabin developed the LIST strategy. LIST includes these steps:

L—*Look* at the word for difficult letter–sound combinations (or clusters).

I—*Identify* those combinations/clusters by underlining or circling them.

S—*Say* the sound you remember from your cue card.

T—*Try* reading the whole word.

TIME SAVERS

Several research-validated secondary reading programs (e.g., *Corrective Reading, Language!,* and *Rewards*) teach students how to divide words into decodable chunks. Using a program that teaches skills similar to those described in this chapter will reduce the need for extensive teacher modeling of each skill. Similarly, teachers can use supplemental resources, such as *Megawords,* which introduce students to syllable types and provide already made student practice sheets. Teachers can also target their intensive instruction to just those syllables—or letter–sound combinations—causing student errors, as noted through informal assessments.

SUMMARY

Marshall is like many secondary students who struggle with decoding. These students frequently do not know how to approach multisyllabic words appearing in their content-area texts. To help students like Marshall, teachers can teach the CLOVER strategy for presenting the six syllable types and vowel sounds associated with each syllable, the DISSECT strategy for unlocking multisyllabic words with prefixes and suffixes, and the LIST strategy for remembering sounds of letters or letter combinations. These strategies use explicit, step-by-step instruction with teacher modeling as an essential component.

CHAPTER APPLICATION ACTIVITIES

Apply your knowledge from the chapter by discussing or completing the following application questions or activities. Suggested answers are provided below.

1. Using the CLOVER strategy, divide the following nonsense words and then label each of the divided syllables as C, L, O, V, E, or R.

   1. durple _____   4. hanner _____
   2. cabcot _____   5. motile _____
   3. disgain _____   6. loplate _____

2. Using the DISSECT strategy, divide these nonsense words:

   undersiktion, disenmenly, reintelment

3. What are some *real* words, serving as key words, that you could provide Marshall to help him or her remember the following letter–sound combinations:

   au, oi, and *tch*

Suggested Responses

Responses will vary, but here are some suggested ideas:

1. CLOVER strategy

    1. dur (R), ple (L)   4. han (C), ner (R)
    2. cab (C), cot (C)   5. mo (O), tile (E)
    3. dis (C), gain (V)   6. lo (O), plate (E) or lop (C) late (E)

2. DISSECT strategy

    un-der-sik-tion; dis-en-men-ly; re-in-tel-ment

3. Key words for selected letter combinations

    au—gaunt, launch, haunted, Austin, August, auto, Paul

    oi—coil, boil, soil, oil, spoil, hoist, sirloin, avoid

    tch—crutch, patch, match, pitch, itch, snatch, sketch, kitchen

SUPPLEMENTAL RESOURCES FOR CHAPTER 6

Birsch, J. R. (2011). *Multisensory teaching of basic language skills.* Baltimore, MD: Paul H. Brooks.

Fisher, P. (1993). *The sounds and spelling patterns of English: Phonics for teachers and parents.* Morrill, ME: Oxton House.

Griffith, L., & Rasinski, T. (2004). A focus on fluency: How one teacher incorporated fluency with her reading curriculum. *The Reading Teacher, 58,* 126–137.

Lebzelter, S., & Nowacek, J. (1999). Reading strategies for secondary students with mild disabilities. *Intervention in School and Clinic, 34*(4), 212–219.

Decoding Curriculum and Teaching Resources

Archer, A., Gleason, M., & Vachon, V. (2000). *REWARDS Reading excellence: Word attack and rate development strategies.* Longmont, CO: Sopris West.

Engelmann, S., Carnine, L., Johnson, G., Meyer, L., Becker, W., & Eisele, J. (1999). *Corrective reading: Decoding.* Columbus, OH: SRA/McGraw-Hill.

Greene, J. (2000). *Language! A literacy intervention curriculum.* Longmont, CO: Sopris West.

Megawords series. Cambridge, MA: Educators Publishing Service (provides supplemental instruction on CLOVER).

Wilson, B. (1996). *Wilson reading system.* Millbury, MA: Wilson Language Training Corporation.

Reading Comprehension: Informal Assessments

7

Comprehension is often tested but seldom taught. In fact, the only instruction some students receive in comprehension skills is in the form of questions about a paragraph or story . . . . When you ask a reader to answer questions to a passage he [she] has read, and the only feedback you give him [her] is that the answer is correct or incorrect, you are *testing* comprehension.

(Shanker & Cockrum, 2009, p. 164)

MEET AMANDA

Amanda is a ninth grader with a mild disability that was identified in fourth grade. At that time she was a slow but accurate reader, but she understood very little of what she had read. Since fourth grade, Amanda has had an IEP goal in reading comprehension. As she advanced in grades, her difficulties with comprehension impacted subjects in which she was expected to "read to learn." Although Amanda was included in general education science, social studies, and math, comprehension difficulties limited her performance even with accommodations such as text-to-speech assistive technology and reader support during tests. She has continued to make growth in reading; however, she is still approximately two years behind her peers in comprehension.

When Amanda entered high school, she was placed in a co-taught general English class rather than given resource instruction. Ms. Wendt, the English teacher, wonders how Amanda will cope with the reading material in her class, which includes Romeo and Juliet, To Kill a Mockingbird, *and short stories and poems by Poe, O. Henry, Frost, and Dickinson.*

CHAPTER OVERVIEW

This chapter provides an overview of reading comprehension by reviewing skills associated with this complex reading task. The chapter also explains different ways to informally assess reading comprehension skills for older readers. Finally, the chapter shows how Amanda's teachers developed her IEP based on informal assessment results.

IMPORTANCE OF READING COMPREHENSION

Comprehension is often described as constructing meaning from print. Readers must set a purpose for reading and synthesize the author's meaning using both print information and their background knowledge. To successfully comprehend, readers need foundational skills such as decoding words, maintaining an appropriate reading rate, making connections within the text and to background knowledge, and recognizing word meanings. Readers also analyze what they read and problem-solve when they encounter difficulties with words, sentences, or larger chunks of text. Finally, readers evaluate the success of their reading comprehension, often by rereading to clarify meaning.

Consequently, comprehension represents a higher order thinking task. Pressley and Afflerbach (1995) noted strategies used by good readers:

- *Before reading,* they construct a goal, overview the text, activate prior knowledge, summarize from the preview, and generate hypotheses about the text's message.
- *During reading,* they repeat or restate what they read, quickly process easy text, read aloud, make notes, pause to reflect, and look for patterns.
- *After reading,* they reread, recite to support memory, self-question, reflect on information, continually evaluate and reconstruct understanding, and change responses as they build understanding.

- To *monitor*, they reread a section, use context clues, substitute synonyms, or use a dictionary.
- To *evaluate*, they use and reflect upon their feelings about the topic and text, decide whether the text has salient information, decide if the content is current and plausible, and reflect on content after reading.

Readers often successfully engage in all these activities with easy text, but as the difficulty of the passage increases, readers often decrease attempts to problem-solve and repair comprehension. This leads to poor comprehension. Further, unless the difficult passage greatly interests the reader, motivation to read decreases. Consequently, students vary in the amount and type of information they understand from any given text.

The most basic comprehension occurs at the literal level, in which readers understand explicit only word meanings. Deeper comprehension occurs as readers make connections between and among chunks or sections of text, to other texts they have read, and to their background knowledge. This implicit comprehension involves making inferences and managing embedded figurative language.

Secondary students are expected to comprehend increasingly complex texts. High school texts are challenging for several reasons, including length, format, plot complexity, number of characters, reliability of the narrator, amount of unknown vocabulary and figurative language, and cultural-language differences between the author and reader. Further, secondary students may be learning concepts related to the study of literature (e.g., theme, tone, symbolism, foreshadowing, etc.), making reading a two-fold challenge—to understand the text *and* literary devices. All of these challenges contribute to the difficulty of comprehending beyond a literal level.

COMPREHENSION OF STUDENTS WITH MILD DISABILITIES

On standardized tests of reading given in eighth grade, *over 60% of students* with disabilities do not meet comprehension standards; that is, their reading is below the basic, literal level. Students with disabilities have difficulty with comprehension for many reasons, some of which relate to weaknesses in decoding, fluency, and vocabulary. Some students equate successful reading with accurate decoding. Their focus on word-level reading absorbs cognitive efforts, making it difficult to derive meaning from what they have read. Consequently, they do not monitor their comprehension or take corrective action when they begin to lose meaning. Further, the effort to reread to construct meaning may overwhelm the resources of readers who struggle, making it unlikely that they will repair comprehension issues. Many teachers address this by providing simplified versions of the text, so readers can focus on meaning.

Even when they decode adequately and have vocabulary support, students with disabilities may not understand a text's meaning. They may interpret both oral and written language literally, have difficulty discriminating between central and incidental details, and need support making connections between parts of the text and their own background knowledge and experience. These issues may relate to problems in working memory and executive functions associated with learning disabilities. Whatever the cause, without the ability to make appropriate connections, students with disabilities have difficulty making inferences.

INFORMAL ASSESSMENT METHODS

When Amanda entered high school, her teachers collected informal assessment data to guide their instruction. Mr. Perkins, the special educator, and Ms. Wendt identified Amanda's strengths and needs. First, Mr. Perkins completed an interest inventory, an informal reading inventory (IRI), and a comprehension maze assessment.

Reading Interest Inventories

Because comprehension depends largely on students' background knowledge, their interests and motivation to read may influence their reading performance. Many IRIs include background knowledge questions to ask before students read a passage. These questions may support comprehension. Reading interviews identify students' interests and motivation and opportunities to read outside of the classroom. Examples of interview questions for secondary students include the following:

1. In the last few days, did you do any reading?

   If so . . .

   What did you read?

   When and where did you read?

   What was the reason you were reading?

   What was your reaction to the reading?

   Share another example if you can . . .

2. If you did not read in the last few days, why not?

3. How often do you read at home?

4. Are there materials available at home for you to read?

5. How do you decide what to read?

6. If you could pick anything you wanted to read, what would it be and why? Tell me as much as you can.

7. Have you ever read a book/magazine/et cetera more than once? Why?

8. In general, how do you feel about reading? What is the best (worst) thing about it?

9. What makes a good reader?

10. Do you consider yourself a good reader? Why or why not?

Mr. Perkins was careful to ask all prereading questions before Amanda read the selection. He also asked her about her favorite authors, interests, and general attitude toward reading before beginning the assessment.

Informal Reading Inventories

When using the IRI, Mr. Perkins first had Amanda read several word lists from the IRI to estimate her instructional reading level. Then he selected a passage from the IRI that he thought Amanda could decode with at least 95% accuracy to complete comprehension measures because he did not want decoding to interfere with her attention to meaning. Amanda had the choice of reading the passage silently, but she chose to read aloud. After reading, Mr. Perkins had several options for assessing comprehension:

- Retells of what she read (oral or written)
- Response to literal and inferential comprehension questions (oral or written, open ended or forced choice)
- Cloze passage (fill-in-the-blank version of the passage)

Mr. Perkins had Amanda complete an oral retell. Amanda told him everything she had read and learned from the passage before orally answering comprehension questions. He could have asked Amanda to write her response, but he believed she would provide more details orally as part of a conversation with general cues such as, What happened next? These statements encouraged Amanda to elaborate and include both within (literal) and beyond the text (inferential) information. Mr. Perkins scored the retell using this rubric:

- 5 = comprehensive retell: follows the general organization of the passage (i.e., sequential, including beginning, middle, and end); explicitly states the gist; clusters all main ideas with sufficient supporting details; and appropriately incorporates the same vocabulary used in the passage.
- 4 = satisfactory retell: contains a beginning, middle, and end; explicitly states the gist or implies the gist; clusters some main ideas with some supporting details; uses some vocabulary from the passage.
- 3 = unsatisfactory retell: no discernible organization; gist is absent; refers to one or more main ideas but does not cluster with supporting details; does not use vocabulary of the passage.
- 2 = minimal retell: consists of collection of random details with no structure.
- 1 = *no retell:* does not provide any details or information related to the passage. (Fountas & Pinnell, 2011)

If Mr. Perkins had used a written format for the retell, he could use the same rubric. Following the retell, Mr. Perkins asked 10 comprehension questions. As with the retell, he had several options including these:

- Written or oral response
- Open-ended, multiple-choice, or true/false response
- With or without passage support
- Literal or inferential questions

He had Amanda respond orally to open-ended questions without passage support, but later he allowed her to search the passage for answers she missed. This allowed Mr. Perkins to determine how well she could use the text to locate information. For a detailed picture of her comprehension, Mr. Perkins asked both literal and inferential questions. Literal or "in the book" questions have a specific, explicit answer that students can identify in one or more sentences. Inferential questions require students to think "beyond the text" by using their background knowledge and making connections to other information sources.

Although Mr. Perkins used open-ended comprehension questions (e.g., What is the main idea of the story?), at other times and with other students, he has used a forced-choice format (e.g., multiple choice or true/false). Forced-choice (or recognition) questions provide students with possible answers to questions and are an alternative for students with memory or language deficits, those who read so slowly that looking in the text is impractical, and those who cannot provide an oral or written response due to physical or speech barriers but who can point to the correct choice or indicate "yes" or "no" when presented with response options.

Mazes

Finally, Mr. Perkins used a maze passage to informally assess Amanda's comprehension. In a maze assessment, students silently read and periodically select one of three word choices to successfully complete a sentence; consequently students primarily use context at the sentence level rather than constructing the meaning of the whole passage. Use of the maze has increased recently because of its ease of use and strong correlation to overall comprehension. Although published versions and norms are available for grades 1 through 8 (e.g., Aimsweb; Spinelli, 2011), teachers can create mazes for any passage level. Mr. Perkins created a maze following steps recommended by Shinn and Shinn (2002).

- Select 200- to 300-word passages from the student's curriculum. Mr. Perkins used Jamestown passages with a known readability level.
- Delete every seventh word and replace it with three word choices (in parentheses).
- If the seventh word is a proper noun, skip it and delete the next word.
- Word choices include these:
  - The original word (correct answer).
  - Two distracter words similar in length to the deleted word. One of the distracter words should not be the same part of speech as the deleted word, and it should not make a complete sentence when replacing the deleted word.

Maze results are reported as the number of words restored correctly (wrc) and are compared to national or district norms. Although this guideline varies from district to district, a good rule of thumb is that students who score below the 25th percentile on these assessments should be considered for comprehension instruction.

Teachers can also gain valuable information by examining students' accuracy of attempted maze responses. For example, readers who score below the norms but have a high rate of accuracy on attempted maze responses (> 80%) likely have strong comprehension with poor reading fluency. Conversely, readers with large numbers of attempts with low accuracy rates likely need assistance in monitoring comprehension and using context clues. Shinn and Shinn reported that typical growth in comprehension as measured with a maze is .4 wrc per week; however, this growth has a ceiling effect due to an upper limit for reading rate.

To prepare for the maze assessment, Mr. Perkins typed the passages, replacing some individual words with a choice of three words in parentheses, making sure that all three choices appeared on the same line of text. Amanda had three minutes to complete the assessment. Mr. Perkins compared Amanda's score (i.e., total words restored correctly, or wrc) to the district median score for eighth graders, which was 20 wrc. The first paragraph of Amanda's maze is included in Figure 7.1.

| **Figure 7.1** | First Paragraph of Amanda's Maze Results (her responses in **bold**) |

Level: Grade 6–8   Passage Title: excerpt–County Fair Remembrance

Whenever I think of my family, (she, **I**, do) can't help but think of county (barns, shone, **fairs**). The smell of the barns and (families, simple, **livestock**) and every kind of fried food. (**The**, One, With) hawkers called to passers-by— "Just fifty (camps, **cents**, lives) a toss!" "Hey, buddy, win a (flip, four, **nice**) prize for your girl." And the (**candidates**, sympathy, happiness) shaking hands. Some nights, tractors or (why, **the**, an) demolition derby or stock cars roared. (The, **But**, Some) always, the gears of the tilt-a-whirl (over, **and**, sun) the excited children riding it squealed. (**Sometimes**, Anyone, Completed) there was sticky-sweet cotton candy.
    Second paragraph continues . . .

RESULTS FROM AMANDA'S ASSESSMENTS

Amanda initially read a ninth-grade IRI passage with only 90% decoding accuracy at a rate of approximately 100 words correctly per minute (wcpm), placing her somewhat below grade-level expectations. Therefore, Mr. Perkins continued the assessment by having Amanda read the eighth-grade IRI passage (e.g., Jamestown, Level H; Blachowicz, 2004). Amanda's comprehension scores on this eighth-grade IRI passage were as follows:

- Oral retell: 2/5 (rubric) score, minimum retell, random details
- Questions without passage: 4/10 (literal/explicit—3/5, inferential/implicit—1/5)
- Questions with passage (look back): same scores

Her low oral retell score suggested that she had difficulty understanding the passage as a whole. Rather than focusing on main ideas, she recalled only random details, and her comments did not reflect the passage organization. That is, Amanda did not follow a beginning, middle, and end format or use connecting terms in the text (e.g., first, second, if-then, because, etc.). Mr. Perkins's use of questions provided scaffolding for comprehension not present in an oral retell, and allowing her to look back in the text eliminated memory issues. In spite of these supports, Amanda did not show a strong understanding of the meaning of the passage as a whole. In addition, she did not use the text effectively to revise initial answers, suggesting that she overrelies on background knowledge or has some obstacle to rereading—perhaps because decoding was difficult, or she did not know how to skim for answers. The reading passage is shown in Figure 7.2, and examples of Amanda's answers are shown in Figure 7.3.

Mr. Perkins assessed Amanda's background knowledge using the following basic rubric: 3 = excellent background knowledge; 2 = good

Figure 7.2 Amanda's Comprehension Passage

Level: Grade 6–8   **Passage Title: County Fair Remembrance**

Whenever I think of my family, I can't help but think of county fairs. The smell of the barns and livestock and every kind of fried food. The hawkers calling to passers-by—"Just fifty cents a toss!" "Hey, buddy, win a nice prize for your girl." And the candidates shaking hands. Some nights, tractors or the demolition derby or stock cars roared. But always, the gears of the tilt-a-whirl and the excited children riding it squealed. Sometimes there was sticky-sweet cotton candy.

　　Even stickier was the summer heat. Always held in the dog days of summer, the fairs were the highlight of our year. My father raised horses that raced at the fairs from June to September. He trained and jockeyed the first one, Alphie himself. My mother sewed the silks. These shiny pieces of fabric were draped over the horse's withers during the races. My father had picked a navy blue square with five silver stars—one for each of his daughters.

　　One summer morning, long before sunrise, he loaded Alphie into the trailer and us into the back of the car for the long ride to the next county fair. He joked that he needed two horse trailers—one for the horses and one for "all these little girls!" I slept in the backseat with my sisters until we bumped into the entrance of the fairgrounds. Morning had come, and the sun was climbing higher into the sky. We tumbled out of the backseat into the damp grass ready for the excitement we knew would greet us. At the fair!

　　But everything was still. The fair itself appeared to be asleep. No one stirred or called. The rides were so quiet that I could hear the crickets and birds. Instead of bright lights, I saw rusty hinges, peeling paint, and cigarette butts scattered around the ticket-takers' booths. My mother handed us each a peanut butter sandwich and some water, "This will do for breakfast. Now you all stay out of your father's way." I watched and chewed and waited for the fair I loved to slowly come to life.

background knowledge; 1 = fair background knowledge with some inaccuracies; 0 = no background knowledge or inaccurate background knowledge. The questions and Amanda's oral responses are shown in Figure 7.3:

| **Figure 7.3** | Amanda's Responses to Comprehension Questions for County Fair Remembrance |

Prereading Questions and Responses (**in bold**)

1. What is a memoir or remembrance? **Something written to tell about a person's life.**
2. What is a county fair? **When there are rides and food and animals. It comes for like a week or so and then goes on to another town. It's a fun time to go and be with friends.**
3. What word would you use to describe how people feel at the fair? **Happy.**
4. What are silks? **Fabric, expensive fabric that is very shiny and pretty.**

Score: 12/12 possible Amanda appears to be familiar with the main ideas in the passage.

Postreading Questions and Responses (+ = correct; – = incorrect)

Question *type* (accepted responses)	Amanda's response with no passage (Mr. Perkins's notes)	Amanda's response with passage available (Mr. Perkins's notes)
What is the selection/passage mainly about? *Implicit* (going to the fair at night and before it opened)	About the fair –	About the fair –
What did the author hear at the fair? *Explicit* (roar of tractors, stock cars, demolition derby, tilt-a-whirl, children squealing, hawkers calling)	The people screaming on the rides +	
What else did the author hear at the fair? *Explicit*	I don't remember –	I don't remember –
What did the horses wear during the race to identify them? *Implicit*	They had numbers –	Numbers –
Why did the children sleep on the way to the fair? *Implicit* (they had left home long before sunrise)	Because they were really tired from riding rides –	I don't know –
What two things made the author believe the fair was "asleep"? *Explicit* (no bright lights, no people or sounds, the rides were quiet or still)	There were no lights or noises from the rides +	

Question *type* (accepted responses)	Amanda's response with no passage (Mr. Perkins's notes)	Amanda's response with passage available (Mr. Perkins's notes)
What color/design did the father pick for his horses' silks? *Explicit* (navy blue with five silver stars)	Navy blue with five silver stars +	
What did her father mean that he needed two horse trailers? *Implicit* (there were five daughters—he needed a big trailer for all of his children)	He had so many horses to take to the fair –	(reading from passage) "He joked that he needed two horse trailers" –
What made the fair the highlight of the year for her family? *Explicit* (her father's horses racing)	Eating food and riding rides –	(reading from passage) "the fairs were the highlight of our year" –
Why do you think the author chose to write a remembrance of this time in her life? *Implicit* (because she enjoyed it, because it made her think about her family)	Because she loved her time at the fair +	

Amanda's score: (no passage) explicit 3/5, implicit 1/5; (with passage) same. Target score: > 8/10

Mr. Perkins noticed that Amanda did use the look back strategy with comprehension questions but did not realize that answers to inferential or implicit questions might not be present in the text. For these questions, she attempted to reread related sentences but failed to find a specific answer. Mr. Perkins also believed that Amanda focused so much on decoding that she could not think about the meaning of the text.

Mr. Perkins also analyzed Amanda's maze results. Because Amanda read an eighth-grade text, her maze score of 12 wrc (18 attempted/ 6 errors; < 67%) was compared to the average score of typical eighth graders, which was 20. Results indicated that she struggled with comprehension at the sentence level because she had difficulty selecting a word that made the maze sentences whole.

AMANDA'S INDIVIDUALIZED EDUCATION PROGRAM

Based on informal assessment, the team targeted reading comprehension as the focus of a continued intervention for Amanda. Her IEP is shown in Figure 7.4.

Figure 7.4 Amanda's IEP

Individualized Education Program

Name: Amanda   Grade: 9   Skill Area: Reading Comprehension

Present Level of Performance: Amanda indicated that she does not enjoy reading and seldom reads for pleasure, but she enjoys reading stories about animals and pets. She currently orally reads eighth-grade materials with 96% decoding accuracy. With these materials, she answered 3 of 5 literal questions and 1 of 5 inferential questions. She earned a "minimum" rubric retell score of 2 out of 5 and recalled random details. Amanda attempted 16 responses on a maze comprehension assessment and provided 12 correct responses.

Annual Goal: After silently or orally reading ninth-grade reading passages, Amanda will correctly verbally answer 4 of 5 literal questions and 3 of 5 inferential questions.

Objective 1: After silently reading a ninth-grade passage and given 10 multiple-choice comprehension questions, (5 literal and 5 inferential) Amanda will correctly verbally answer 8 out of 10 by the end of the first quarter.

Objective 2: After silently reading a ninth-grade passage, Amanda will verbally summarize the main idea, state at least two questions about the text, verbally clarify those two questions, and state one prediction by the end of the second quarter.

Objective 3: After silently reading a ninth-grade passage and being asked to provide an oral retell, Amanda will state a satisfactory retell and earn a rubric score of 4 by the end of the third quarter.

Objective 4: Given a maze assessment based on a ninth-grade text and 3 minutes for completion, Amanda will correctly restore 24 words (24 wrc) by the end of the fourth quarter.

SUMMARY

Students' current level of performance on comprehension tasks forms the basis for selecting and teaching reading strategies. Students who accurately and quickly decode grade-level text may spend so much attention at the word level that they fail to understand what they read. These "automatic word callers" often need assistance in comprehension tasks such as building and using background knowledge relevant to a passage, identifying main ideas, and using the organization of the passage to support comprehension. For Amanda, these strategies will foster improved understanding of narrative text in her high school classes.

CHAPTER APPLICATION ACTIVITIES

Apply your knowledge from the chapter by discussing or completing the following application questions or activities. Suggested answers are provided below.

1. In the spring of the academic year, several of Mr. Perkins's ninth graders with IEP goals in comprehension completed a maze assessment. All students read sixth-grade text with at least 95% accuracy (instructional level). The benchmark for the 50th percentile in sixth grade is 25 words restored correctly. Based on these results, did the students with each of the scores in the list below have satisfactory comprehension of sixth-grade text? Explain your answer.

   a. Raw score of 11 (lowest 10th percentile), attempted 26, < 50% accuracy

   b. Raw score of 14 (lowest 25th percentile), > 90% accuracy

   c. Raw score of 24 (50th percentile), attempted 50, < 50% accuracy

   d. Raw score of 32 (75th percentile), > 90% accuracy

   e. Raw score of 21 (below 50th percentile), attempted 50, < 50% accuracy

2. Mr. Perkins had his students read a sixth-grade passage silently. He then removed the passage and asked students to tell him "everything you read and learned" in the passage. All scored either a 1 or 2 out of 5 on Mr. Perkins's retell rubric. What are several accommodations he could make for the oral retell to make sure results accurately reflect students' understanding of the passage?

3. Find the expected end-of-year score for students in Question 1 who did not have satisfactory comprehension. Remember that typical growth on the maze is 0.4 words restored correctly (wrc) per week. A ceiling effect occurs around 40 wrc due to limits to reading rate. A typical academic year is 36 weeks; however, intervention may not occur during each week. We use 30 weeks as a reasonable estimate of the number of intervention weeks.

Suggested Responses

1. Students a and b both fall below the 25th percentile; therefore, they do not have satisfactory comprehension of sixth-grade text. Students c and e had scores close to the benchmark for sixth-grade text; however,

they had low accuracy on the maze. Further assessment is recommended to determine the source of this low accuracy. Student d had satisfactory comprehension.

2. Mr. Perkins can scaffold the readers' oral retell by (a) using general verbal prompts such as What else can you tell me? (b) using specific oral prompts or comprehension questions such as Who was the main character? (c) phrasing questions as yes/no or true/false statements, or (d) allowing students to look back in the passage to support memory. If Mr. Perkins believes students will do better with written than oral tasks, all of these supports can be used for a written retell.

3. 30 weeks x .4 wrc/week = 12 wrc increase over the academic year. For students working on accuracy, rate of growth may be somewhat lower.

   a. 11 + 12 = 23 wrc

   b. 14 + 12 = 26 wrc

   c. 24 + 12 = 36 wrc

   d. not applicable

   e. 21 + 12 = 33

SUPPLEMENTAL RESOURCES FOR CHAPTER 7

Atwell, N. (1998). *In the middle: New understandings about writing, reading, and learning* (2nd ed.). Portsmouth, NH: Heinemann.

Johns, J. (2011). *The basic reading inventory*. Chicago, IL: Harcourt.

Kennedy, J. (2011). *Administration and scoring of reading maze for use in general outcome measurement*. Retrieved from http://www.aimsweb.com/uploads/pdfs/MAZE6pp.pdf

Maze Passage Generator. (2011). http://www.interventioncentral.org/tools/maze-passage-generator

Reading Comprehension: Methods and Strategies

8

While this questioning [question-respond-evaluate] may help some students to develop a strategy for comprehending on their own, it does not teach those students who most need to learn how to comprehend. . . . When you give the reader more feedback than if the answer is correct or incorrect, when you explain why his answer is correct or incorrect, you are starting to *teach* comprehension.

(Shanker & Cockrum, 2009, p. 164)

CHAPTER OVERVIEW

This chapter describes Ms. Wendt's instructional approach and choice of strategies as she considered the rigorous comprehension demands in the curriculum and the weak comprehension skills of many students. Her array of instructional strategies include individual, small group, and large group venues, so students have opportunities to work alone, discuss their thinking processes with peers, and receive whole group modeling instruction from the teacher.

Specifically, after working with Mr. Perkins and reflecting on the challenges facing readers in their class, Ms. Wendt decided to teach a set of

(Continued)

(Continued)

comprehension strategies that students could use across texts. Because she knew comprehension involves activities students complete before, during, and after reading, she chose one strategy primarily focused at each point in the reading process. She believed that students would be more successful mastering and applying a small number of interrelated strategies.

FEATURED METHODS AND STRATEGIES

Chapter Strategies	Corresponding Common Core State Standards
ANCHOR Reciprocal Teaching Question-Answer-Relationships	Cite strong and thorough textual evidence to support analysis of what the text says explicitly as well as inferences drawn from the text. Determine a theme or central idea of a text and analyze in detail its development over the course of the text. Read and comprehend literature including stories, dramas, and poems at grade-level complexity with scaffolding as needed.

Source for standards: Common Core State Standards Initiative, 2012

BEFORE READING: ACTIVATING BACKGROUND KNOWLEDGE

Activating background knowledge assists students in making connections between critical parts of the author's message and their own lives and experiences. One research-based method of activating background knowledge is the ANCHOR strategy (Deshler & Schumaker, 2005).

The Anchor Strategy

Anchoring concepts are concepts from students' background knowledge that are established, familiar, and analogous to the new material that students will read. The mnemonic ANCHOR helps students and teachers remember the steps:

A—*Announce the new concept.*

N—*Name the known concept (the anchor).*

C—*Complete known information.*

H—*Highlight characteristics of the known concept.*

O—*Observe the new concept.*

R—*Reveal shared characteristics.*

Ms. Wendt introduced the ANCHOR strategy with *Romeo and Juliet.* She knew that the previous year drama students had performed *West Side Story,* and many of her students participated or attended the play.

To begin ANCHOR instruction, Ms. Wendt activated students' background knowledge. She showed them a know/want/learn (KWL) chart (Ogle, 1986) that they had used previously, explained that an ANCHOR chart would help them in similar ways, shared a rationale for learning and using ANCHOR, obtained students' agreement to learn and use the strategy, and agreed to teach them to the best of her ability.

Next, Ms. Wendt briefly explained the ANCHOR chart and modeled how to use each step in the chart contrasting the traditional story of *The Three Little Pigs* with *The True Story of the Three Little Pigs.* These stories were familiar to students, easy to read, and fun, and they provided an excellent context for focusing on strategy steps. She rehearsed the ANCHOR mnemonic and the meaning of the steps to support students' memorization.

In the next lesson, Ms. Wendt provided students with copies of the ANCHOR chart and modeled filling in some columns. She *announced* the new concept: the literary elements of *Romeo and Juliet,* and then she *named* the known concept: the play *West Side Story.* For this lesson, she focused only on the first two scenes, in which the main characters are introduced and have an initial meeting.

Ms. Wendt had already listed elements in the far left column of the chart that she wanted students to emphasize. The class brainstormed and *completed* prereading sections. She modeled by adding details about main characters in *West Side Story.* Students added information about the setting, how the characters met, and problems in the opening scenes. Ms. Wendt showed several 1- to 3-minute video clips from the high school musical to further enhance background knowledge and encourage discussion.

Ms. Wendt then read aloud the opening monologue from *Romeo and Juliet*. She paused and thought aloud about similarities between the two stories, adding these to the second column of the chart; *highlighting* elements common to both. Ms. Wendt cautioned students that although there were parallels between the two plays, they should also notice differences. Students then read the first scene of *Romeo and Juliet* in small groups.

During and after reading, students collaborated with Ms. Wendt to *observe* the new concept, completing the far right column. She modeled identifying one similarity (written in the center column) and one difference (written in the far right column). After the modeling, students added more detail to the chart and considered matches between the anchoring concept and what they read.

Finally, Ms. Wendt asked students to *reveal* their understanding of the new concept by independently writing a summary of the first scene in the Summary section at the bottom of the ANCHOR chart. She reminded students to use notes they made in the ANCHOR chart. She then assigned completion of the second scene as independent practice with the ANCHOR chart (see Figure 8.1).

Figure 8.1 Partially Completed ANCHOR Chart for *Romeo and Juliet* (Act I, Scenes 1 and 2)

Known Information *West Side Story*	Known Concept: *West Side Story*		New Concept: *Romeo and Juliet*
Two gangs that hate each other: the Jets and the Sharks	Characteristics	Characteristics Shared (similarities)	Characteristics of New Concept (differences)
There is a school dance and everyone comes.	Characters: Maria, Tony, Anita, Doc, Riff, Chino	Tony = Romeo Maria = Juliet Chino = Paris	
Girl (Maria) from one gang and boy (Tony) from the other fall in love at the dance.

Maria is supposed to marry Chino. | Setting: city, New York? in the 1960s; store where Tony works, bridal shop where Maria works, apartment and fire escape. | | |

Known Information *West Side Story*	Known Concept: *West Side Story*		New Concept: *Romeo and Juliet*
Friends and family (Anita, Riff, Bernardo) try to keep them apart, warn them about the trouble. The gangs have a fight, and two people are killed.	Problem 1: Maria is supposed to marry Chino, but she doesn't love him.	Both girls are supposed to marry someone their families picked for them.	
	Problem 2: The gangs don't get along and try to kill each other.		
	Problem 3: Maria and Tony fall in love but can't be together because of their cultures and the gangs.		Romeo and Juliet are from the same culture; their families just dislike one another.
Summary of assigned reading:			

Ms. Wendt continued to use ANCHOR charts for *Romeo and Juliet,* selecting anchoring concepts and literary elements to emphasize in each scene or act. She continued to anchor some scenes in *Romeo and Juliet* by showing short video clips of *West Side Story.* Ms. Wendt helped students memorize steps, encouraged partner, small group, and large group discussion to consider similarities and differences from multiple perspectives, and assigned written summaries at the end of each section.

In summary, the ANCHOR strategy teaches students to use background knowledge, make relevant connections, monitor understanding of new concepts during and after reading, self-question, and summarize.

DURING READING: RECIPROCAL TEACHING

After success with ANCHOR charts, Ms. Wendt wanted to support Amanda's strategy use *during* reading. She decided to teach students to monitor and self-question during reading. Ms. Wendt found several research-based multi-step comprehension strategies that secondary students can use during reading. As shown in Figure 8.2, these strategies contain comprehension monitoring and self-questioning steps.

Ms. Wendt selected reciprocal teaching (RT) which has wide research support for improving the reading comprehension of secondary students

Figure 8.2 Multistep Comprehension Strategies

Strategy	Authors	Steps

Reciprocal Teaching	Palincsar & Brown (1984)	Teacher reads aloud and models
		    Summarizing
		    Questioning
		    Clarifying
		    Predicting
		Teacher transfers control to students
		working in small groups

Collaborative Strategic Reading	Klingner & Vaughn (2002)	Preview the text
		    Say what I know
		    Predict
		Click and clunk (during reading)
		    Clicks (tell what makes sense)
		    Clunk (what doesn't make sense)
		Fix up strategies (reread, read on, word analysis)
		Get the gist (restate main idea and supporting details)
		Wrap up (self-question and answer)

TWA	Mason (2004)	Think before reading
		    State author's purpose
		    Tell what I know
		    Tell what I want to learn
		Think while reading
		    Adjust reading speed
		    Reread
		    Link knowledge
		Think after reading
		    Find main idea (highlight)
		    Summarize
		    Tell what I learned

RAP	Schumaker, Denton, & Deshler (1984)	Read the paragraph Ask yourself the main idea and details Paraphrase (put main ideas and details in your own words)
POSSE	Englert, Tarrant, Mariage, & Oxer (1994)	Predict Organize Search and summarize Evaluate (were predictions, etc. correct?)

Strategy	Authors	Steps
ASK IT!	Clark, Deshler, Schumaker, Allen, & Warner (1984)	Attend to clues during reading State questions (self-question) Keep predictions in mind Identify answers Talk about answers
DR-TA (Directed Reading Thinking Activity)	Stauffer (1969)	Teacher divides text into identifiable sections Preview text Predict for first section Read and think aloud Confirm/correct prediction Predict for next section Continue to end Summarize what I learned

with mild disabilities. RT, developed by Palincsar and Brown (1984), includes explicit instruction in four critical skills (or strategies) that good readers complete spontaneously:

Summarizing—identifying and paraphrasing main ideas, first in one paragraph and then across paragraphs

Questioning—posing questions about the passage such as questions about unclear parts, puzzling information, unknown vocabulary, et cetera

Clarifying—addressing confusing parts and attempting to answer questions just posed

Predicting—hypothesizing what may happen next

Before students can use RT, they must learn and have much practice with these four skills. Lessons typically last for 30 minutes daily for 20 days. Eventually, in groups of four, students take turns assuming the role of teacher as they lead discussions using the four reading skills.

Ms. Wendt used RT with her poetry unit because poems often mean different things to different people, and the complex figurative language, symbolism, and descriptive vocabulary provide a context for questioning and clarification. For daily RT sessions, Ms. Wendt arranged mixed ability groups to orally read poems. She chose poems that were divided into multiple sections (couplets or stanzas) which created natural breaks in the reading for group members to complete RT steps and then change readers.

Cue Cards

As shown in Figure 8.3, Ms. Wendt created various cue cards for students to use in their groups.

Figure 8.3 Two Reciprocal Teaching Cue Cards

Poem Title:	Reciprocal Teaching Strategy			
Poetry features	Summarize	Question	Clarify	Predict
Rhyme, alliteration				
Five senses				
Metaphors, similes				
Personification				
What this poem means to me:				

Passage:	Day 1	Day 2	Day 3	Day 4
Student names	Question	Question Clarify	Question Clarify Summarize	Question Clarify Summarize Predict
1.				
2.				
3.				
4.				

She explained that RT would help them understand and enjoy the poems. Ms. Wendt modeled use of RT and the cue card using the first stanza of *The Snake*, by Emily Dickinson:

A narrow fellow in the grass

Occasionally rides;

You may have met him, — did you not?

His notice sudden is.

Modeling Use of Cue Cards

Ms. Wendt modeled use of the cue cards as follows:

My goal is to understand this stanza. To do that, I will read the stanza, think about what I have read, clarify tough parts, and predict what will come next. [Ms. Wendt read aloud and *summarized* the first stanza of the poem].

This stanza tells us that the poem is about a thin snake slithering up in the grass and surprising someone. I know that because the title is *The Snake,* the snake is narrow, or thin, it is in the grass, and it does something suddenly. OK—I think I have done a good job summarizing the stanza by finding the main idea.

But I have a *question*: I am not sure I understand some of these terms like "occasionally rides." I need to think about this and ask myself, How can a snake ride? Well, *(clarifies)* maybe the snake is gliding on top of the grass like a car rides on the road. Also, *(questions)* that last line has an unusual word order. It says: "His notice sudden is." What could that mean? I'm not sure, but I'll think about what those words mean. *(clarifies)* Maybe his notice is sudden, like, you notice him suddenly, and it surprises you. I think that is a good clarification because it makes sense in the poem. I'll keep going.

Next, I *predict* that the poem will tell more about what snakes are like, maybe that snakes are frightening. I think the snake will be green because it is hidden in the grass.

In subsequent stanzas, Ms. Wendt either confirmed or rejected her prediction. She checked off steps on the cue card as she completed them. Finally, Ms. Wendt thought aloud to orally summarize what she understood from the entire poem by connecting the poem to figurative language *like a snake in the grass* referring to someone who suddenly betrays you.

Instructional Ideas

After she believed students understood each RT skill, Mrs. Wendt grouped students, so they could work collaboratively using RT cue cards and a new poem. After the group read each stanza, a different student took the teacher role to facilitate RT. Co-teachers moved from group to group providing assistance and correction.

When using RT, teachers can adjust the rate at which they introduce each individual skill/strategy and the amount of practice they provide before students independently participate in small groups. For example, some teachers have introduced each individual RT skill during a different lesson and used cue cards that each have a different RT skill. As students used these cards and took the leader role, they practiced just one RT skill before leadership passed to another student.

Teachers can scaffold student learning by controlling the text readability, coherence, and content. Students may successfully focus on all four strategy steps if they can decode approximately 95% of the words. The full text should contain only one or two new vocabulary terms or concepts that students can solve through questioning and clarification.

Teachers should examine the text to ensure sufficient context information is available to support students' questioning and clarification. If not, students may conclude that RT strategies are unhelpful in solving comprehension issues. Also, consider introducing students to self-questioning techniques including Question-Answer-Relationships prior to beginning RT. Self-questioning may assist students in asking a variety of questions that help them distinguish between important and incidental information.

AFTER READING: SUMMARIZATION AND MAIN IDEAS

As Ms. Wendt taught RT to her class, she realized that some students could not consistently summarize the main idea. Instead, they focused on incidental information and often missed the gist, or overarching message. Therefore, Ms. Wendt needed to teach strategies to identify the gist and main ideas that would help students summarize.

Ms. Wendt decided to teach a strategy recommended by Jitendra, Hoppes, & Yin (2000) who identified several types of main ideas that answer questions about *who, what, when, where, how,* and *why.* However, simply identifying *who* or *what* is insufficient as a main idea. The main idea also includes *actions* or *descriptions* of the person or thing. As Ms. Wendt planned her lessons on main ideas, she used a cue card, shown in Figure 8.4, which reminded students of possible main idea choices.

Figure 8.4 Cue card for Identifying Main Idea

The main idea is about . . .	Doing, thinking, happening, described (looks like, smells like, etc.)	My paraphrase
Who?		
What?		
When?		
Where?		
How?		
Why?		

Adapted from Jitendra et al. (2000).

She selected short stories by Edgar Allen Poe as the texts for strategy instruction. As Jitendra et al. (2000) suggested, Ms. Wendt began Lesson 1 by selecting three paragraphs with an *explicit* main idea that answered the question *Who?* or *What?* She then read one paragraph to the class and applied the rule: "Name the person (or thing) and tell the main thing the person did in *all* the sentences" (Jitendra et al., p. 130). Ms. Wendt modeled finding the main idea by thinking aloud to ask herself who or what the paragraph was mostly about. She identified that the main idea in Paragraph 1 was *who* but then noted that this was not enough to be the main idea—*What is the character doing or thinking in this paragraph? Is this a description of the character?* Ms. Wendt clarified that the main idea includes actions or relationships between or among persons or things. Consequently, students learned to ask themselves not only *who* and *what* but also what *actions, relationships,* or *problems* are explained in a piece of writing. She concluded by paraphrasing her main idea and thinking aloud about whether most sentences in the paragraph related to this main idea.

In this lesson, students completed guided practice with the other two paragraphs, collaborating to find and summarize main ideas. Ms. Wendt later introduced more complex passages in which

- the main idea was the action(s) of multiple people (groups) or things.
- there were several options for the main idea.
- the main idea was implicit (no explicit identifiable main idea in the text).

These complicating features required students to critically evaluate choices for the main idea. This was completed in small groups, so students could discuss and refine ideas. Because main ideas are not always persons and their actions, Ms. Wendt also provided instruction on generating main ideas for passages "describing where, why, and when something occurred and how something looked or was done" (Jitendra et al. p. 131). Descriptions of the settings of stories provided good context for *when* and *where* main idea statements.

AFTER READING: ANSWERING COMPREHENSION QUESTIONS

Summarization, or telling what was learned, is one important after-reading strategy. Summarization assists students in solidifying comprehension, tying sections of text together, and revising previous understandings. Researchers indicate that directly teaching summarization improves the comprehension of students with mild disabilities.

Question-Answer-Relationships (QAR)

After reading, self-questioning helps students consolidate their comprehension of passages. Students with disabilities often focus on the literal meaning of the text; consequently, they have difficulty answering the range of comprehension questions asked by teachers or included on comprehension tests. Raphael and Au (2005) provided perhaps the best known analysis of question types.

These authors noted that all question types appear on standardized tests; therefore, students need experience asking and responding to each type. Ms. Wendt used QAR to explicitly teach students how to identify the question type and use different sources of information to answer each type.

Raphael and Au divided QAR into "In the Book" and "In my Head" questions. In the Book questions have an explicit answer in the text, either in a specific sentence ("Right There") or derived by combining information across two or more sections of text ("Think and Search"). In the Book questions ask

- *Who*
- *What*
- *Where*
- *When*
- *How*

and answers include names of persons, concrete and abstract nouns, places, dates, and procedural steps, respectively.

In contrast, answers to In my Head questions are not in the text and require readers to use their personal knowledge and experiences ("On my Own") or synthesize what they understand from the text with this knowledge ("Author and Me"). The source of information needed to answer questions differs for each type of question. During QAR instruction, Ms. Wendt explicitly named the question type and the source of information to answer the question, and she modeled how to answer the question.

Specifically, she modeled how to mark key terms with highlighters or highlighter tape. She then modeled how to scan a section of text to locate the target word and thought aloud as she read around the word to find the answer. She restated the question in her answer using the information she located and wrote the page and paragraph numbers next to her answer, which helped students determine whether their answer made sense.

With Think and Search questions, Ms. Wendt first thought aloud about the question and how it differed from a Right There question. Usually, these differ in that the Think and Search questions require several answers (e.g., What factors made Romeo and Juliet decide to run away?) found in different sections of text. Ms. Wendt then modeled the process for analyzing the question and skimming for target words, scanning several sections of text, and highlighting. She also thought aloud about signal words that helped her answer Think and Search questions (e.g., *first, second, third, if/then,* etc.).

For In my Head questions, Ms. Wendt similarly modeled how to select the key or target terms from the question and think aloud about what the question asks. For example, she asked the In my Head question, "How do you think the story would have been different if Romeo and Juliet had told their parents they were in love after they first met?" She thought aloud about the fact that the answer is not in the book and that she needed a different strategy for answering. Ms. Wendt continued to think aloud about similar situations from her background and encouraged her students to do so as well. She emphasized that the key component for this In my Head question was the students' personal connection between the text and their own knowledge of how parents react when children break a family rule or rebel against family beliefs.

Ms. Wendt modeled this connection between her background and what she knew about the families from the text.

Raphael and Au recommended that teachers provide explicit instruction in each type of question that includes naming the type of question, stating whether the answer is explicitly found in the text, and providing text support for the response. QAR can be used with other strategies (see Reciprocal Teaching) to enhance students' skills in responding to questions.

TIME SAVERS

Reading comprehension strategies are useful in all subjects. Teachers can be more efficient if they communicate with each other regarding which comprehension skills or strategies they will teach and if they share instructional responsibilities. Teachers on grade-level teams, for example, can decide which few comprehension strategies will be introduced or reinforced across all subjects in a given year or semester and who will be responsible for initial strategy instruction. As with other strategies, having examples prepared, scripting the model/think-aloud ahead of time, and having charts ready and prepared for students in ways that reduce unnecessary student copying of answers are time savers.

SUMMARY

Many secondary students need systematic, explicit instruction in strategies that good readers routinely and automatically use. Without this instruction, they will not comprehend what they read or experience the assigned reading as relevant, interesting, or important. Comprehension instruction needs to occur before, during, and after reading, and supports such as cue cards and peers foster success for struggling readers. ANCHOR charts, RT, main idea identification, and QAR are evidence-based practices that improve the comprehension skills of secondary students with mild disabilities.

CHAPTER APPLICATION ACTIVITIES

Apply your knowledge from the chapter by discussing or completing the following application questions or activities. Suggested answers are provided below.

1. Ms. Wendt used the ANCHOR strategy to prepare her students to read novels, poems, and short stories. For the following examples, what step of the ANCHOR strategy was Ms. Wendt using?

a. Ms. Wendt took familiar nursery rhymes like *Mary had a little lamb* and substituted words with related meanings (went = strolled, dashed, wandered, zipped; white = pale, colorless; snow = cotton, ivory, clouds). She then led a discussion of how the word choices changed the *tone* of the nursery rhyme.

b. After the illustration in item a, students read poems by Poe, Dickinson, and Shelley to identify words that set the poems' *tone*.

c. Ms. Wendt told her students that they were going to learn an author technique similar to *prediction* (a known concept). She had them brainstorm what they already knew about predicting when reading.

d. After the illustration in item c, Ms. Wendt wrote *foreshadowing* on the board and briefly defined it with an example.

e. Ms. Wendt had students make and throw paper airplanes from a fixed point in the class and mark where each landed. Students wrote how this illustrated the difficulties of locating a plane lost at sea.

f. Ms. Wendt had students read a short story about the search for a plane lost in the Pacific Ocean. They used a graphic organizer to compare their paper airplane experiment to the search for the plane.

g. After reading and taking notes in item f, students wrote a summary of the short story.

2. Label the questions below as Right There, Think and Search, Author and Me, or On my Own.

a. What lesson do you think the author was trying to teach by telling this story?

b. In what ways are asteroids and moons the same? Different?

c. Which character in the story would you most like to have as a friend? Explain.

d. Based on the front cover and title, what do you think will happen in the story?

e. When was the Declaration of Independence signed?

f. Who was the most important person in the American Revolution?

3. Why is it important that students be able to identify main ideas?

Suggested Responses

1. a. Highlight, b. Observe, c. Announce, d. Name, e. Highlight, f. Observe, g. Reveal

2. a. Author and Me, b. Think and Search, c. On my Own, d. On my Own, e. Right There, f. Think and Search and On my Own

3. Main ideas provide a structure for organizing information and remembering details. Like a key ring keeps keys together, main ideas hold a story together by helping to create coherence and support written and oral retelling of the passage information. Without main ideas, details have no connecting concept and overall comprehension suffers.

SUPPLEMENTAL RESOURCES FOR CHAPTER 8

Bremer, C., Vaughn, S., Clapper, A., & Kim, A. (2002). Collaborative strategic reading (CSR): Improving secondary students' reading comprehension skills. *Research to Practice Brief, (1)2*. Retrieved from http://www.ncset.org/publications/viewdesc.asp?id=424

Jones, R. (2009). *Making sense in social studies*. Retrieved from http://www.readingquest.org/home.html

Reading strategies to help high school students and middle school students understand their textbooks. (2011). Educational Research Newsletters & Webinars. Retrieved from http://www.ernweb.com/public/1056.cfm

San Juan Unified School District. (2011). *QAR: Take questioning across Bloom's taxonomy*. Retrieved from http://www.sanjuan.edu/webpages/gguthrie/resources.cfm?subpage=124122

The Literacy Web. (2007). Retrieved from http://www.literacy.uconn.edu/index.htm

Comprehension Curriculum and Teaching Resources

Accelerated Reader. (1986). Wisconsin Rapids, WI: Renaissance Learning.

All about adolescent literacy: Classroom strategies. (2012). Washington DC: Washington Education Television Association. Retrieved from http://www.adlit.org/strategy_library/

Corrective reading. https://www.mheonline.com/programMHID/view/0076181804

Herczog, M. M., & Porter, P. (2010). *Strategies for struggling readers: A teacher resource guide*. Washington DC: U.S. Department of Education, Center for Civic Education.

Read 180. (2005). New York: Scholastic.

Written Language: Informal Assessments 9

Written expression is a fundamental skill for today's high school students. Those who lack the ability to adequately demonstrate conceptual knowledge and communicate their thoughts and beliefs in writing are at a grave disadvantage.

(Chalk, Hagan-Burke, & Burke, 2005, p. 85)

MEET VIOLETTE

Violette is an eighth grader who hates to write. She has good ideas, wide background knowledge, and legible writing, and she applies basic capitalization and punctuation rules, but the task of putting words on paper is almost torture. Therefore, Violette avoids writing as much as possible. She even analyzes writing demands on study guides and other class assignments before even attempting them.

Violette enlists the help of friends, parents, and her special education teacher, who write her dictated responses for reports and essays, but this accommodation does not help her improve her writing skills. Her resource teacher, Mr. Fielder, believes that Violette can become an effective writer with carefully chosen strategies for writing instruction.

CHAPTER OVERVIEW

This chapter provides an introduction to teaching written language. The chapter emphasizes why writing is difficult for many students and discusses informal writing assessments for secondary students. Finally, the chapter shows how Mr. Fielder linked Violette's writing assessments to her IEP.

WRITTEN LANGUAGE

Many experts maintain that written language is the most complex form of language. Writing requires students to use correct capitalization, punctuation, and spelling; apply the correct amount of physical force when writing or typing; and produce a legible document—skills not required during verbal interactions. Skilled writers generate ideas, organize and elaborate on their ideas, choose words to convey their content, consider the needs of their audience, constantly monitor their writing and what they plan to write, and monitor their physical writing and mechanics. Students with disabilities can have difficulties in any of these skills.

Writing is an important part of our everyday life, from writing texts and e-mails to generating resumes and cover letters to writing editorials and business letters. Although the Internet has added more informality to writing tasks, teachers are still accountable for teaching students how to write in a wide range of writing genres such as stories, reports, essays, and themes. Secondary teachers can infuse student writing into all subjects through writing journals, responses to specific prompts, or reflections on what they learned in class or what they read.

Writing is a process. Experts note different steps in this process, but according to Scott and Vitale (2003) the process generally includes: (a) *planning* (providing students with rich experiences, collecting information through brainstorming, reading further on the topic, taking notes, organizing information into an outline or graphic organizer), (b) *drafting* (developing thoughts and ideas into meaningful words, sentences, and paragraphs without concern for grammar and mechanics), (c) *revising* (receiving feedback; adding, deleting, and moving text), (d) *editing* (addressing spelling, mechanics, and grammar; peer editing; self-editing), and (e) *publishing* (sharing the final draft with others through an anthology, website, bulletin board, gifts, etc.).

INFORMAL ASSESSMENTS

Teachers can begin the term or semester by having students complete writing tasks to assess existing skills. Spending several days assessing student writing helps pinpoint student strengths and needs.

One method of informally assessing student writing skills is to administer three versions of a standard writing task, which means the student completes the same type of writing activity, under the same time limits, and without assistance. Three samples provide the greatest reliability for baseline data. Mr. Fielder wanted to assess Violette's skills with writing an opinion essay, which was the writing outcome required on the district writing exam. Therefore, Mr. Fielder provided Violette class time on three separate occasions to write each essay. She could take as much time as she needed. Mr. Fielder and Violette brainstormed several writing topics. For each essay, Mr. Fielder instructed Violette to plan her essay, include all the components of a good essay, and write as much as she could (Jacobson & Reid, 2010).

Mr. Fielder collected and analyzed all three essays. Based on district outcomes and the strategy he planned to teach, Mr. Fielder was especially interested in these components:

- Topic sentence
- Reasons that support an opinion
- Examples that support each reason
- Ending/conclusion
- Variety of sentence types
- Use of transition words
- Mechanics (spelling, capitalization, punctuation, grammar)

Teachers can use checklists, rubrics, rating scales, or score sheets to summarize data. Mr. Fielder used the basic checklist in Figure 9.1.

With other writing samples, Mr. Fielder might be more interested in calculating (from three samples) the median (or mean) (a) total number of words, (b) total number or percentage of words correctly spelled, (c) average number of words per sentence, (d) average number of sentences in the passage, or (e) number and percentage of mature words based on all three writing samples. Teachers can also calculate the number of writing units in correct sequence and correct letter sequences for words. Mather, Wendling, and Roberts (2009) explained these and other components to assess in *Writing Assessment and Instruction for Students With Learning Disabilities.*

Combining product with process information provides a fuller understanding of students as writers and helps with planning interventions (Gunning, 2010). Therefore, while she was writing, Mr. Fielder observed Violette to note whether she used prewriting strategies to help her plan her writing, whether she consulted any available references, and how much time she devoted to the writing process. He asked Violette how she feels about writing, writing activities she completes in and out of school, what she likes and dislikes about writing, her strengths and challenges in writing, and how teachers could help her more in writing (Gunning, 2010).

Finally, Mr. Fielder reviewed permanent products such as Violette's weekly spelling tests, daily written work, and writing portfolio and journal

Figure 9.1 Violette's Opinion Essay Checklist

Component	Essay 1	Essay 2	Essay 3	Number of essays that met criteria
Did essay begin with a topic sentence that stated a position/ opinion?	No	✓	✓	2/3
Did essay include at least three reasons?	Two reasons	Two reasons	Two reasons	0/3
Did each reason have at least one example?	No	No	No	0/3
Did essay conclude with ending statement?	✓	✓	No	2/3
Did essay include a combination of simple, compound, complex, and/or compound/complex sentences?	Five simple	✓ Three simple and three compound	Six simple	1/3
Did essay use transition words?	None	None	None	0/3
Did essay have three or fewer spelling, capitalization, punctuation, or grammar errors?	Four (Two spelling, one punctuation, one grammar)	Six (Three spelling, two capitalization, one punctuation)	Four (Two spelling, one punctuation, one grammar)	0/3
Other notes (overall length)	Five sentences	Six sentences	Six sentences	Five to six sentences

entries. Using such products, teachers can categorize spelling errors into phonic elements such as consonants, initial digraphs, initial consonant blends, initial digraph blends, final consonant blends, final digraphs and trigraphs, final diagraph blends, short vowels in closed syllables, long vowels in open syllables, long vowels in silent *e* syllables, *r* controlled syllables, vowel digraphs, vowel diphthongs, common prefixes, and common suffixes (Mather et al., 2009). Also, IEP or grade-level teams can review written work for completion, neatness, reoccurring errors, organization, or other elements. In addition, Violette's self-assessments, writing goals, and reflections should be considered when developing her IEP.

VIOLETTE'S INDIVIDUALIZED EDUCATION PROGRAM

Information from these informal assessments helped the IEP team craft Violette's writing goals and objectives. Violette's IEP is noted in Figure 9.2.

Figure 9.2 Violette's IEP

Individualized Education Program

Name: Violette   Grade: 8   Skill Area: Written Language

Present Level of Performance: Violette currently writes opinion essays containing five or six sentences with two reasons, no examples or only one, no transition words, and five capitalization, punctuation, spelling, or grammar errors. Over 80% of her sentences are simple sentences. She does not use any prewriting planning strategies or classroom resources. She indicates that she forgets her ideas once she begins writing, so she stops. She maintains 80% accuracy on weekly spelling tests. Her handwriting is legible.

Annual Goal: Violette will write an opinion essay containing at least eight sentences (topic sentence, three supporting reasons, an example for each reason, a concluding statement), at least four transition words, and three or fewer capitalization, punctuation, spelling, or grammar errors.

Objective 1: By the end of the first quarter, upon teacher request, Violette will write simple, compound, and complex sentences containing at least eight words with correct punctuation (commas, semicolons, periods).

Objective 2: By the end of the first quarter, when given a template of an opinion essay with five to eight missing transition words, Violette will write an appropriate transition word for each blank.

Objective 3: By the end of the third quarter, when provided with a paragraph at her independent reading level containing 10 capitalization, punctuation, spelling, and grammar errors, Violette will cross out errors and write in corrections with at least 90% accuracy.

Objective 4: By the end of the school year, when given a graphic organizer for an opinion essay and a topic, Violette will write a topic sentence that indicates a position, three reasons for the position, an example for each reason, and an ending and score at least 20 of 25 points on a writing rubric.

SUMMARY

For a variety of reasons, written language is difficult for students with disabilities. Informal assessments typically involve gathering three standard writing samples to determine baseline data. Observations and student interviews often glean additional valuable information about how the students feel about writing and their approach to writing tasks. Reviewing permanent products, such as writing portfolio entries, weekly spelling tests, homework assignments requiring writing, and essays often reveals patterns and skill areas to target for intensive instruction.

CHAPTER APPLICATION ACTIVITIES

Apply your knowledge from the chapter by discussing or completing the following application questions or activities. Suggested answers are provided below.

1. Assume that on three separate occasions, you provided Suzanne time to write a good paragraph. On those writing samples, respectively, she wrote 40, 42, and 46 words; spelled words with 90%, 95%, and 92% accuracy; wrote (on average) 5, 6, and 7 words per sentence per paragraph; wrote 2, 3, and 3 mature words; and wrote only simple sentences in all paragraphs. Using the median scores from these data, write a present level of performance for Suzanne.

2. Beyond the questions suggested in the chapter, what are some additional questions you could ask a student (who is a reluctant writer) as part of the writing assessment process?

3. What are some prewriting strategies you might hope to see students use in their writing process?

Suggested Responses

Responses will vary, but here are some suggested ideas:

1. Suzanne currently writes paragraphs containing about 42 words, with six words per sentence and three mature words per paragraph. She spells 92% of the words accurately. She writes only simple sentences.

2. What are some topics you would like to write about? What technologies have you used—or would you like to use—with your writing? How can teachers make writing more enjoyable for you?

3. Students might use some of these prewriting strategies: brainstorming, webbing/mapping, outlining, sketching, talking with a peer, or checking reference materials.

SUPPLEMENTAL RESOURCES FOR CHAPTER 9

Fisher, D., & Frey, N. (2004). *Improving adolescent literacy.* Upper Saddle River, NJ: Pearson–Prentice Hall.

Graham, S. (2006). Strategy instruction and the teaching of writing: A meta-analysis. In C. MacArthur, S. Graham, & J. Fitzgerald (Eds.), *Handbook of writing research* (pp. 187–207). New York, NY: Guilford.

Graham, S., & Harris, K. R. (2003). Students with learning disabilities and the process of writing: A meta-analysis of SRSD studies. In L. Swanson, K. R. Harris, & S. Graham (Eds.), *Handbook of learning disabilities* (pp. 383–402). New York, NY: Guilford.

Graham, S., & Perin, D. (2007). A meta-analysis of writing instruction for adolescent students. *Journal of Educational Psychology, 99,* 445–476.

Green, S. K., Smith, J., & Brown, E. K. (2007). Using quick writes as a classroom assessment tool: Prospects and problems. *Journal of Educational Research, 7,* 38–52.

Mason, L., Kubina, R., Valasa, L., & Cramer, A. M. (2010). Evaluating effective writing instruction for adolescent students in an emotional and behavior supports setting. *Behavioral Disorders, 35*(2), 140–156.

Mercer, C., Mercer, A., & Pullen, P. (2011). *Teaching students with learning problems.* Upper Saddle River, NJ: Pearson.

Written 10 Language: Methods and Strategies

Writing strategy instruction that uses the self-regulated strategy development (SRSD) model is a powerful instructional tool.

(Graham & Harris, 2003)

CHAPTER OVERVIEW

Results from Violette's informal writing assessments helped Mr. Fielder and IEP team members identify skills for intensive instruction. First, Mr. Fielder decided to teach Violette three writing preskills—various sentence types, transition words, and editing. He also decided to later teach Violette the POW + TREE writing strategy. Because POW provides a structure that students can use for various types of writing assignments, and TREE helps students organize expository writing, Violette can use this strategy for many writing tasks.

This chapter describes how Mr. Fielder and Violette worked collaboratively to identify writing goals and target specific skills for improvement. The chapter notes critical preskills that Violette needed to review, includes a think-aloud for the POW + TREE strategy, and includes Violette's individualized checklists, graphic organizers, and cue cards.

FEATURED METHODS AND STRATEGIES

Chapter Strategies	Corresponding Common Core State Standards
Sentence Types Transition Words	Produce clear and coherent writing in which the development, organization, and style are appropriate to the task, purpose, and audience.
COPS, SCOPE	With some guidance and support . . . develop and strengthen writing as needed by planning, revising, editing, and rewriting.
POW + TREE	Write arguments to support claims with clear reasons and relevant evidence.

Source for standards: Common Core State Standards Initiative, 2012

SENTENCE TYPES

Because Violette's pretests indicated that she wrote mostly simple sentences with one subject and one verb (i.e., Selah moved to Oregon), Mr. Fielder reviewed simple, compound, complex, and compound/complex sentence types. On the first day, he reviewed and provided activities with subjects and verbs. Reviewing subjects and verbs continued as a daily routine on the Smart Board even as various new sentence patterns were introduced. Similarly, by the third day, Mr. Fielder contrasted complete sentences (those that contain at least one subject and one verb) with sentence fragments. These were also frequently reviewed as part of the daily warm-up writing activity.

After reviewing these preskills, Mr. Fielder introduced simple, compound, and complex sentences in that sequence over the course of several weeks. He chose this sequence because each sentence type builds on the previous one. For each sentence type, Mr. Fielder named the type of sentence, indicated what that type of sentence included, provided examples and non-examples of that sentence type, and provided activities for Violette to identify and write that sentence type. The sentence types included the following:

- *Simple*—sentences with an independent clause (subject and a verb) that express a complete thought. The sentence writing strategy (Schumaker & Sheldon, 1985), from the University of Kansas Center for Research on Learning (KU-CRL), includes these patterns:
  o S-V such as: Myrna drove to her exercise class.
  o S-S-V such as: Fern and Frank ate hot dogs.

- ○ S-V-V such as: The musicians sang and danced all night.
- ○ S-S-V-V such as: Dawn and Rachel ate lunch and walked around their neighborhood.

- *Compound*—sentences with two or more independent clauses (each of which could be a sentence on its own) joined with a coordinating conjunction. The conjunctions include *for, and, nor, but, or, yet,* and *so.* (Use the mnemonic FANBOYS to remember them). Except in very short sentences, coordinating conjunctions are preceded by a comma as is shown in the following example: Walt drove to Des Moines, and Joel fished at Lake McBride. A different kind of compound sentence uses two independent clauses, no conjunction, and a semicolon; an example is this: Walt drove to Des Moines; Joel fished at Lake McBride.
- *Complex*—sentences with one independent clause joined by one or more dependent clauses. A complex sentence always has a subordinating conjunction such as *because, since, after, although,* or *when* or a relative pronoun such as *that, who,* or *which.* When a complex sentence begins with a subordinating conjunction, place a comma at the end of the dependent clause. (Example: Because she studied, Violette earned an A on her test.) When the sentence begins with an independent clause and the subordinating conjunction is in the middle, do not include a comma. (Example: Violette earned an A on her test because she studied).
- *Compound/Complex*—sentences that include various variations of compound and complex sentences using punctuation rules specific to the clause.

To help Violette remember to use a variety of sentence types, Mr. Fielder taught this fun mnemonic:

Simple, compound, complex

All these I should use.

They will help my writing

And my grades improve!

TRANSITION WORDS

Before teaching the POW + TREE writing strategy, Mr. Fielder introduced Violette to transition words. Violette did not use any transition words in her initial essays, so Mr. Fielder read short essays to Violette with and without transition words to illustrate how they connect ideas and maintain flow. Mr. Fielder made cue cards (see Figure 10.1) to remind Violette of transitions for the opinion essays that she would soon be writing.

He indicated that when she writes her opinion essay, she must use a transition word to introduce each new reason (card 1) and the ending (card 3). He strongly suggested she use transition words to also introduce at least some (but not necessarily all) examples (card 2). As a frequent

Figure 10.1 Cue Cards for Transition Words

Transition Words: Reasons
    First
    Second
    Third
    Another
    In addition
    The most important
    Next
    Finally
    Lastly

(1)

Transition Words: Examples
    For example
    For instance
    To illustrate
    Specifically

(2)

Transition Words: Ending
    In conclusion/ To conclude
    In summary/ To sum up
    In brief
    In closing
    For these reasons
    Thus, we can see

(3)

practice activity using the Smart Board, Mr. Fielder provided Violette with a short essay paragraph containing no transitions. He used a modified cloze technique by placing a blank (_____) where Violette inserted a transition word or phrase from her cue card, as shown in this example for a "reasons" paragraph:

> There are three reasons why I need an allowance. _____, I need money for clothes. _____, I want to save money for summer camp. _____, I would like my own spending money to do fun things.

This activity helped Violette become more skilled at choosing a transition word from her cue card. Also, reading short persuasive essay paragraphs helped Violette become more aware of this writing structure genre.

PROOFREADING USING COPS AND SCOPE

Violette's preassessments also indicated that she made several editing errors. Two well-known editing strategies include (1) the error monitoring strategy known as COPS (Schumaker, Nolan, & Deshler, 1985) and (2) SCOPE (Vaughn & Bos, 2009). As shown in Figure 10.2, the two strategies share similar elements.

Mr. Fielder chose to teach COPS because Violette did not make syntax or expression errors as noted in SCOPE. He presented essays with

Figure 10.2 COPS and SCOPE

COPS	
Step	**Question**
C	Have I capitalized the first word and proper nouns?
O	Have I made any handwriting, margin, messy, or spacing errors?
P	Have I used end punctuation, commas, and semicolons correctly?
S	Do the words look like they are spelled right? Can I sound them out, or should I use a dictionary?

SCOPE	
Step	**Question**
S	Is the spelling correct?
C	Are first words in sentences and proper nouns capitalized?
O	Is the syntax or word order correct?
P	Are there punctuation marks where needed?
E	Does the sentence express a complete thought? Does the sentence contain a noun and a verb?

numerous mechanical and appearance errors to emphasize the importance of first impressions and correct editing. He reviewed basic capitalization and punctuation rules and reminded Violette to check her spelling by asking someone and using classroom and online resources, which he modeled. Then he modeled COPS using a think-aloud by orally reading short paragraphs with numerous errors. For each COPS step, he started at the beginning of the essay and edited only for that particular skill. He and Violette practiced COPS with additional paragraphs, and Mr. Fielder provided additional proofreading exercises for Violette for independent practice.

Mr. Fielder knew that reviewing these critical writing preskills was important before teaching the actual writing strategy. Therefore, he and Violette spent several weeks on each preskill before applying those skills to the POW + TREE strategy.

POW + TREE

Mr. Fielder decided to teach Violette the POW + TREE writing strategy because (1) it is an age-appropriate writing strategy, (2) it connects to common core state standards, (3) students in Violette's school are being assessed on their persuasive writing skills, and (4) it teaches thinking skills as well as writing skills.

As shown below, POW frames the entire writing process, and TREE helps students organize essential writing components.

P—*Pick an idea.* Sometimes the teacher provides a topic, but other times, students have a choice. Remind students to write about a topic they know and care about.

O—*Organize notes.* Have students use a graphic organizer to organize their thoughts before they write. The graphic organizer should include these reminders:

T *refers to Topic sentence:* In one sentence, tell what you believe.

R *refers to Reasons:* Include at least three convincing reasons for your position.

E *refers to Examples:* Provide a specific example for each reason.

E *refers to Ending:* Conclude the paragraph and restate your opinion.

W—*Write and say more.* Write the paragraph and then go back and add more details or examples.

As Mr. Fielder taught the strategy, he followed these self-regulated strategy development (SRSD) instructional steps:

- *Stage 1: Develop background knowledge.* As previously mentioned, Mr. Fielder completed the informal assessments described in Chapter 9, analyzed Violette's writing strengths and needs, and taught her necessary preskills. After he taught these preskills, he and Violette discussed components of a good opinion essay (e.g., tells readers what you believe, provides at least three reasons, includes examples of the reasons, includes an ending sentence, and makes sense). Mr. Fielder introduced the TREE strategy (topic sentence, reasons, examples, ending), and together they read exemplar opinion essays and identified these parts.
- *Stage 2: Discuss it.* Mr. Fielder described the purpose, benefits, and strategy steps in greater detail. He indicated that the topic sentence needs to tell what you believe; it must make your opinion clear. The essay must include three or more reasons to support that position, and each reason must be supported with at least one example. Mr. Fielder presented the prompts: *Why do I believe this?* and *Will my readers believe this?* as questions to consider when providing examples (Reid & Lienemann, 2006). The ending signals the essay's end and repeats the opinion using slightly different words than the topic sentence. Violette and Mr. Fielder reviewed her three previous essays to determine what parts she included and omitted. The two reviewed differences between effective and ineffective writing such as word choice, sentence variety, and transition words. They also reviewed Violette's IEP goal for writing a quality opinion essay.
- *Stage 3: Model it.* Mr. Fielder modeled POW + TREE using a think-aloud that included self-questioning, self-monitoring, and self-reinforcing statements. His model is described in the following section.

Modeling POW + TREE

The assignment: Write an opinion essay on one of the following:

1. Should middle school students be allowed to have cell phones at school?

2. Is it better to attend a public school or be home schooled?

3. Should middle school students in public schools be required to wear uniforms?

In class today, Ms. Svoboda gave choices on topics for our opinion essay.

I remember that an opinion essay states what I believe, and I should pick a topic I know something about. The P in POW stands for pick an idea, so I will read over these three topics. Hmm . . . cell phones, OK—I know about those; homeschooling—no, not so much; and school uniforms—I have an opinion on that, too. I know I need to write three good reasons for my position, and I am not sure I know three reasons for or against school uniforms, but I think I can write three reasons for allowing students to have cell phones at school, so I will pick that one. OK, I have the first step done because I picked a familiar topic, and I can think of three reasons for my position.

What do I do next? O stands for organize notes. How do I organize my notes? I use a graphic organizer (see Figure 10.3) to

Figure 10.3 Graphic Organizer

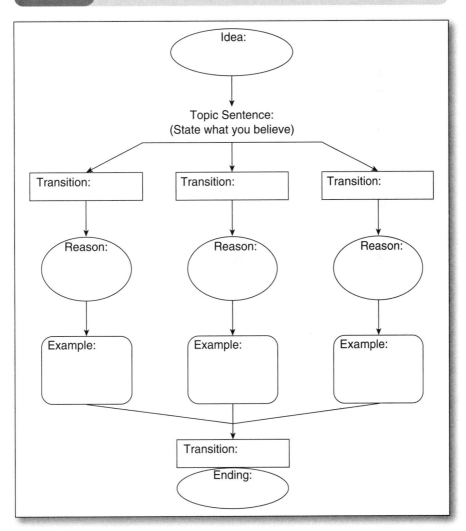

plan my essay, so I don't forget anything, and so I stay organized and on track.

In my graphic organizer, I will write "middle school students and cell phones" in the idea circle because that is the topic. Those words came directly from the prompt, so I know I have the correct idea to write about. Now, for the T step, how will I write my topic sentence? It needs to clearly state my opinion: what I believe. I believe students *should* be allowed to have their cell phones with them, so that is what I will write. That statement names the topic or topics (students and cell phones) and states my opinion (they can have them), so it is a good topic sentence.

Now I am ready for the R step—reasons. What do I do in this step? I think of and write three reasons why students should be allowed to have their cell phones at school. I also see on my graphic organizer that I need to indicate which transition word I will use to introduce each reason. I will think of my reasons first. I think students should be allowed to have cell phones with them because (1) there might be a family emergency, (2) the student might be in danger, and (3) cell phones are convenient. I will write those on my graphic organizer in the circles. I will use the words *first, next,* and *finally* from my cue card as transitions, so I will write those in these boxes on my graphic organizer, so I do not forget. OK—let me stop and think. Do I have three reasons and three different transitions? Yes. OK—I have marked those in my graphic organizer, and I believe I have done a good job so far, so I am ready for the E step, examples.

Now I need to tell more about the reasons with some examples. I ask myself: *Why do I believe this?* and *Will my readers believe this?* I want my examples to really support my reasons. The first reason for having a cell phone in school is that there might be a family or school emergency. What would be an example of this? Maybe someone was hurt or sick, someone was in a car accident, a storm hit the town, or there was a safety issue—all those are emergencies. Which one would my readers believe? I think I will pick the car accident. If a parent or family member was in a serious car accident, and that person was rushed to the hospital, everyone in the family should know right away. I'll write that in the graphic organizer. The next reason is the student might be in danger. Someone could be bullying her, wanting to fight her, she could be tempted to do something she knows is wrong, she could be sick or hurt, or maybe her school bus had an accident. Which should I pick? I like the example about peer pressure best because that has happened to me. If a student had a cell phone, she could get help immediately and avoid doing something she knows is wrong. The last reason is convenience. Sometimes students stay after school for activities, they do not have a ride home, and the school does not have any phones available. Having a cell phone keeps everyone connected and the lines of communication open in these situations. Wow—I came up with an example for every reason, so I am going to write those in the example circles on my graphic organizer, so I do not forget them. I think these are good examples because they have actually happened to me and my friends.

The next E in TREE is for ending. I need to use a transition word and conclude my essay. I will use "in summary" as the transition. I will close by writing that cell phones are especially helpful when there is an emergency, when students are in danger, or when students need a ride or have changed their regular plans.

The W helps me remember to write and say more. So now I will write out my essay. I think I can write more about students doing other things after school and their parents wondering where they are. I'll expand that example and tell more.

Mr. Fielder and Violette also discussed and used Violette's personalized checklist, shown in Figure 10. 4, based on her IEP goals, which she could use to guide her persuasive essay writing.

Figure 10.4 POW + TREE Checklist

Step	Check When Completed
1. If I have a choice for a topic, did I pick an idea that I know and care about?	
2. Did I use a graphic organizer to organize my notes?	
3. Does my topic sentence clearly tell what I believe?	
4. Did I include three good reasons?	
5. Did I include at least one example for each reason?	
6. Did I include an ending sentence?	
7. Did I include transition words to introduce each reason and to end the essay?	
8. Did I write and say more?	
9. Did I use simple, compound, and complex sentences?	
10. Did I proofread using COPS?	

Finalizing POW + TREE

After modeling, Mr. Fielder finished the SRSD instructional steps as follows:

- *Stage 4: Memorize it.* Violette memorized the POW+ TREE steps.
- *Stage 5: Support it.* Mr. Fielder decreased his support as Violette practiced writing several opinion essays. Initially, the two worked together, or Violette wrote with a partner. At times, Violette used a cue card, checked her work against an exemplar, or asked for help when she needed more reasons or more examples.
- *Stage 6: Independent use.* Eventually, Violette wrote her essay independently.

THEME WRITING

The POW + TREE strategy can be used with minimal modifications to teach other writing structures such as descriptive, comparison/contrast, or persuasive essays, but students also write longer compositions, or themes. Teaching students that paragraphs have a topic or main idea sentence, reasons or lead-off sentences, examples or follow-up sentences, and a concluding sentence helps prepare them for writing longer papers.

The theme writing strategy (Schumaker, 2003) uses such a structure with the support of graphic organizers to teach students how to write a five-paragraph theme. This KU-CRL strategy teaches numerous interesting ways to introduce a topic and catch a reader's attention in the introductory paragraph by providing a definition, describing a scene, using a quotation, posing a question or problem, et cetera. Students are taught that the middle three paragraphs should each begin with a topic sentence, followed by a series of lead-off and follow-up sentences until the summary sentence. Students also learn interesting ways to write the concluding paragraph by offering a summary, suggestions, a moral, opinions, or cautions or using a combination of these methods.

To support other students on his caseload as they wrote similar five-paragraph themes and based on the district's writing process, Mr. Fielder developed the theme-writing cue cards shown in Figure 10.5.

He used the SRSD approach to teach theme writing to these students just as he did to help Violette learn opinion essays.

Figure 10.5 Cue Cards for Five Paragraph Theme

Introductory Paragraph

- Use an attention grabber or general statement.
- Include thesis/topic sentence that explains purpose or opinion.
- Introduce three main points about the topic.

Second Paragraph (Body)

- Restate first main point.
- Write three sentences that support it.
- Conclude by finishing main thought of paragraph.

Third Paragraph (Body)

- Restate second main point.
- Write three sentences that support it.
- Conclude by finishing main thought of paragraph.

Fourth Paragraph (Body)

- Restate third main point.
- Write three sentences that support it.
- Conclude by finishing main thought of paragraph.

Concluding Paragraph

- Summarize essay.
- Use words similar to (but not exactly like) thesis/topic sentence.
- Write two to three sentences that support it.
- Tie together final thoughts.

Other Reminders

- Proofread using COPS.
- Use transition words.

TIME SAVERS

Writing is difficult for many students, and students need sufficient time to write. To save some time teaching some of the methods described in this chapter, teachers can be selective regarding which skills to emphasize with a student. For example, based on informal assessment results, Violette needed only a quick refresher on simple sentences, so her instruction would emphasize compound and complex sentences. Other students might need only extensive teacher modeling of certain steps of a strategy and reminders of other steps. If students had already received instruction on some of the components of POW + TREE, such as writing topic sentences or writing a good ending, teachers could reduce the amount of time devoted to those parts to pinpoint their instruction.

SUMMARY

Writing is very difficult for many students with disabilities. The good news is that numerous resources are available for teachers to promote evidence-based writing practices. Teachers can use the six-stage SRSD instructional process for teaching any type of writing genre. Teacher modeling is a critical component of effective writing instruction. Researchers have developed various strategies that make the writing process explicit for students. Most writing strategies use prewriting steps, graphic organizers, cue cards, and checklists to encourage students to plan, monitor, and evaluate their work.

CHAPTER APPLICATION ACTIVITIES

Apply your knowledge from the chapter by discussing or completing the following application questions or activities. Suggested answers are provided below.

1. Students with disabilities often include little variety in their sentence structure. Teaching various sentence types can add much needed variety in their writing. Assume you want to teach simple, compound, and complex sentences in your writing class. Reorder these sentences to reflect the instructional sequence noted in the chapter:

   A. Vicki moved to Georgia; Antonis moved to South Carolina.

   B. Greg likes to eat lasagna.

   C. Because he prepared for his solo, Joe sang perfectly.

   D. Erika and Sheldon watched the fireworks and ate pizza.

2. Assume you have taught the COPS strategy, and you want to provide a practice sheet for students to apply the strategy. Write a short paragraph that contains several capitalization, overall appearance, punctuation, and spelling errors for students to edit.

3. One step in the POW + TREE strategy is to write a "convincing" reason for your position. Students often have difficulty distinguishing between convincing and nonconvincing reasons. Assume you are modeling this part of the strategy using the prompt: Why I should receive an allowance? Provide two convincing and two not-so-convincing reasons that you could discuss with your students.

Suggested Responses

Responses will vary, but here are some suggested ideas:

1. Teach the sentences in this order: B D A C. B and D are simple sentences, A is a compound sentence, and C is a complex sentence.

2. The Sumer of 2012 was one of the hottist on record. Many states broak records for days ina row.Some peapl e died because of the heat I stayed cool by swiming drinking cold water and staying in the house with AC.

3. Why I should earn an allowance? Convincing reasons: (1) so I can learn how to handle money and (2) so I do not have to bother my parents for money all the time. These are convincing reasons because parents want their children to become more responsible and independent. Not-so-convincing reasons: (1) so I can get a tattoo and (2) so I don't have to get a part-time job. These are not good reasons because most parents would not want their child to get a tattoo, and most parents don't want to be a substitute for an employer for their children.

SUPPLEMENTAL RESOURCES FOR CHAPTER 10

Brice, R. (2004). Connecting oral and written language through applied writing strategies. *Intervention in School and Clinic, 40*(1), 38–47.

Harris, K., & Graham, S. (1996). *Making the writing process work: Strategies for composition and self-regulation.* Cambridge, MA: Brookline Books.

Harris, K., Graham, S., Mason, L., & Friedlander, B. (2008). *POWERFUL writing strategies for all students.* Baltimore, MD: Brookes.

Lienemann, T., & Reid, R. (2008). Using self-regulated strategy development to improve expository writing with students with attention deficit hyperactivity disorder. *Exceptional Children, 74,* 471–486.

Marchisan, M., & Alber, S. (2001). The write way: Tips for teaching the writing process for resistant writers. *Intervention in School and Clinic, 36*(3), 154–162.

Mason, L., & Graham, S. (2008). Writing instruction for adolescents with learning disabilities: Programs of intervention research. *Learning Disabilities Research & Practice, 23*(2), 103–112.

National Center on Accelerating Student Learning. (n.d.). *POW + TREE writing strategy*. Retrieved November 19, 2012, from http://kc.vanderbilt.edu/casl/powtree.html

University of Oregon Center on Teaching and Learning. (2010). *Self-regulated strategy development instruction for the struggling adolescent writer part 2.* Retrieved from http://ctl.uoregon.edu/node/1023

Spelling and Writing Curriculum and Teaching Resources

Dixon, R., & Englemann, S. (2001). *Spelling through morphographs.* Columbus, OH: SRA/McGraw-Hill.

McCabe, D. (2008). *Sequential spelling.* Birch Run, MI: AVKO Educational Research Foundation.

Scarborough, M. (2004). *Target spelling.* Austin, TX: Steck Vaughn.

Schumaker, J. (2003). *Fundamentals in the theme writing strategy.* Lawrence, KS: Edge Enterprises.

Schumaker, J., & Lyeria, K. (1991). *The paragraph writing strategy.* Lawrence: The University of Kansas.

Schumaker, J., & Sheldon, J. (1985). *The sentence writing strategy.* Lawrence: The University of Kansas.

Swann, K. (2007). *More basic paragraph practice—2.* San Antonio, TX: PCI Education.

Wier-Cavazos, B. (2007). *Types of writing workbooks.* San Antonio, TX: PCI Education.

Study Skills: Informal Assessments   **11**

Study skills are the key to independent learning, and they help students gain and use information effectively.

(Vaughn & Bos, 2012, p. 347)

MEET DON

Don is a cooperative, pleasant, and well-liked high school freshman who has some attention, organization, and learning challenges. He and his family recently moved to a much larger school district, and Don is not used to the noise and activity level of a large suburban high school. His first semester midterm progress reports indicated several missing assignments and low test scores. In the past, Don relied on his ability to remember information from lectures and class discussions, which served him well on most exams, but now the amount of information in multiple rigorous classes is too great for him to rely on memory alone. Don's IEP team members have decided to meet and add a study skills goal to his existing IEP. First, special educator Mr. Hartson gathers some informal assessment data to share with the team.

CHAPTER OVERVIEW

This chapter provides an overview of study skills by defining study skills, listing various study skills, and introducing informal tools teachers can use to assess study skills. The chapter concludes by presenting the study skills goal and objectives Mr. Hartson suggested be added to Don's IEP.

STUDY SKILLS

Study skills are tools associated with acquiring, recording, organizing, synthesizing, remembering, and using information and ideas in school (Hoover & Patton, 2007). This broad definition includes numerous skills such as listening, note taking, outlining, organizing materials, using mnemonics, test taking, completing and submitting work, using reference materials, interpreting charts and graphs, varying one's reading rate, managing time well, and many others.

Many students with mild disabilities have poor study skills. They often do not attend to or remember the main ideas of a presentation; take good classroom notes; maintain organized backpacks, binders, and lockers; complete or submit all assignments; know how to use reference materials; and know how to study for upcoming tests. However, these skills are critical for school success—especially at the secondary level. Many teachers expect secondary students to use effective study skills even though few of these skills are formally taught.

Students without disabilities often develop these skills without much formal instruction, but students with mild disabilities do not. In contrast, students with disabilities often require extensive explicit instruction in study skills before they are able to execute the skills independently (Mastropieri & Scruggs, 2010). They benefit from study skill supports as well as explicit instruction in study skills. The study skill supports listed here provide routines, organizational strategies, and accommodations, but they do not replace instruction. Examples of study skill supports include the following:

- Provide a set of textbooks at home.
- Color code folders to corresponding colored book covers.
- Provide the student with a locker without a locker mate.
- Have the student identify someone in each class to contact for support.
- As needed, allow extra time on tests, more time for lengthy assignments or projects, and reduced penalties for submitting work late.
- Use checklists or cue cards and have the student check off items after completion.
- Have specified folders or places in the binder or backpack for homework to do as well as finished homework to submit.
- Daily, check and help the student organize belongings, including backpack, folders, and pockets.
- Help organize loose papers by color coding folders and showing the student how to hole-punch and file.

- Maintain a consistent and specific time and distraction-free location for homework.
- Allow study breaks about every 10–20 minutes or after completion of a specified task.
- Maintain a homework procedure at school through the use of an assignment notebook with adult signatures, as necessary.
- Maintain weekly communication checks among teachers, parents, and the student.
- Pair a newly learned yet easily forgettable task within a routine. (For example, after you brush your teeth before bed, set out materials you need to take to school in the morning.)
- Have the student check in with a teacher or counselor at the beginning and end of each day to plan and review organizational structures and tasks for the next day.

INFORMAL ASSESSMENTS

Teachers can assess study skills through several informal assessments such as observations, analysis of student work samples, teacher grade books, pretests, and student interviews. Mr. Hartson used various informal assessment instruments to gather baseline data for Don's study skill goal and objectives. Figure 11.1 provides examples of these different instruments as well as Don's data. Prior to the IEP meeting, Mr. Hartson gathered this information by observing Don, requesting information from general education teachers, reviewing Don's work samples and other artifacts, checking Don's notebook and locker, and having Don complete a questionnaire.

Figure 11.1 Various Informal Study Skills Instruments

Instrument/Tool	To Assess	Don's Results
Observation	Time on task in class, time on task studying independently, compliance with teacher directions	On task 10 of 25 minutes when told to study for an upcoming science test
Checklists/ rubrics	Notebook/locker organization	Notebook checklist: 5/10 points Locker rubric: 2/6 points
Grade book data	Percentage of homework submitted, average homework grade, average test score	Submitted 6/10 homework assignments, average homework grade D, average test score D

(Continued)

Figure 11.1 (Continued)

Instrument/Tool	To Assess	Don's Results
Work sample/ artifact analysis	Assignment notebook completion, assignment completion, errors on tests/ assignments	Written work messy, does better with multiple choice and matching exams, inconsistent with assignment notebook
Pretests	Establish baseline data in skill or strategy (can student take notes, use resources, use test taking skills)	Pretest score on WATCH strategy 8/18, mnemonics pretest score 8/17
Self-assessments/ interviews	Student's awareness of strengths and needs	Don admits to losing things, does not know how to use assignment notebook, relies on memory, does not understand why he is earning low grades, cannot recall grading procedures for classes, does not have a system for memorizing items on a list other than "going over and over it"

Questionnaires

After Don completed the Study Skills Self-Questionnaire (see Figure 11.2), Mr. Hartson was especially interested in gathering more information about Don's approach to organizing and submitting homework and reviewing for a test—skills Don acknowledged as weaknesses.

Figure 11.2 Study Skills Self-Questionnaire

Directions: Read each question and place a check mark in the box that indicates how frequently you complete each task or activity.

Skill . . . Do I	All of the Time	Most of the Time	Sometimes	Seldom/Never
Attend every class?				
Arrive on time for every class?				
Ask questions in class if I do not understand?				

Skill ... Do I	All of the Time	Most of the Time	Sometimes	Seldom/Never
Write homework assignments in a convenient place?				
Have a set time and place to do homework?				
Check over homework before submission?				
Know what to do if I get stuck on homework?				
Preview the chapter before I begin reading?				
Take notes, outline, highlight, or make a web as I read?				
Reread when I do not understand?				
Take study breaks every 15 minutes?				
Review notes every week?				
Develop mnemonics or memory tricks to remember things?				
Read test directions carefully?				
Look for clues in tests?				
Use flashcards or other study aids to prepare for a test?				
Submit homework assignments on time?				
Have an organized notebook/binder/ backpack?				
Have an organized locker?				
Keep track of my grades?				
Set goals for improving grades?				

The WATCH Strategy

Therefore, he developed specific pretest assessments targeting these skills. As shown in Figure 11.3, the first pretest targeted Don's knowledge and use of the WATCH strategy, which helps students complete and submit homework assignments. The steps of WATCH include the following:

W—*Write down the assignment and the due date.*

A—*Ask for clarification or help on the assignment if needed.*

T—*Task-analyze the assignment and schedule tasks over available days.*

CH—*Check all work for completeness, accuracy, and neatness.*

Mnemonics

Mr. Hartson developed the second assessment to determine whether Don could memorize lists of items for a test. On Wednesday, he presented Don with three lists of items to be memorized and told Don to study these lists, and he quizzed Don on these lists on Thursday. The quiz had three questions: (1) What are the steps of mitosis in order? (2) What are

Figure 11.3 Pretests for WATCH Strategy and Mnemonics

WATCH Pretest

In this class, we may learn the WATCH strategy. Do your best to answer these questions. Use legible printing or handwriting.

Part 1: WATCH Steps

What do the letters W, A, T, and CH represent in the WATCH strategy?

W—

A—

T—

CH—

Part 2: Application

Suppose you were assigned to research and then write a one-page summary of the work of a famous scientist. The assignment is due on April 3rd. With this in mind, complete the following tasks:

1. On the assignment sheet attached, create an entry for the assignment listed above. Spell out and define any abbreviations that you think you might use in the assignment.

---

2. Imagine that you forgot what resources (books, Internet, handouts, and so on) you are allowed to use to research your scientist. In two to three sentences below, write the *exact words* you would say to ask your teacher for clarification about the use of resources for this assignment.

What I would say to the teacher:

3. Now it is time to begin. Use the table below. In the left-hand column, indicate each step that you would follow to complete the assignment. Write the steps in their proper order. In the right-hand column, estimate how long each step will take. Include at least four steps. Add more steps to the table if needed.

Step	Time (in minutes) to Complete the Step

4. Now you think your paper is ready to submit to your teacher. What would you do to check over your paper to make sure it is ready?

Mnemonics Pretest

Assume you have to remember the items in each list below for a science quiz tomorrow. Study these lists and be prepared to be tested on each list tomorrow. Remember the items **in their order** in each list.

Steps of mitosis:

Prophase

Metaphase

Anaphase

Telephase

Steps of the scientific method:

Ask a question

Do background research

Construct a hypothesis

Conduct an experiment

Analyze data

Draw conclusions

Communicate results

Qualities of living things:

Contain cells

Metabolize

Respond

Grow

Reproduce

Adapt

the steps of the scientific method in order? and (3) What are the qualities of living things in order? Mr. Hartson also asked Don to explain how he memorized these lists.

DON'S INDIVIDUALIZED EDUCATION PROGRAM

Don's IEP team, which included Don, his parents, several general educators, and Mr. Hartson, reviewed the data and developed goals. Team members agreed that helping Don with study skills would require frequent communication among all parties. Team members also agreed to

Figure 11.4 Don's IEP

Individualized Education Program

Name: Donald   Grade: 9   Skill Area: Study Skills

Present Level of Performance: According to informal assessments, Don submits 60% of homework assignments, earns Ds on homework assignments and tests, has made complete and accurate entries in his assignment notebook for 4 out of 10 assignments, maintains on-task study behavior 40% of the time, has a messy notebook and locker, and earned 8 out of 18 points on the WATCH pretest and 8 out of 17 points on a mnemonics pretest. Don admits that he loses things, has no system for studying for a test, and does not know how to use his assignment notebook.

Annual Goal: Don will submit 80% of his assignments on time and earn at least a C average on homework assignments, projects, tests, and quizzes in his inclusion classes.

Objective 1: By the end of the first quarter, after being assigned a homework assignment in an inclusion class, Don will correctly write entries in his assignment notebook for 4 out of 5 assignments.

Objective 2: By the end of the second quarter, after being given a verbal prompt, Don will write study note cards for tests and quizzes, orally read the note cards, and verbally answer questions based on the content of the note cards with 80% accuracy.

Objective 3: By the end of the third quarter, after being given a verbal prompt and a list of items to memorize for a test or quiz, Don will verbally state a mnemonic for the list and state or write items in the list with 80% accuracy.

Objective 4: By the end of the school year, after being told the instructions and due date for an assignment in an inclusion class, Don will submit 8 out of 10 homework assignments on time.

emphasize assignment completion and submission as well as test preparation through the use of study note cards and mnemonics. They felt that Don's grades would improve if he met objectives in these areas.

SUMMARY

Study skills involve numerous subskills that are critical for school success. Many students without disabilities acquire these with minimal explicit instruction, but this is not the case for most students with mild disabilities. Because few formal tests directly and authentically assess study skills, teachers can use informal tools or instruments such as observations, rubrics, checklists, self-assessments, work sample analyses, and grades as indicators of study skills. Results of these assessments help IEP teams target relevant goals and objectives. Students benefit the most from a consistent study skills program that collaboratively involves teachers, parents, and themselves in purposeful and relevant goal setting.

CHAPTER APPLICATION ACTIVITIES

Apply your knowledge from the chapter by discussing or completing the following application questions or activities. Suggested answers are provided below.

1. Develop a short rubric or checklist that you could use to informally assess locker organization.

2. You have noticed that Bertram has a personal digital assistant (PDA). How could you informally assess whether or not Bertram knows how to use his PDA to record homework assignments?

3. The A step of the WATCH strategy stands for *Ask for clarification or help on the assignment, if needed.* Design a short scenario for Don to role-play that could be used as part of a pretest.

Suggested Responses

Responses will vary, but here are some suggested ideas:

1. Locker Organization Checklist:

   Are jackets, sweaters, backpack, et cetera, hanging on hooks? Are books stacked neatly on the shelf and arranged by subject, schedule, or some other priority? Is the bottom of the locker clean and void of wrappers, paper, et cetera? Are loose papers tucked away in folders, notebooks, or the backpack? Are shoes or sports equipment et cetera on the floor of the locker?

2. Ask Bertram to show you the features of his PDA and how he uses it. If he says he uses it to record homework assignments, have him show you one of his more recent entries, so you can assess it for completeness and accuracy.

3. Don, I want to know what you would say to Mrs. Klondike if you did not understand the math assignment on finding the lowest common multiple. Pretend I am Mrs. Klondike, and I have just assigned the homework assignment, but you did not hear what page or what problems to do or when it was due. What would you say to Mrs. Klondike to better understand these requirements of the assignment?

SUPPLEMENTAL RESOURCES FOR CHAPTER 11

Benz, C., Fabian, M., & Nelson, W. (1996). Assessing study skills of students with learning disabilities. *The Clearing House, 69*(6), 349–353.

Carter, C., Bishop, J., Block, J., & Kravits, S. (2005). *Keys to effective learning.* Upper Saddle River, NJ: Merrill/Prentice-Hall.

Study Skills: Methods and Strategies

12

Students who are taught to use efficient study and organizational strategies perform better and are more likely to succeed in school.

(Berry, Hall, & Gildroy, 2004)

CHAPTER OVERVIEW

Don's team agreed that he needed the most immediate support with completing and submitting homework assignments and learning systems for preparing for tests and quizzes. Teaching effective homework approaches is one of the most efficient ways to improve academic performance (Cancio, West, & Young, 2004). Therefore, Mr. Hartson decided to teach Don the WATCH strategy, a system for developing and using note cards, and various mnemonic methods. The chapter describes each of these methods and includes the think-aloud Mr. Hartson used as he taught Don the WATCH strategy. The chapter concludes with test-taking strategies and tips.

FEATURED METHODS AND STRATEGIES

Chapter Strategies	Corresponding Common Core State Standards
WATCH	Conduct short as well as more sustained research projects to answer a question (including a self-generated question) or solve a problem; narrow or broaden the inquiry when appropriate; synthesize multiple sources on the subject, demonstrating understanding of the subject under investigation.

(Continued)

(Continued)

Chapter Strategies	Corresponding Common Core State Standards
CD, RD, WD Mnemonics PIRATES SPLASH	Cite strong and thorough textual evidence to support analysis of what the text says explicitly as well as inferences drawn from the text.
ANSWER	Produce clear and coherent writing in which the development, organization, and style are appropriate to task, purpose, and audience.

Source for standards: Common Core State Standards Initiative, 2012

THE WATCH STRATEGY

The WATCH strategy (Reid & Lienemann, 2006) teaches students critical homework and task–completion skills. Before teaching Don WATCH, Mr. Hartson and Don discussed Don's WATCH pretest scores, his assignment completion rates, and how and when Don uses an assignment notebook. Mr. Hartson explained how other students have benefitted from the WATCH strategy. Here's what Mr. Hartson shared in each step:

- W—*Write down the assignment and the due date.* Mr. Hartson explained the importance of writing the assignment the moment it is assigned. Some teachers write assignments on the board, but others only verbally state the assignment. Don needs to be prepared for both. Mr. Hartson showed Don how to write the assignment in his assignment notebook on the due date, using abbreviations that Mr. Hartson included on a cue card. If students need more support for this first step, they can learn the mnemonic TRICK BAG (Scott & Compton, 2007):

  - T—*Take* out your assignment book.
  - R—*Record* the assignment.
  - I—*Insert* important details.
  - C—*Circle* materials you need.
  - K—*Keep* materials in your homework folder.
  - B—*Be* sure you can read it.
  - A—*Ask* a partner to check it.
  - G—*Go* put it in your backpack.

- A—*Ask for clarification or help on the assignment if needed.* Sometimes students do not understand assignment details. They can ask friends, but sometimes friends are unsure of the assignment also, and they offer poor advice. Therefore, Mr. Hartson emphasized asking the teacher for help. If students have a question requiring a short teacher response, they can raise their hand in class and ask the question. If the teacher's response may be lengthy because the question is detailed or complex, Don should (a) go to the teacher's classroom before or after school, (b) ask if the teacher has a few minutes to explain the assignment, (c) indicate that he wants to do well on the assignment, (d) ask the question or questions one at a time and wait for a response, (e) take notes on what the teacher said, and (f) thank the teacher for helping. When asking the teacher for clarification, students should bring any necessary materials, have questions prepared in advance, and if possible, show completed work thus far to receive helpful feedback.

- T—*Task-analyze the assignment and schedule tasks over available days.* Some assignments are large projects best completed over an extended period of time and in steps. Completing large projects in steps over time reduces stress and allows for opportunities for teacher, peer, or parental feedback before final submission. Mr. Hartson and Don discussed ways to break large projects into smaller steps and consider the length of time each step would take. Similarly, they discussed ways to strategically prepare for a test by applying this system. Frequently, students have homework for multiple subjects each night and assignments due at various days during the week. Mr. Hartson and Don discussed ways to plan studying time by dividing the evening into blocks of time and deciding what task to do during each time block.

- CH—*Check all work for completeness, accuracy, and neatness.* The last step asks students to check their work, which helps with self-monitoring. Students can ask themselves questions such as, Is the assignment complete? Are my answers accurate? Is my paper or project neat? In this step, Mr. Hartson taught Don to (a) reread his assignment notebook entry and double-check the assignment to ensure he completed all of it; (b) pick at least one-fifth of his math answers to double-check for accuracy and make changes, as needed; and (c) edit, recopy, or retype any written paper, if needed. Students should use teacher-provided rubrics to guide their work and remember feedback given earlier by the teacher on previous, similar types of assignments.

NOTE CARDS AND THE CD, RD, WD STRATEGY

Because Don did not have a consistent method for organizing and studying information for a test, Mr. Hartson taught a basic note card method. Together, using the social studies study guide provided by the social studies teacher, Don and Mr. Hartson practiced writing the question on one side of a card and the answer on the back. Mr. Hartson developed this basic strategy to help Don remember the steps:

C—*Copy* the question (from the study guide or other source).

D—*Double*-check that you copied the question correctly.

R—*Read* your social studies passage for the answer.

D—*Double*-check the question and answer. (Does it make sense?)

W—*Write* the answer and page number on the back of the note card.

D—*Double*-check that you wrote the correct answer and the page number where you found it.

The front of each card includes only one question, and the back includes the answer and page number where the answer was found. Adding the page number now saves time when double-checking or rereading later on. Note cards prepared in this way are especially useful for facts—or questions that begin with *who, what, when,* and *where.*

The note card system is also useful for learning vocabulary (Rooney, 2010). Rooney advised that students write the vocabulary word on the front and the meaning on the back by (a) listing important parts of the definition (rather than copying the definition); and (b) providing an example, rephrased definition, drawing, or diagram to support later retrieval.

One concern of the note card system is that it does not work for higher-level skills. One way to address this is by having students write the higher-level question on the front and bulleted points, a short outline, or a graphic organizer on the back, all of which serve as discussion points for short answer or essay responses or sufficient memory prompts for objective questions. Examples of the three types of note cards that Mr. Hartson modeled are included in Figure 12.1.

Making note cards is an important step in the test preparation process. However, students also need to learn how to use note cards as a study tool. Therefore, Mr. Hartson modeled this by (a) taking no more than five completed note cards from the completed stack, (b) reading each question and each answer slowly and perhaps more than once, (c) rereading just the question from Card 1 and, without looking at the answer, verbalizing the answer and then checking the answer on the back for accuracy, and (d) completing this same step for the remaining four cards. When the student can supply the correct answer without looking three consecutive times, the card goes in the "I think I know this" pile. Students review these less frequently than cards in the "I am not sure of this" pile. Another,

Figure 12.1 Note Card Examples

Who was a famous conductor of the Underground Railroad?	Harriet Tubman p. 149
Fact Card	

martyr	People who die for something they believe Nat Turner was a martyr for leading a slave rebellion. p. 148
Vocabulary Card	

Using the Inuit tribe as an example, explain how their environment influenced their culture. (This was the short answer question given in advance by the general education teacher.)	Climate: cold, harsh Tundra: cannot farm Lived near sea Animals for hunting, clothing, shelter Igloos Used seal oil for warmth
Short Answer Card	

more difficult way to review is to look at the answer and recall the question. Students can review both ways and have others quiz them.

MNEMONICS

Don did not have a systematic method of memorizing items for an upcoming test other than "going over items over and over." Therefore, Mr. Hartson decided to teach Don some mnemonic methods.

Mnemonics are memory aids or tricks that help students recall items. Most of us have used these to help us remember the colors of the rainbow

(Roy G. Biv—red, orange, yellow, green, blue, indigo, violet), coordinating conjunctions (FANBOYS—*for, and, nor, but, or, yet, so*), or a math fact (7 and 7 are mighty fine; when multiplied, they are 49). A mnemonic can be a rhyme, rule, phrase, diagram, or acronym—or anything that aids memory. Usually, students use mnemonics to help remember factual information. Researchers have found that mnemonics are especially helpful and effective for students with mild disabilities who have memory and processing issues.

Probably the most well-known and researched mnemonic approach used by special educators is the first letter mnemonics strategy (Nagel, Schumaker, & Deshler, 1986). The FIRST strategy from the University of Kansas Center for Research on Learning (KU-CRL) teaches students five ways to remember items that appear in a list. These include the following:

F—*Form a word*. Take the first letter of each word in the list to form a word such as HOMES for the Great Lakes (Huron, Ontario, Michigan, Erie, Superior). Assume these lakes were noted in this order in the text, so students do not need to change order to construct their mnemonic.

I—*Insert a letter*. Insert a letter or letters to make a word while maintaining the order of the items such as CIT(Y) to remember the first level of the administrative divisions of the United States (commonwealth, Indian reservation, territories). The letter *Y* was inserted to create a real word, but order was still preserved. Students need to remember that the *Y* is the "filler" letter that does not represent a part of the answer.

R—*Rearrange letters*. Rearrange letters to make a word when order is not important such as ADMIT for the five ways that people solve a problem (accommodating, dominating, moving, inventing, and tolerating). These solutions were listed in a different order in the text, but if order is not important, students can rearrange these to form a word.

S—*Shape a sentence*. Make a sentence using the first letter of each list item such as **N**eat **A**nswers **A**lways **H**elp for the last four U.S. states to join the union (New Mexico, Arizona, Alaska, Hawaii). Do not add any additional words; use only the first letters of the words in the list and develop a complete sentence.

T—*Try different combinations*. Use two or more of the previous steps to make the mnemonic such as rearranging letters and shaping a sentence. Four large cities in Illinois (Chicago, Aurora, Rockford, Naperville) becomes **N**ate **C**an **R**est **A**nywhere.

In addition to forming words and shaping sentences, students can develop and use other types of mnemonics as well as noted in Figure 12.2.

Figure 12.2 Different Types of Mnemonics

Type of Mnemonic	Description	Use	Example
Acronyms	Word that is formed by taking the first letters of items in the list	To remember items that are familiar to the student and concrete	COPS (capitalization, overall appearance, punctuation, spelling)
Acrostics	Sentence in which the first letter of each word is used	To remember items that cannot be formed using an acronym	My very eager mother just served us nachos (to remember planets in order from the sun)
Keyword	Method that associates the word to be remembered with a similar-sounding word (the keyword) and links them in an interactive image (see Chapter 4)	To remember unfamiliar information, to remember vocabulary words (keyword must be something that is easily drawn)	Vocabulary word: plantation Key Word: play station Interactive Image: People playing with their play stations while sitting in the middle of a plantation
Snapshot (also called mimetics)	Pictorial representation of all the items to be remembered	When items can be easily drawn and associated into one picture, and the content is already familiar and meaningful to students	Four things Iowa is known for: corn, hogs, good schools, RAGBRAI (the annual bike ride across the state) Snapshot: picture with a big corn field, pigs in a pig pen, several schools in the background, and people riding bikes along the side of a highway
Story Method	Original story that includes items to be remembered	For items that are difficult to form into acronyms or acrostics	For the Iowa example above: On my way to school, I took a short cut through a corn field, saw pigs in a farmer's pig pen, and cheered for the RAGBRAI bike riders.
Pegword	System that associates rhyming peg words (one–bun, two–shoe, three–tree, four–door, five–hive, six–sticks, seven–heaven, eight–gate, nine–vine, ten–hen) with a fact or item associated with that number	To remember information that is numbered or ordered	Fact: George Washington was the first U.S. president (number one) Pegword: one–bun Image: Washington eating a hot dog bun

Teachers need to present and help students develop the type of mnemonic that best matches the information to be memorized. Not all mnemonics are equally appropriate or effective for a particular memory task. Similarly, students will be most successful if teachers teach one type of mnemonic to mastery and then introduce a different type. Mnemonics are best taught to students through an explicit instructional approach that includes teacher modeling, guided practice, and independent practice.

Modeling Mnemonics

Mr. Hartson knew that Don was talented at drawing, so he introduced Don to the snapshot method first, which is a system that incorporates items to be memorized into a picture or visual, as noted in Figure 12.2. His model step went something like this:

The snapshot method is a mnemonic, or a memory trick, that uses your drawings to help you remember items. Think of a camera taking a snapshot picture. In the snapshot method, the picture or drawing does not have to be perfect or detailed; it just needs to include items you need to memorize. The steps of this method include these:

T—*Take the list* of the items you need to memorize.

I—*Include all the items* together in a simple drawing.

N—*Note whether* all items have been included.

T—*Test yourself* to see if you can remember all the items.

You can remember the steps by recalling TINT—which is an art term, and this process uses art, or drawings.

The first step is T—*take the list* of items you need to memorize. Let's assume your social studies teacher wanted you to know the five parts of the first amendment, which states our five freedoms. In the first step, we take those five items and write them, so they are handy for our drawing. On one side of this large index card, I will write a title: The Five Parts of the First Amendment. On the back toward the bottom, I neatly list the five answers—the freedoms of religion, press, assembly, petition, and speech. I double-check my answer once more just to be sure—yes, my list matches exactly what I have on my review sheet, so I know I have correctly completed the first step.

The second step is I—*include all the items* together in a simple drawing. This is where our art skills come in handy, but our drawing does not need to be perfect. Our picture must integrate all the items from our list. Let me see—we have freedom of religion, speech, press, assembly, and petition. All of these deal with people doing something they could do in their town or city, so I can draw all of those in a single picture showing people in a city.

Let's see—I'll start with freedom of religion. I'll draw a church in the background of my city. That will be enough to help me remember freedom of religion.

Next we have freedom of press—this deals with ways information in our country is shared. I think of media such as the newspaper or TV, so down the street from the church is the newspaper office. I'll draw a tall building and on top of the building draw a little newspaper as my reminder.

Next is freedom of assembly, which means people may gather as a group to protest or march for rights, et cetera. How can I include that in my drawing in this city? Hmmm . . . I'll draw some people with signs protesting against unfair hiring practices. Where can I place these people? I'll draw them by the newspaper building as they are assembling against unfair hiring practices that have been occurring at the newspaper office. OK—that works because they have a right to assemble peacefully and gather as a group to protest civil wrongs.

What is next? The next item is freedom of petition, which allows people to gather signatures to appeal laws or government policies or actions. I remember people coming to our house to gather signatures about a new local zoning law, so in my picture, I'll draw a house. Someone is at the door with a petition, and the homeowner is signing it. That helps me remember freedom of petition.

Finally, we have freedom of speech. This means that people may speak openly without censorship about their opinions. There are some restrictions, but for our picture, I will show someone speaking. I will show the person in a local park exercising freedom of speech.

Alright, I have my drawings integrated into a picture, so I am ready for N—*note whether* all items have been included. This step means I double-check to make sure I included every item in my picture. Let's double-check [double checks for all items]: Yes, I have them all. I followed the steps so far and have done a good job.

The final step is T—*test yourself* to see if you can remember all the items. To study this, I read the prompt on the front of the card,

which states, The Five Parts of the First Amendment. Next, I turn
the card over and look at my picture and ask myself what each
drawing represents. The church represents freedom of religion,
and so forth. . . . When I think I can remember all five items,
I turn the card over and quiz myself. Thinking of my picture, can
I state the five parts of the first amendment? If I cannot state all
five, I turn the card over, study the picture once more, and test
myself until I can state all five items without looking. I need to be
able to do this three times successfully before I place my card in the
"I think I know this" pile.

The completed visual is shown in Figure 12.3.

Figure 12.3 Snapshot Mnemonic Notecard

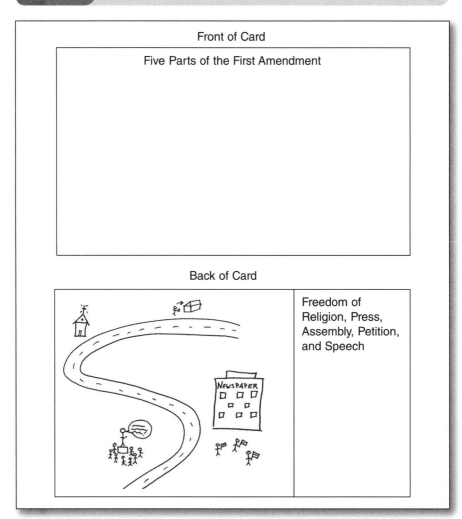

TEST TAKING

Although Don did not have test taking as a targeted IEP goal, many students benefit from learning test-taking skills or strategies. Students with disabilities tend not to be test-wise; they often do not catch clues in tests that help them select the best choice nor do they approach assessments in a strategic manner.

As an ongoing practice, students benefit from reflecting on past test performances and experiences in order to improve future performances. Therefore, as soon as possible after a test, teachers can discuss with students what worked and did not work for them regarding their test-taking approach. Students can discuss questions such as, Did you study the wrong material? Did you run out of time? Did you remember to underline key terms? Did you change your answer only if you were sure? Were there any surprises on the test? What can you do differently next time? Discussing these issues, especially in groups, may uncover successful and unsuccessful test-taking practices. Students should be encouraged to share their successful tips with others.

The PIRATES and SPLASH Strategies

Students remember these tips better when they are placed within the context of a strategy. Fortunately, researchers have developed strategies that incorporate many of these tips. Steps of two commonly used test-taking strategies are listed in Figure 12.4. PIRATES and SPLASH share similar steps such as numbering the test sections in the sequence they will be taken, returning later to answer difficult questions, eliminating choices whenever possible, and reviewing answers before submitting the test. After comparing and contrasting these two strategies, teachers could decide which one would be more appropriate to teach their students.

The first step of PIRATES (Hughes, Schumaker, Deshler, & Mercer, 1988) reminds students to write their name and the acronym *PIRATES* on the test (which serves as a handy reminder of the remaining steps), allot time, order test sections, say positive self-talk affirmations, and begin within two minutes. Don has a 50-minute science test containing three parts: 20 multiple choice items (1 point each), 5 fill-in items on a diagram (1 point each), and two short answer responses (5 points each). As he begins, he decides which test section to complete first. He does not like to write, and he remembers from past tests that sometimes words from multiple choice items have helped him with the short answer section, so he decides to maintain the order of the test and spend 20 minutes on the multiple choice items, 5 minutes on the diagram, and 20 minutes on the

Figure 12.4 Two Test-Taking Strategies

PIRATES	SPLASH
P—*Prepare* to succeed (write your name and the mnemonic *PIRATES* on the test, allot time, order sections, say affirmations, begin within two minutes).	S—*Skim* the test (read over everything to get a sense of the test).
I—*Inspect* the instructions (read instructions carefully, underline what to do and where to respond, notice special requirements).	P—*Plan* your strategy (where to begin, consider point values and time constraints).
R—*Read* the whole question, remember what you studied, and reduce the choices.	L—*Leave* out tough questions (place a dot or bullet by unknown questions and return to these later).
A—*Answer* or abandon the question for the moment.	A—*Attack* questions you know (answer these first).
T—*Turn* back to answer unknown questions.	S—*Systematically guess* (pick your best response).
E—*Estimate* answers for remaining questions (avoid absolutes, choose the longest and most detailed choice, eliminate similar choices).	H—*House clean* (reserve 5–10% of your time to review answers, proofread essay responses, ensure you have answered all questions, etc.).
S—*Survey* your test.	

short answer questions. This also leaves him with 5 minutes to look over the test before submitting it. He takes a deep breath, says to himself that he can do this, and begins.

Before he reads the first multiple choice item, Don reads the directions for this section, which note to darken in the oval on the Scantron sheet indicating your answer. He dislikes Scantrons as he sometimes loses his place, so as he progresses, he continually double-checks his question number and corresponding answer sheet number to make sure they match.

Throughout the test, Don applies the next steps of PIRATES. If he does not know an answer after reading the question, he skips the question (and skips that number on the Scantron) and moves to the next question. He remembers to turn back and guess at those unknown questions. He also reads each question in its entirety and every response before choosing a response.

The SPLASH strategy is unique in that it teaches students to first skim over the entire test to get a sense of its length, sections, and requirements.

This provides an overall context and mentally prepares students for taking the test. After surveying, students are better prepared to sequence the order in which they will take the test. As they take the test, students answer easiest questions first, return later to questions they skipped, make a good guess on unknown questions, and survey the test before they submit it.

The ANSWER Strategy

When Don approaches the essay section, he uses the ANSWER strategy (Hughes, Schumaker, & Deshler, 2005), which includes these steps:

A—*Analyze* the situation (read the question carefully, underline key terms, gauge the time you need)

N—*Notice* requirements (scan and mark the parts of the question, ask and say what is required, tell yourself to write a quality answer)

S—*Set up* an outline (set up main ideas, assess whether they match the question, make changes if necessary)

W—*Work in* details (remember what you learned, add details to the main ideas using abbreviations, indicate order, decide if you are ready to write)

E—*Engineer* your answer (write an introductory paragraph, refer to your outline, include topic sentences, tell about details for each topic sentence, employ examples)

R—*Review* your work (look to see if you answered all parts of the question, inspect to see if you included main ideas and details, touch up your answer)

As Don reads the essay question, he studies the question and notices requirements. (The first question states, "In four complete paragraphs compare and contrast animal cells and plant cells . . ."). He underlines the words four paragraphs, compare and contrast, animal cells, and plant cells. He remembers that *compare and contrast* means to write about how the items are similar and different. Before he begins writing, he jots down a few main ideas in a graphic organizer (which serves as his outline), then he adds some details about plant cells and animal cells, and then he begins writing. Don decides to write a short introductory paragraph stating that he will be comparing and contrasting plant and animal cells. His second paragraph will note similarities between the two. His third paragraph will describe differences between animal and plant cells, and his last paragraph will summarize.

He rereads his answer for clarity, punctuation, and whether he answered the question before moving on to the next question.

Although students with disabilities often have test accommodations such as a reader, extended time, or someone to write their responses, they still need to know how to systematically approach a test and apply effective test-taking skills based on the specific question type. Each question type is unique and requires a different approach. Also, short answer or essay questions contain prompts such as *compare and contrast, analyze, prove, describe,* and *state,* and not all students know the meaning of these terms. Therefore, students should learn common tips and strategies based on item types that may help them during testing situations. Appendix B includes several test-taking tips (Conderman & Pedersen, 2010; Hoover & Patton, 2007). Teachers can prioritize which of these tips to discuss with and teach to their students, based on common student test errors. These tips obviously do not replace the need for sustained study and test preparation.

TIME SAVERS

Teachers can consult the internet for supplemental resources that will help them save some instructional time. For example numerous youtube clips provide information about assignment notebooks, note cards, mnemonics, and test-taking tips. With some supervision, students can view preselected clips and then practice each chosen study tip as an in- or out-of-class assignment. These clips do not provide the explicit instruction many students need, though, so they should not replace careful teacher instruction. They are helpful for students who need a refresher or who do not need intensive teacher modeling.

SUMMARY

Students who lack effective study skills are at a clear disadvantage, especially in the secondary grades when courses become more rigorous, organizational skills are critical for success, and students can no longer rely on their auditory memory for satisfactory performance in a course or on a test. Results from informal assessments help teachers pinpoint specific study strategies to teach. Teachers can teach (a) the WATCH strategy to students who experience difficulty completing and submitting homework, (b) a basic note card system to those who do not know how to prepare for a test, (c) various mnemonic strategies to students who lack a systematic method for remembering factual information, and (d) test taking tips and strategies to students who are not test-wise. These—and other study skills—promote student responsibility and engagement while directly teaching skills that students can also use in future educational and employment settings.

CHAPTER APPLICATION ACTIVITIES

Apply your knowledge from the chapter by discussing or completing the following application questions or activities. Suggested answers are provided below.

1. One of your students, Elaine, is overwhelmed that she has to research a famous psychologist, write a short paper on that person, and give a speech on that person in her psychology class. How could you help Elaine with the T step of WATCH— task-analyze the assignment and schedule tasks over available days? She has four days during social studies class to complete this assignment, and she will be giving her speech on the fifth day.

2. Another student, Arnold, needs to memorize the four kinds of tissue in the human body: muscle, nerve, connective, and epithelial. Based on the first letter mnemonic strategy, develop a mnemonic to help Arnold remember these. Order is not important.

3. A third student, Roger, wants to improve his essay responses on tests, but he does not like setting up an outline, which is the S step in the ANSWER strategy. What other tasks could he do in this step rather than set up an outline?

Suggested Responses

Responses will vary, but here are some suggested ideas:

1. Here are some possible steps and a timeline for Elaine:

   Day 1: Decide on your psychologist, begin basic research, and take some basic notes (Internet search, check school library, glance through psychology texts in social studies lab)

   Day 2: Continue researching topic by taking more notes, completing an outline, or filling in a graphic organizer

   Day 3: Start writing paper by ordering your notes in a logical sequence

   Day 4: Finish writing paper and rehearse speech

   Day 5: Give speech in class

2. Using the S—shape a sentence step from the FIRST strategy, one mnemonic is, Exciting cartoons need music!

3. Roger could make a bulleted list, make a graphic organizer, write down abbreviations for ideas of concepts he wants to include in his answer, brainstorm everything he remembers about the topic and then order his thoughts, or even glance through the rest of the test and see if other questions and answers might help him craft some ideas.

SUPPLEMENTAL RESOURCES FOR CHAPTER 12

Conderman, G., Bresnahan, V., & Pedersen, T. (2009). *Purposeful co-teaching: Real cases and effective strategies.* Thousand Oaks, CA: Corwin. (Chapter 4 is on mnemonics, and Chapter 6 is on study skills and learning strategies.)

Conderman, G., Hartman, P., & Johnston-Rodriguez, S. (2009, May). Mnemonics to the rescue: Strategies for memory and recall. *LD Forum*, 6–8.

Landsberger, J. Study guides and strategies. http://www.studygs.net/tsttak3.htm

Mastropieri, M., & Scruggs, T. (1998). *Enhancing school success with mnemonic strategies.* Retrieved from http://www.ldonline.org/article/5912/

Scruggs, T., & Mastropieri, M. (2000). The effectiveness of mnemonic instruction for students with learning and behavior problems: An update and research synthesis. *Journal of Behavioral Education, 10,* 163–173.

Test taking tips. http://www.testtakingtips.com/

Study Skills Curriculum and Teaching Resources

Archer, A., & Gleason, M. (2002). *Advanced skills for school success.* Billerica, MA: Curriculum Associates.

Hoover, J., & Patton, J. (2007). *Teaching study skills to students with learning problems.* Austin, TX: Pro-Ed.

Klemstein, P., & Hawkes, B. (2000). *Guide to study skills and strategies.* Upper Saddle River, NJ: Globe-Fearon.

Kruger, S. (2006). *SOAR study skills curriculum.* Lake Orian, MI: Soar Study Skills Publishers. Available from http://studyskills.com/

Mangrum, C. (2000.) *Learning to study.* Logan, IA: Perfection Learning.

Mangrum, C., & Strichart, S. (2011). *Study skills and strategies for students in high school.* Loveland, CO: Mangrum-Strichart Learning Resources. Available from http://www.mangrum-strichart.com/index.asp

Textbook Skills: **13**
Informal
Assessments

Important and relevant diagnostic information can be informally acquired from the students themselves and from their textbooks, the major content source used in secondary classrooms for instruction.

(King-Sears & Duke, 2010, p. 284)

MEET LYNN

Lynn is a sixth grader who has avoided textbooks (except for math) throughout elementary school. During those years, he remembered information from class discussions and retained most of what he heard from taped materials. Therefore, he did not think it was important to learn about how textbooks are organized, their various parts, or how to locate information in them. He was excused from much of this instruction, or his teachers did not provide it.

As Lynn entered middle school, though, he quickly discovered that most of his teachers rely on and use textbooks almost every day. Mr. Story, Lynn's resource teacher, noticed that Lynn does not independently complete study guides and other textbook-based assignments. Because Lynn was never taught how to use a textbook, he is at a disadvantage. Although he still benefits from class discussions and taped materials, these supports have not helped Lynn become more independent in using and understanding resource materials or thinking strategically about the material.

CHAPTER OVERVIEW

This chapter describes some issues and challenges associated with textbook reading for students with disabilities. Specifically, the chapter describes why students find textbooks challenging, explains why secondary students need to learn how to effectively use textbooks, describes five ways to informally assess students' knowledge and use of textbooks, and provides an example of an IEP associated with textbook use based on Lynn's informal assessment data.

TEXTBOOKS

Despite the availability of various resources, instructional approaches, and technology-based or electronic tools, most teachers still depend on textbooks as their primary instructional tool (Lenz, Deshler, & Kissam, 2004). In fact, secondary students spend as much as 75% of classroom time and 90% of homework time interacting with textbooks, and student use and dependence on textbooks increase at each grade level (Saenz & Fuchs, 2002). Therefore, students like Lynn should learn how to successfully navigate textbooks if they are to become independent learners.

Navigating textbooks, though, presents some unique challenges—especially for students with disabilities. First, students may experience difficulty with the reading level and concept load. Many textbooks are written above students' reading and grade level, and students may not have sufficient background knowledge to independently navigate a text, especially if authors do not present vocabulary terms, timelines, "big ideas," key events, or prerequisite concepts (Friend & Bursuck, 2012). Second, students are most familiar with narrative, rather than expository text. As they begin to read textbooks, they may expect a story line and become frustrated with new writing structures such as compare and contrast, problem and solution, or cause and effect—all of which require specific thinking and reasoning skills. Finally, students may be unaware of the significance of features such as boldface print or multicolored headings that support comprehension. Similarly, some texts lack organizational and writing formats such as headings and subheadings, graphic aids, transitions, easy-to-follow chronological sequences, clear pronoun references, and explicit conjunctions that support comprehension (Friend & Bursuck, 2012). Generally, teachers choose textbooks without considering these issues and the needs of students with disabilities in their classrooms (Sabornie & deBettencourt, 2009). Even with the increased use of hypertext and electronic books (e-books), students still need to be taught how to use the e-books and access the hypertext and other helpful book components (Boyle & Scanlon, 2010). Consequently, students like Lynn may become frustrated with textbook-related activities and assignments.

INFORMAL ASSESSMENTS

As with academic skills, the first step in knowing how to support students with their texts is to gather informal assessment data. Teachers can use (a) skill-based assessments, (b) interviews, (c) inventories, (d) activities, and (e) pretests to gather baseline data.

Skill-Based Assessments

One initial step in assessing a student's use of a textbook is to determine if the student can comfortably read the textbook. If the text is written at a frustrational reading level (in which the student decodes less than 90% correctly), he or she will need considerable support. Weiser Educational (www.wiesereducational.com/) offers numerous high-interest low reading level materials in the content areas for secondary students who read considerably below grade level.

To quickly assess the reading appropriateness of a text, develop an informal reading inventory, such as the one described in Chapter 5, by identifying several 100- to 200-word passages from the most recently taught chapter in a content-area text. Have the student orally read each passage while you record oral reading errors. Gather timed and untimed oral reading information such as how many words the student accurately reads in one minute (King-Sears & Duke, 2010) and ask literal and inferential questions to assess comprehension.

To assess vocabulary, gather critical vocabulary words from previous, current, and upcoming chapters in the text. Neatly print terms on note cards or type them in a list and ask the student to orally read each word and provide a definition. Use a recording form to indicate the student's responses.

Results from these assessments provide helpful information such as answers to these questions:

- Is the text at the student's independent, instructional, or frustrational reading level?
- What types of oral reading errors does the student make?
- What is the student's reading rate on textbook materials?

- Can the student answer factual and inferential questions based on the text?
- Can the student pronounce and provide the meaning of various vocabulary terms?
- What is the student's approach to decoding new vocabulary terms?

Interviews

Individualized interviews provide an opportunity for the student and teacher to get to know each other, discuss how classes are going, and then address the student's perception of their textbook use. During this interview, focus on the student's use of content-area texts (e.g., science and social studies rather than math or English) as they tend to provide more continuous expository text and include more traditional textbook features. Students should bring their textbooks and study guides to the interview to show their work and explain how they use their text. King-Sears and Duke (2010) provided questions to consider during an interview:

- Show me the last chapter you completed in [subject]. How did the teacher use the textbook during this unit?
- Which textbook parts do you find easier to use? Why?
- Which textbook parts do you find more difficult to use? Why?
- When you need to remember vocabulary definitions, how do you study those words?
- What do you do if you have to read a chapter and answer questions?
- While you are reading your text, what do you do if you do not know how to pronounce a word, or you do not know its meaning?

If students have experience with e-books or other technology tools related to textbook use, ask them to share their experiences with e-books and the features they find helpful and not so helpful.

Sammons & Davey (1993/94) developed a longer and more comprehensive interview procedure for students in fourth grade and above to help identify how they learn from textbooks. Their assessment is called The Textbook Awareness and Performance Profile (TAPP), and it includes three parts: (a) a metacognitive interview consisting of open-ended questions; (b) authentic textbook tasks, such as having the student take notes, provide oral summaries of passages, and use textbook features; and (c) a summary sheet. The individual evaluation takes about 45-60 minutes and can (and should be) administered in several settings. The authors noted that results help teachers design an individualized instructional program based on student strengths.

Inventories/Questionnaires

Student inventories or questionnaires are another effective informal assessment tool to use *if* students provide honest responses. Therefore, emphasize the importance of being truthful. Teachers can administer inventories by (a) orally reading questions to the whole class and having each student mark responses, (b) having students read questions silently and mark responses, (c) reading questions aloud to individuals or small groups and having them mark responses, or (d) taping the material or providing it in electronic form and having students respond on paper or electronically. Orally reading questions allows teachers to pause and explain or clarify questions. Figure 13.1 provides an example of a textbook questionnaire.

As with interviews, teachers can develop a system, such as an Excel spreadsheet, to efficiently save and organize student responses and tailor interventions to students with specific identified needs.

Figure 13.1 Example of a Textbook Inventory/Questionnaire

Directions: Read each question and place a check mark in the box that indicates how frequently you complete each task or activity.

Skill . . . . Do I . . .	All of the time	Most of the time	Sometimes	Seldom/ Never
Read my textbook in a place and time that is best for me?				
Preview the chapter before I begin reading by looking over the chapter introduction, conclusion, objectives, vocabulary terms, headings, subheadings, and end-of-chapter questions (if these are present) before I begin reading?				
Think about what I already know about the information before I begin reading?				

(Continued)

Figure 13.1 (Continued)

Skill . . . . Do I . . .	All of the time	Most of the time	Sometimes	Seldom/ Never
Take notes, underline, highlight, outline, or make a graphic organizer as I read?				
Know what is important and less important from each paragraph?				
Go back and reread when I am confused?				
Use the table of contents?				
Use the glossary?				
Use the index?				
Use the book's appendix?				
Consider why some words are in bold or italics or are written larger or in a different color than others?				
Stop and make sure I understand charts, graphs, and other visual aids?				
Consider what do if I come across an unknown word or one I cannot pronounce?				
Use the teacher's study guide (if provided) to help me focus on important ideas?				
Look for answers to questions as I read?				
Keep track of questions I have as I read?				

Skill . . . . Do I . . .	All of the time	Most of the time	Sometimes	Seldom/ Never
Quiz myself when I am done reading by answering end-of-chapter questions?				
Retell or summarize the chapter to myself or someone?				
Consider what to study after I have completed all the activities associated with the chapter?				
Consider how to use features of my e-book (if I use one)?				
Consider how to use hypertext features?				

Textbook Activities

Textbook application activities, also referred to as textbook quests or textbook exploration activities (Conderman & Elf, 2007), engage students in authentic textbook-related tasks. Typically, these are used as individual or small group activities after the teacher has reviewed textbook parts. If teachers plan to use an activity as a pretest, students must complete the activity independently and without support. An example of a textbook exploration activity is shown in Figure 13.2.

Pretests

As shown in Figure 13.3, teachers can also design and/or administer informal pretests to assess student knowledge of their textbooks. Typically these indicate if the student knows the names and uses of various textbook parts.

Although results from these assessments provide some helpful information, their use is somewhat limited. Typically, results do not indicate if the student can successfully *use* parts of the textbook. In other words, how helpful is it to know that Lynn can identify on a quiz that the glossary lists words, their pronunciations, and their definitions? Just because Lynn *knows* the purpose of a glossary does not necessarily mean that he can *use*

Figure 13.2 Textbook Exploration Activity

Directions: Use your social studies text to answer the following questions. This is a pretest, so your score will not count toward your class grade. Do your best to answer each question.

1. What are the last names of the two authors of our text? _____ and_____

2. On what page does Chapter 7 begin? _____

3. Define the word *membrane*: _____

4. How many chapter objectives are included in Chapter 3? _____

5. List all the pages that reference Thomas Jefferson: _____

6. On what page does the appendix begin? _____

7. What three features are included in the appendix? _____, _____, and _____

8. What chapter is the shortest? _____ longest?_____

9. How did you find the answers to question 8? _____

10. What visual aid from Chapter 9 indicates how many years passed between the Albany Congress and when the Constitution was ratified? _____

Figure 13.3 Textbook Pretest

Directions: This pretest is intended to determine what you know about your textbook. Do your best to answer each question. This is a pretest, so your score will not count toward your class grade. Read each question and circle the correct answer.

1. What part of his textbook should Kenny look at to determine how many chapters are included in the book?

A. The glossary

B. The table of contents

C. The appendix

D. The index

2. Where, in his history textbook, should Justin look if he wants to know which pages explain the Dred Scott decision?

A. The table of contents

B. The index

C. The appendix

D. The introduction

3. Brandi does not know the meaning of *nullify,* which is a term used frequently in her reading. Where should she look to find a definition?

    A. The glossary

    B. The index

    C. The appendix

    D. The table of contents

4. Which part of a history textbook would contain maps and copies of important charters or treaties?

    A. The table of contents

    B. The glossary

    C. The appendix

    D. The references

5. Stephanie wants to know the names of the authors of her biology text. Where should she look?

    A. The table of contents

    B. The glossary

    C. The title page

    D. The copyright page

6. Wanda wants to know where and when (what year) her *Introduction to Religion* book was published. Where should she look?

    A. The table of contents

    B. The glossary

    C. The title page

    D. The copyright page

7. How are items in the index listed?

    A. By page number

    B. By chapter

    C. By date

    D. In alphabetical order

8. Why do textbook authors bold, italicize, or use a different color for some words or headings?

    A. To show that these are foreign words

    B. To show that these are difficult to pronounce

    C. To show that these are on the test

    D. To show that these are important

the glossary. Similarly, some students use the various parts of their text appropriately, but they cannot recall the specific name of that part on a quiz. Therefore, this assessment should be supplemented with information from other sources.

A second kind of pretest assesses whether or not the student can *apply* selected study skills to a textbook chapter or part of a chapter. To develop this pretest, provide students with the necessary materials and ask them to complete the task. Do not provide examples or assistance. For example, assume Mr. Story wanted to know if Lynn could take notes from his science textbook. He could provide Lynn with a photocopied page or pages of the science text or an e-book if Lynn used this format, paper/pencil or a computer, and a reasonable amount of time and ask Lynn to read the textbook page(s) and write good notes that would prepare him for a quiz on this information. He would remind Lynn to do his best, that he could not provide any help, and that he wanted to know if Lynn could take good notes. Mr. Story could assess Lynn's notes with a basic checklist, such as that shown in Figure 13.4. Because these quizzes are more authentic as

Figure 13.4 Taking Notes Checklist

Appearance

_____ Were the notes neat and easy to read?

_____ Did the notes have an appropriate organizational structure?

_____ Did the notes contain sufficient white space between different ideas or topics?

_____ Did the notes contain bold or underlined features to emphasize terms, dates, proper nouns, et cetera?

Components

_____ Did the notes include the student's name, date, subject, topic, and page number?

_____ Did the notes include main ideas?

_____ Did the notes include important details?

_____ Did the notes include visuals, bullets, numbers, diagrams, et cetera, if appropriate?

_____ Did the notes include abbreviations, if appropriate?

Overall Evaluation

_____ Did the notes summarize critical information from the text?

_____ Are the notes presented in a format that is conducive to study and review?

they parallel classroom demands, their results provide teachers with helpful data. If Lynn has experience using an e-book or hypertext features, the pretest would require him to use the various features, thus assessing his competencies with accessing additional text, data, graphics, or audio bites, for example.

Mr. Story can assess Lynn's use of a textbook-related learning strategy in a similar manner. Perhaps Mr. Story wants to know if Lynn is familiar with and can use the PQRST textbook strategy, which includes the steps: preview the whole chapter, question (turn headings into questions), read that section, summarize what you have read, test yourself on the whole chapter. The pretest would be specific to this strategy and, like other strategy pretests presented in this book, include two parts: one that assesses Lynn's ability to list the steps of the strategy and a second that assesses his ability to apply those steps to a textbook passage. An example of a pretest for the PQRST strategy is in Figure 13.5.

Figure 13.5 Pretest for the PQRST Strategy

PQRST Strategy Pretest   Name_____

In this class, we may learn the PQRST strategy. Do your best to answer these questions. Use legible printing or handwriting.

Part 1: PQRST Steps

What do the letters *P, Q, R, S,* and *T* represent in this strategy?

P—

Q—

R—

S—

T—

Part 2: Application

You were assigned to read, take notes, and prepare for a quiz covering pages 107–115 of Chapter 5 of your science text. A photocopy of these pages is included. Use these pages and the materials provided (paper, pencil, and highlighter) to complete the following:

   1. Before you begin reading and taking notes from these pages, list anything from the chapter that you would glance over first.

(Continued)

Figure 13.5 (Continued)

2. Take each heading from pages 107–115 and turn it into a question that will serve as a purpose for reading and taking notes on that section. Write the heading and your question for each heading below:

Heading	Question
Example: The Industrial Revolution	*Example:* What is the Industrial Revolution?

3. Now it is time to begin reading. As you read, use your highlighter to highlight important ideas.
4. Indicate how you would review this information.
5. Indicate how you would quiz yourself on this information.

LYNN'S INDIVIDUALIZED EDUCATION PROGRAM

Mr. Story administered an interview, inventory, and the PQRST pretest to Lynn to assess Lynn's knowledge and use of a textbook. Mr. Story had previously conducted informal curriculum-based reading measures with Lynn using the science and social studies texts and determined that the texts were written two years above Lynn's instructional reading level. Mr. Story invited members of Lynn's IEP team to review the assessment data and plan interventions that would help Lynn more independently access the general education curriculum. Lynn's IEP goals and objectives related to these assessments are noted in Figure 13.6.

Figure 13.6 Lynn's IEP

Individualized Education Program

Name: Lynn   Grade: 6   Skill Area: Study Skills/Textbook Skills

Present Level of Performance: On informal assessments, Lynn earned 10 out of 25 points on the textbook strategy pretest by providing questions for all seven chapter headings, listing two items he would preview before reading, and highlighting one main idea. Lynn was not able to list the steps of the PQRST strategy or indicate how he would review or test himself on information he had read. He indicated that he is familiar with the table of contents but finds using the glossary difficult, seldom/never underlines in a book, and answers about one-fourth (25%) of his study guide questions on his own. This fact was verified by his parents, who help him with homework.

Annual Goal: Lynn will independently correctly complete 75% of assigned study guides and other textbook-based assignments from his inclusion classes.

Objective 1: By the end of the first quarter, after receiving instruction and after completing activities on the different parts of a textbook, Lynn will independently locate information in his science and social studies textbooks using the title page, author page, table of contents, index, appendix, and/or glossary with 90% accuracy.

Objective 2: By the end of the second quarter, given removable highlighter tape (or using the highlighting option in his e-book), Lynn will highlight 4 of 5 main ideas and details from his content-area textbooks.

Objective 3: By the end of the third quarter, after being assigned a textbook note-taking assignment and being allowed to use a computer, Lynn will type notes earning 80% of possible points on a teacher-made checklist.

Objective 4: By the end of the school year, when given a study guide, removable highlighter tape, and use of a computer, Lynn will independently highlight or type 75% of the study guide answers.

SUMMARY

As more students with diverse learning, language, and social-emotional needs receive more of their instruction in general education settings, they will be expected to be wise users of general education resources, which include textbooks. Many textbooks are not designed or chosen with students with disabilities in mind; therefore students often experience frustration using a textbook due to the reading and language load, organizational structure, and lack of instruction regarding its use. Teachers can gather informal data from various sources to assess students' knowledge and use of textbooks. Results from textbook-based informal reading inventories, interviews, textbook inventories, pretests, and activities provide IEP team members with valuable data to plan and design interventions.

CHAPTER APPLICATION ACTIVITIES

Apply your knowledge from the chapter by discussing or completing the following application questions or activities. Suggested answers are provided below.

1. Assume your student, Joshua, has some experience with electronic textbooks (e-textbooks). How might you modify the assessment in Figure 13.4 to determine if he can use features of the e-book?

2. Assume that one of your students, Teri, a ninth grader, reads at a fourth-grade level. Your school has various assistive technologies (e.g., Kurzweil) to support students as they access the general education curriculum. While these supports are helpful, what are some possible disadvantages of using such materials?

3. Many teachers use a version of the textbook exploration activity shown in Figure 13.5. How might you use it with students?

Suggested Responses

Responses will vary, but here are some suggested ideas:

1. Some of the questions are relevant, regardless of whether the student is using a traditional textbook or a digital one. However, additional questions could ask Joshua to show how he used features of the digital book such as highlighting text, taking notes, finding terms in the glossary, accessing videos or custom animation, et cetera.

2. Some schools do not have the technology budget or support to provide many options for students. Some teachers are not well trained in the use of various assistive technologies. If students use only taped materials or materials in other formats, they are not getting any reading practice with materials at their own level. These accommodations do not replace the need to provide sustained reading interventions.

3. The textbook exploration activity can be used as a pretest to determine students' knowledge about their textbook. After introducing and surveying the text with the whole class, some teachers have students in pairs or groups complete the activity. Other teachers assign it as a homework assignment.

SUPPLEMENTAL RESOURCES FOR CHAPTER 13

Strichart, S., & Mangrum, C. (2011). *Study skills for learning disabled and struggling students grades 6–12.* Upper Saddle River, NJ: Merrill.

Textbook Skills: 14
Methods and
Strategies

Textbooks can be daunting to students with disabilities; however, we can assist them in tackling the material by using strategies.

(Gore, 2004, p. 97)

CHAPTER OVERVIEW

After interviewing Lynn and reviewing his assessments, Mr. Story developed a plan. His plan involves working with Lynn (and other students) on using the textbook as well as consulting with general education teachers on ways they can support students like Lynn in accessing the general education curriculum, especially with respect to textbook-related assignments. Therefore, this chapter first describes various kinds of textbook supports that teachers can provide for students like Lynn. Next, the chapter describes several note-taking and textbook-reading strategies that help students navigate through their textbooks.

FEATURED METHODS AND STRATEGIES

Chapter Strategies	Corresponding Common Core State Standards
READ Note taking Note cards PQRST	Determine the central ideas or information of a primary or secondary source; provide an accurate summary of the source distinct from prior knowledge or opinions.
	Identify key steps in a text's description of a process related to history/social studies.
	Read and comprehend science/technical texts independently and proficiently.

Source for standards: Common Core State Standards Initiative, 2012

TEXTBOOK SUPPORTS

In addition to receiving instruction on using classroom resources, students need and benefit from additional supports that promote their success with accessing the general curriculum. These supports help all students, and they can be developed by the general or special educator or, ideally, both teachers collaborating. As Mr. Story consults with his general education colleagues, he explains the use and benefits of anticipation guides, guided notes, graphic organizers, cue cards, study guides, highlighted text, electronic text, and taped material.

Because more students are listening to taped materials, Mr. Story reminded teachers to (1) record verbatim only those passages relevant to objectives—summarize or omit other material; (2) insert statements to model think-alouds or to call attention to illustrations, graphs, comprehension questions, summaries, and other textbook aids; (3) use four different symbols (e.g., a star, a circle, a square, and a rectangle), as appropriate, in the text to cue students where the tape has (a) summarized material, (b) omitted material, (c) provided material recorded verbatim, or (d) when they need to stop the tape to complete an activity; (4) enlist the help of others to complete the taping.

Teachers can also consult the following:

Audible.com, www.audible.com (this is a subscription service)

Books Aloud, Inc., www.booksaloud.org

National Library Service (NLS), www.loc.gov/nls/reference/factsheets/playback.html

Learning Ally, www.learningally.com/

Talking Books, www.loc.gov/nls/tbt/

Talking Tapes/Textbooks on Tape, www.talkingtapes.org

When instructing students to highlight text, Mr. Story reminded teachers to consider three different colors: (1) key terms in green, (2) important information and facts in yellow, and (3) definitions in pink. If all teachers on a grade-level team agree to be consistent in their taping procedures and use of textbooks, students like Lynn will likely encounter fewer difficulties.

STUDY GUIDES

Secondary teachers frequently provide study guides to students as a reading support. Well-developed study guides help students access the curriculum as they provide cues about important concepts, organize information for studying purposes, introduce new content-specific vocabulary, and provide a structure for students for thinking about the unit of study (Gore, 2004; Salend, 2008; Vaughn, Bos, & Schumm, 2003). Because some teachers may be unfamiliar with ways to write student-considerate student guides (in other words, study guides that provide maximum success, structure, and clarity for students) and ways to differentiate study guides, in Appendix C, we offer tips for teachers for developing effective study guides (Conderman & Bresnahan, 2010).

Some teachers have also explored the use of electronic or hypertext study guides. These allow students to access hypertext links when they need specific assistance. For example, the hypertext can be linked to strategies, definitions, or graphics that supplement the reading. Because these study guides have supplemental learning resources, students need to learn how and when to use them and how to monitor their activity and time in accordance with the task and learning objectives. Although researchers have noted some promising learning results using electronic study guides for students with disabilities, they agree that more research is still needed.

Some students experience difficulty locating answers, understanding exactly what kind of response is required, or paraphrasing responses and may need teacher modeling of each different question type using a highlighted text. They may need support understanding that each question type requires a different reading-response approach.

Students may also benefit from a basic study guide strategy that applies to all questions. We developed the READ strategy, which includes these steps:

- R—*Read the study guide question.* Read it a few times to ensure you know what it is asking.
- E—*Examine the question word or task.* Focus on what the question is asking and the task (e.g., matching, true-false).
- A—*Analyze the text for the answer.* Look for words or sentences in the text that have some of the same words as the question.
- D—*Double-check the answer.* Before you answer, double-check by asking: Did I follow the steps for this type of question? and Does the answer make sense?

NOTE-TAKING APPROACHES

Well-written study guides are an invaluable study resource for students, but not all teachers provide them, some are poorly written, and students might skim only for answers and mistakenly think nothing else in the chapter is important. Therefore, students may need to write their own notes on reading material. Further, note taking is an important skill for completing research or summarizing other written accounts. Grade-level team members or teachers in an entire school can determine which note-taking approach or approaches they will teach and expect students to use.

Two-Column Systems

For students who are already familiar and successful with two-column study guides, the two-column note-taking system is an appropriate first step to note taking. This system requires students to divide their paper in half lengthwise, assign different components to each of the two resulting columns, use only the front side of the paper, and use abbreviations, when possible. Two-column notes are especially helpful for reviewing because students can cover one column and quiz themselves. Because this system is flexible and dependent upon the text structure used in the reading, teachers can model several two-column note-taking formats. Some of those include the following:

- *The question-answer system*—Students write questions in the first column and corresponding answers in the second column. They turn chapter headings and subheadings into questions and read carefully to locate answers.
- *The notes and question format*—Students write notes in the left column (i.e., bullet points, phrases, statements) and questions based on those notes in the right column. Questions later serve as study questions. This format is opposite of the question-answer format.
- *The keywords and explanation system* (*the Montana plan*)—Students write keywords, concepts, proper nouns, and important dates in the left column and provide a definition or explanation of their importance in the right column.
- *The main ideas and detail format*—Students write the main idea or ideas in one column and details in the second column.

Figure 14.1 provides examples of two-column notes based on a passage about gold from a social studies text.

Other popular two-column note-taking approaches include conclusion (left column) and support (right column) and cause (left column) and effect (right column).

Figure 14.1 Examples of Two-Column Notes

Question-Answer Format

Question	Answer
Why is gold so valuable?	Quantities are limited, and it cannot be destroyed easily.

Notes and Questions Format

Notes	Questions
Natural state is nuggets	What is gold's natural state?
Refined by treating it with nitric acid	How is gold refined?
Exchanged for goods and coins and used in jewelry and dentistry	What are common uses of gold?

Keywords and Explanation Format

Keywords	Explanation
Ore	Metal-bearing mineral or rock
Nugget	Lump
Alloyed	Substance composed of two or more metals

Main Ideas and Details Format

Main Ideas	Details
There is a process of changing nuggets into gold. Gold is valuable.	Natural state is nuggets, contains more or less silver, refined by treating with nitric acid
	Gold is in limited quantities and cannot be destroyed easily
Gold has several uses.	Some uses include these: exchange for goods and coins, jewelry, dentistry

Cornell System

The Cornell system is a long-standing and well-known version of the two-column system. Students divide their paper vertically by drawing a line from top to bottom about 2 inches from the left side of the page. They write their name, course, date, and page numbers across the top. As they read, they write main ideas and concepts in the right column, which is the notes column. Students can write paragraphs, sentences, definitions, or a combination of these in the notes column. As soon after reading as possible, students review their notes and clarify information by checking other resources. Then they summarize what they have written in the notes column by writing short phrases, dates, key ideas, et cetera in the left column, which is the recall column. This step helps students clarify meanings, understand relationships, and remember information. As a review step, they cover up the notes column, look only at the recall column, and quiz themselves by stating what they remember. As Figure 14.2 shows, they also summarize main ideas from the reading at the bottom of their paper.

Figure 14.2 Cornell Notes

Cindy Knapp	2/22/13
Foods 1	pp. 106–108
Food pyramid (three facts)	Outline of what to eat daily General guide for nutrients and calories Based on dietary guidelines
Number of main food groups	Five main groups (not including fats, oils, and sweets group)
Serving size in each group	One serving size in each group is as follows: Dairy—1 cup of milk or yogurt Meat—2–3 ounces of lean cooked meat Vegetable—1 cup of raw leafy vegetables Fruit—1 medium sized piece of fruit Bread—1 slice of bread

Summary: The food pyramid is an outline of what to eat daily. It includes five main food groups with daily serving sizes for each group.

Three-Column Systems

Sometimes the material to be learned is more effectively summarized through a three-column system, or summary chart. An example is a text that describes several features of several related items; Figure 14.3 shows note-taking systems for reading such a text.

In the first column, students write the major subjects or topics, and in the remaining columns, they indicate specific categories to be described. Before students complete three-column systems independently, provide

Figure 14.3 Examples of Three-Column Notes

Three-Column Chart

Climate and Natural Resources of the Three Early Colonies

Colonies	Climate	Natural Resources
New England Colonies	Coldest of all colonies; long, harsh winters; short, mild summers	Fish, forests, wild animals
Southern Colonies	Warmest of all colonies; long, hot summers; mild winters	Rich farm land, forests, fish along ocean coast
Middle Colonies	Cold but moderate winters; warm summers	Rich farm land, timber, furs, iron ore, coal

Personal Connection

The Three Branches of the U.S. Government

Branch	Main Responsibilities	My Question or Connection
Executive	Carries out laws and recommends new ones President, VP, and Cabinet Members	What different cabinets make up the executive branch?
Legislative	Writes bills Includes two groups (100 senators and 435 representatives)	I recently heard that Congress cannot agree on several new bills. What does that mean for us?
Judicial	Interprets and applies laws In charge of court system (district courts, court of appeals, Supreme Court)	Can anyone appeal a case all the way up to the Supreme Court?

(Continued)

Figure 14.3 (Continued)

Vocabulary, Notes, and Summary		
Comets		
Vocabulary	Notes	Summary
Comet	Swirling ball of light with a long flashing tail	Edmund Halley was the first to believe that comets were not separate and distinct objects but were the same ones reappearing about every 76 years. At first, people made fun of his predictions, but now we know comets revolve around the sun and come near the earth about every 76 years.
Edmund Halley	First to believe comets reappeared about every 76 years	
Scoff	Make fun of	

several practice opportunities by first presenting a template with horizontal and vertical headings already labeled, and after modeling, have students work in groups or pairs to complete the remaining parts.

Three-column formats are flexible and can include a column for a personal connection or columns for vocabulary, proper names, dates, et cetera; notes associated with those terms; and a summary.

Note Cards

Some students like making note cards that they can easily manipulate rather than writing notes in columns. Rooney (2010) provided numerous examples of note card systems from various disciplines. She suggested that students first read the text between the main title and the first subtitle as an introduction to support background knowledge. At the first subtitle, students should follow these steps:

1. Read the subtitle and the section under the subtitle and on separate index cards write names (e.g., people and places), terms (words they do not know plus bold-print words), and numbers related to time. Only the word(s) or number should appear on each card. The back of each card (at this point) is blank. These are detail cards. After reviewing (see Step 4), students write on the back *only* if they could not recall the information.

2. Return to the subtitle and turn it into a good test question by writing that question on one side of a card and the answer (in a bulleted

list) on the back. The finished product for this step is a card to help answer questions about the main idea.

3. Repeat steps 1 and 2 for the entire assigned reading section.

4. Review cards by recalling information from memory, going from the front to the back and back to front of each card. If the student is unsure of an answer to a detail question, *at this point*, the student returns to the text to find the answer or have someone help find the answer, *and then* the student writes the answer on the back. Therefore, detail cards have writing on the back *only* if the student could not recall the information. This reduces time and energy in writing.

Webs and Wheels

Students can make webs or other visuals in combination with other note-taking systems or as a stand-alone system. Probably the most common is the web in which they place the main idea of the paragraph or passage in the middle and draw lines and include connectors from the main idea to subordinate ideas or details. Webs are helpful, but often student webs are messy, crowded, or difficult to use for review. Students therefore may need to develop several webs for a particular reading assignment, such as one per paragraph.

Wheels are another effective, structured approach to traditional note taking (Rooney, 2010). Wheels use an oval (called a wheel) in a column or vertical flow map to note main ideas and details. Like webs, wheels have a main idea in the center and related details included in a spoke-like manner around the wheel. A reading assignment may contain several wheels, often one for each subtitle or even one per paragraph. The student uses these steps to develop wheels:

1. Draw an oval and place the first main idea (which might be the subtitle) in the oval.

2. Write related information around the oval in a spoke-like fashion.

3. Draw another oval right beneath the previous wheel for the next idea.

4. Write the main idea in the oval and write related information around that oval.

5. Continue this process until you finish the reading assignment.

Figure 14.4 includes a web and wheel based on the same reading material. The wheel includes fewer memory cues for students, and the web includes some visuals. Students should limit their time creating icons or illustrations for their webs.

Figure 14.4 Web and Wheel

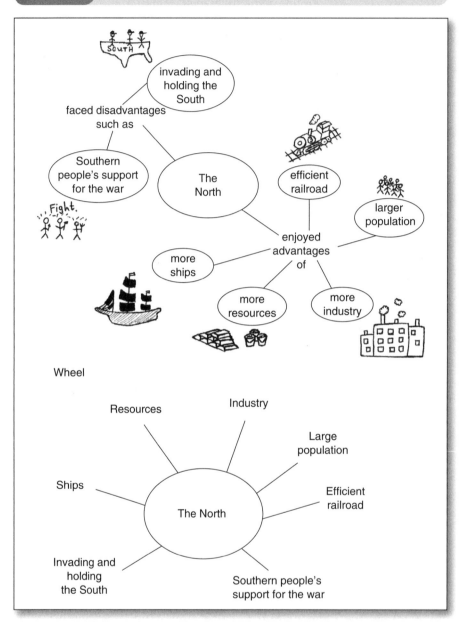

Regardless of which note-taking system students use, Vaughn and Bos (2012) provided helpful tips for students when taking notes from lectures or texts. Some of those tips include the following: Use a two- or three-column system, take notes on only one side of paper, skip lines to note changes in ideas, use abbreviations, write words the teacher writes on the board or overhead, underline or asterisk items emphasized by the teacher, and if you miss an idea, draw a blank line and return to it later.

FOUR COMMON TEXTBOOK READING STRATEGIES

Students like Lynn also benefit from learning a textbook-reading strategy. Four textbook strategies (PQRST, SQRRR, SCROL, and PQRW) are frequently described in the literature, and their steps are included in Figure 14.5.

They all share several common steps. They begin with a preview or survey step in which students look over the reading assignment to get the big picture of the material. They read the title, headings, subheadings, introduction, summary or conclusion, chapter objectives, end-of-chapter questions, bolded or italicized words, charts, graphs, and other visuals and their captions to prepare for reading and say to themselves, This chapter will be about [topic]. While previewing, students ask themselves, What do I already know about this topic? What information might the writer present? This warm-up helps students understand the chapter's

Figure 14.5 Four Textbook Strategies

PQRW	SQRRR
Preview	Survey
Question	Question
Read (just that section)	Read (just that section)
Write answers to each question	Recite (just that section). Then, repeat SQRR steps for the remaining sections.
	Review (the whole chapter)

SCROL	PQRST
Survey	Preview
Connect (look *at all the headings* within the selection, ask how headings relate to one another, and write words from headings that might provide connections among them)	Question
Read (just that section)	Read (just that section)
Outline (just that section)	Summarize (just that section by recalling important ideas from the section and taking notes). Then, repeat PQRS for the remaining sections.
Look back (over just that section)	Test (yourself on the whole chapter) by making a web or wheel, self-quizzing orally or in writing, making mnemonics, creating charts, or having someone quiz you.

organizational structure, primes their background knowledge, and prepares them for reading.

Next, three strategies teach students to take one or two minutes to change the heading or subheading into a question by asking who, what, where, when, why, or how. If the heading is already a question, they use that question. If the heading contains more than one idea, students write a question for each idea. They write their question(s) on their note-taking page and leave space to write answers later. Students do not write questions for the chapter introduction, summary, and conclusion. Typically, students focus on just one heading or subheading.

All four strategies contain "read" as the third step. Now students read *just the section that applies to the heading(s) for which they created questions.* They may mark the text, highlight, or use sticky notes to pinpoint important ideas and details and note answers to previously posed questions; monitor comprehension and reread or apply other fix-up strategies if they do not understand the material; and break long sections into smaller, more manageable segments. Students should notice bolded, underlined, or italicized words or phrases, study visual aids, and make a note card with each new or unfamiliar word.

The four strategies also include versions of summarizing what was read by reciting, outlining, or taking notes and reviewing what was read. In PQRW, students write answers to each question they wrote for the reading section. In SQRRR, students recite by asking themselves questions and answering questions about what they have read, or alternatively, summarize. In SCROL, students outline and look back to check the accuracy of their information. In PQRST, students summarize and then self-test.

Modeling the PQRST Strategy

After considering all four strategies, Mr. Story taught Lynn the PQRST strategy. We abbreviate his model step below:

I'll use the PQRST strategy to help me read today. This chapter is titled "Development of the United States' Economy." I'll start with the first step P for *preview* the whole chapter to get an idea of what is covered. Based on the title, I think the chapter will be about how our economy got started many years ago. I already know that farming was important to our economy and certain inventions made the economy grow, so I think the chapter will include those ideas. As I preview, I notice the chapter does not have an introduction, chapter objectives, or vocabulary; it starts immediately with the first heading, Factors That Influence an Economy. I also see that **economy** is bolded, and I see a timeline of dates and events from

1785 to 1848, so the chapter must focus on that time frame. The next heading is The Seven Factors of an Economy. **Labor force** is bolded; it must be important. The next page has subheadings: Natural Resources, Equipment and Tools, Transportation, and Money and Credit; **surplus** and **census** are bolded, and the margin has pictures with captions that are the same as those headings. I also see a chart showing . . . [continues through chapter].

Alright, I have previewed my chapter. I noticed a lot of things, and I think I did a good job previewing. Now I am ready for Q, *question*. I'll go back to the beginning and look *only* at the first heading. It reads, Factors That Influence an Economy. I will turn that heading into a question using words like *who, what, when, where, why,* and *how.* I'll turn this heading into this question: What factors influence an economy? The other question words would not make sense. I'm going to also add the question, What is an economy? because I do not know the definition of *economy,* and *economy* is part of the chapter title and this heading, so it must be important. Now I have two questions for that heading. I'll write those in my two-column notes. Those questions serve as a purpose for my reading.

In the R or *read* step, I *only* read this section. As I read, I keep my two questions in mind. [Teacher orally reads section.] I see one bolded word: **economy.** I am going to reread that sentence again to make sure I understand. The sentence reads, "The process of producing, buying, and selling goods and services is called an **economy."** I understand this, so now I can summarize.

To complete the S step, *summarize,* I locate answers, find additional main ideas, and write notes. The sentence I just reread answers my second question exactly. So—I will write that answer in my notes. My first question was, What factors influence an economy? The second paragraph reads, "Many factors influence an economy such as (1) how many people live there, (2) available resources, (3) what skills and machinery workers have to use, (4) what people want to buy, and (5) how much profit people can make selling goods and services." I like how those are numbered. I'll write those (abbreviated) in my notes. Let me see . . . is there anything else that seems important to include in my notes? In two different sentences, I read about how the agricultural economy met most of the basic food needs of people in the 13 colonies. Because this is stated twice, it must be important. In my notes, I will write, What economy met the basic food needs of people in the 13 colonies? I will write Agricultural in the answer column. OK—before I go onto the next heading, I summarize [teacher summarizes] and make a connection. My connection is the new iPhone. We need resources to make it, people to buy it, skilled workers to make it, and the company needs to make a profit. All of these influence our economy.

When I have completed these steps with the whole chapter, I do the T step—*test* myself. How could I do that? One way is to read my two-column notes again, cover up the answer column, and see if I can state in my own words the answer to each question in the question column [teacher models this]. So, one question is what economy met the basic food needs of people in the 13 colonies? I cannot remember the answer. I'll reveal the answer side again. Oh, yes, agricultural. That's right. OK. I might need to know that for the quiz. [Teacher continues to model other self-testing strategies.]

TIME SAVERS

Teachers who know or think that they may be teaching the same strategy to several students across class periods or semesters can videotape themselves completing the model step and provide access to that video to students. This saves considerable time and ensures consistency in the model step. Students can also view the model step whenever they need a refresher rather than having the teacher demonstrate the strategy again.

SUMMARY

Reading, understanding, retrieving, and retaining information from textbooks is difficult. Many students need considerable support and much practice before they can independently perform these skills. Teachers can prepare students for textbook material by using a variety of textbook supports. Students should learn several note-taking approaches and explore which ones work best under which circumstances. Finally, students benefit from explicit strategy instruction on navigating through a textbook. Textbook strategies typically involve the steps of previewing, questioning, reading, summarizing, and testing.

CHAPTER APPLICATION ACTIVITIES

Apply your knowledge from the chapter by discussing or completing the following application questions or activities. Suggested answers are provided below.

The PQRST strategy integrates various reading strategies into one comprehensive strategy. The following activities allow practice with that strategy using this chapter as the text.

1. Using the PQRST strategy, what would you preview from this chapter?

2. Using the PQRST strategy, turn the section titled Study Guides into a question that would provide a purpose for reading.

3. Using the PQRST strategy, summarize the section on Study Guides from this chapter.

Suggested Responses

Responses will vary, but here are some suggested ideas:

1. While previewing the chapter, you might read the chapter title, read the chapter overview, read headings and subheadings, notice websites, glance at words in italics, read the summary, and look over the figures.

2. To turn the heading Study Guides into a question, you might consider, What are study guides? What is the value of study guides? How do teachers make study guides?

3. Study guides are helpful for students, but they need support in completing them. A strategy such as READ can help students answer study guide questions.

SUPPLEMENTAL RESOURCES FOR CHAPTER 14

Boyle, J. R., & Rivera, T. Z. (2012). Note-taking techniques for students with disabilities: A systematic review of the research. *Learning Disability Quarterly, 35*(3), 131–143.

Ellis, E. S. (1994). An instructional model for integrating content-area instruction with cognitive strategy instruction. *Reading and Writing Quarterly: Overcoming Learning Difficulties, 10*(1), 63–90.

Goodman, A. (2005). The middle school high five: Strategies can triumph. *Voices from the Middle, 13*(2), 12–19.

Grant, R. (1993). Strategic training for using text headings to improve students' processing of content. *Journal of Reading, 36*, 482–488.

Jones, R. (2006). *Reading quest: Strategies for reading comprehension.* Retrieved from http://www.readingquest.org/strat/pto.html

Santa, C., Havens, L., & Macumber, E. (2004). *Creating independence through student-owned strategies.* Dubuque, IA: Kendall/Hunt.

Schumaker, J., Deshler, D., Alley, G., Warner, M., & Denton, P. (1982). Multipass: A learning strategy for improving reading comprehension. *Learning Disability Quarterly, 5*(3), 295–304.

Wood, J. W. (2006). *Teaching students in inclusive settings: Adapting and accommodating instruction* (5th ed.). Upper Saddle River, NJ: Merrill/Prentice-Hall.

Wood, K. D. (1995). Guiding middle school students through expository text. *Reading and Writing Quarterly: Overcoming Learning Difficulties, 11*, 137–147.

Textbook Curriculum and Teaching Resources

Abbamont, G., & Brescher, A. (1997). *Test smart! Ready-to-use test taking strategies and activities for grades 5–12.* Hoboken, NJ: John Wiley and Sons.

Active reading: Comprehension and rate. (2012). Hanover, NH: Dartmouth College. Retrieved from http://www.dartmouth.edu/~acskills/success/reading.html

Davis, L., & Sirotowitz, S. (1996). *Study strategies made easy: A practical plan for school success.* Champaign, IL: Research Press.

Palomares, S., & Schilling, D. (2006). *Studying, test taking, and getting good grades.* Austin, TX: Pro-Ed.

Romain, T., & Verdick, E. (1999). *True or false? Tests stink!* Minneapolis, MN: Free Spirit.

Rozakis, L. (2002). *Super study skills: The ultimate guide to tests and studying.* New York, NY: Scholastic.

Self-Regulation: Informal Assessments $\quad$ **15**

Collecting self-regulation baseline data provides the student with a rationale for participating in the intervention, may motivate the student to try self-monitoring, and may prompt self-evaluation.

(Maag, 2004)

MEET JAMES

James is a pleasant tenth grader who has been receiving special education services since fifth grade for learning and attention issues. Even with accommodations and adjusted assignments, James's work is messy, incomplete, and/or inaccurate. Further, he quits when the work gets challenging and frequently says that he is "no good at school." Although he does not display disruptive behaviors, Mrs. Harris, James's special education teacher, has noticed that he does not always "track" the teacher during teacher-led instruction, and he frequently looks around the classroom during teacher-led instruction. Despite various interventions, James's grades are suffering. Mrs. Harris wonders if James would benefit from self-regulation instruction.

CHAPTER OVERVIEW

This chapter provides an overview of self-regulation by defining self-regulation, explaining three components of self-regulation, offering a rationale for teaching self-regulation, and illustrating various self-monitoring recording forms. The chapter also includes self-regulation IEP goals and objectives based on informal assessment results.

WHAT IS SELF-REGULATION?

James is like many students with mild disabilities who need support with self-regulation. Students who are unable to regulate their behavior often have difficulty monitoring their performance, changing strategies or approaches when a change is warranted, completing tasks independently, controlling inappropriate behaviors, and engaging in positive self-talk.

Self-regulation is the process of continuously monitoring progress toward a goal, checking outcomes, and redirecting unsuccessful efforts (Berk, 2003). Students who are self-regulated are aware of their own thought process and are motivated to actively participate in their own learning process (Zimmerman, 2001). Consequently, the goals of self-regulation are for *students* to become more aware of and take more responsibility for their thinking processes, task approaches, and self-reinforcement. Self-regulation is typically composed of three components: self-monitoring, self-evaluation, and self-reinforcement (Mercer & Pullen, 2008).

Self-monitoring occurs when individuals (a) self-assess whether or not they have engaged in a particular behavior, (b) record the occurrence of that behavior, and (c) chart or graph the data. Graphs provide a visual representation and summary of data and are helpful to show the student and IEP team members when discussing the effectiveness of the intervention. Because several subskills are involved in self-monitoring, researchers often consider self-monitoring as an intervention in and of itself. Similarly, because critical skills are associated with self-monitoring, often this intervention leads to *reactivity*, which means that observing and recording one's behavior promotes changing that behavior in the desired direction (Maag, 2004). Typically, students self-monitor productivity, accuracy, or strategy use. Because self-monitoring does not teach or create new behaviors, students must already have the targeted behavior in their repertoire.

The target behavior should represent the appropriate, desired behavior rather than a negative one. For example, a common intervention to help students monitor their attention is to have them mark on a card whether or not they were paying attention at certain intervals, such as when a tape recorder beeper signaled, as shown in Figure 15.1. For an independent work period of 15 to 20 minutes, intertone intervals should average 45 seconds and range from 10 to 90 seconds. These amounts may be doubled for work periods lasting 30 to 40 minutes (Maag, 2004).

Teachers need to be very clear about what behaviors show—and do not show—the desired outcome, and model examples and nonexamples of those behaviors prior to the intervention. Sometimes, teachers also

Figure 15.1 Linda's Paying Attention Chart

Directions: When you hear the beep, ask yourself if you were paying attention. Remember, during teacher instruction, paying attention means you were (1) staying in your seat, (2) watching Ms. Woods, and (3) being quiet. If you were doing *all* of these, check the yes column associated with the time segment. If you were not doing *all* of these, check no in the column associated with the time segment.

Time Segment	Yes	No
1.		
2.		
3.		
4.		
5.		
6.		
7.		
8.		
9.		
10.		

My performance today: _____ (e.g. 4/10 yes boxes checked)

My goal: _____ (e.g., 7/10 yes boxes checked)

assess the student's behaviors, and then both student and teacher compare and discuss results; however the goal of self-monitoring is to improve behavior rather than emphasize accurate self-recording. The student's data do not need to be perfect for improvement to occur; the student's increased self-awareness of the behavior, rather than accurate recording, changes behavior. Examples of various self-monitoring formats are shown in Figure 15.2.

Self-instruction refers to using self-talk to navigate through a task or activity. Self-talk is an important aspect of the thinking process because language enhances thinking and affects behavior. This is why teacher modeling, using think-alouds, is so important—especially for students with language-based disabilities. Teachers who make their thinking explicit through think-alouds model appropriate and positive thinking. Jacobson and Reid (2010) as well as Graham, Harris, and

Figure 15.2 Various Self-Monitoring Cards

Jack's Class Card

Directions: For each class, place a check mark in the column indicating if you were on time or tardy. On time means you were sitting in your chair in the classroom before or when the bell rang.

Class	On Time	Tardy
Personalized Writing		
American Government		
Biology 1		
Geometry		
Resource		
Ceramics		

Vanessa's Tally Card

Directions: Make a tally mark beside each class listed below every time you say a positive comment to a peer or the teacher during that class.

American Literature _____

Concert Choir _____

Sociology _____

Chemistry _____

Calculus _____

French _____

Lu Ann's Journal Writing

Directions: After 10 minutes of journal writing in your Personalized Writing class, count how many words you wrote and write that number by the day. Remember, your goal is to write 50 words each day.

Monday: _____

Tuesday: _____

Wednesday: _____

Thursday: _____

Friday: _____

Sandra's Spelling Form

Directions: After correcting your weekly spelling test, write on the line for each week the number of words you spelled correctly. Your goal is to spell at least 20 words correctly.

Week 1: _____

Week 2: _____

Week 3: _____

Week 4: _____

Week 5: _____

Julia's Editing Strategy Cue Card

Directions: Check off each step of the COPS strategy as you complete it.

Step	Question to ask yourself	Check when you complete this step
C—*Capitalization*	Have I capitalized the first word in every sentence and all proper nouns?	
O—*Overall appearance*	Is my writing neat and easy to read, and did I write in the margins?	
P—*Punctuation*	Did I use end punctuation such as periods, question marks, exclamation marks, and semicolons?	
S—*Spelling*	Did I sound out words, check the dictionary, or check with someone?	

MacArthur (2006) noted that think-alouds should contain statements related to the following:

1. Defining the problem or task (e.g., What am I expected to do?)

2. Planning (e.g., What do I do next?)

3. Staying on task (e.g., I am going to keep going)

4. Monitoring performance / self-evaluating (e.g., Does that make sense?)

5. Coping with frustration / self-reinforcing (e.g., I can do this)

Some students, like James, often use negative self-talk, especially when encountering challenging tasks. In some cases, some self-criticism can be helpful, but it should not overpower efforts or cause discouragement. For example, after receiving only partial credit on an essay, James might say to himself, I did not organize my essay well, and I left out some details. Although this sounds negative, it may help James improve future efforts. Students often need encouragement regarding ways to use negative feedback to plan future efforts.

Because some students forget what to say to themselves, they benefit from a cue card that includes statements they can use when completing tasks. Students and teachers can brainstorm statements to include on the cue card. Reid and Lienemann (2006) provided these examples:

- *Problem definition*—What do I need to do now? What's my next step?
- *Focusing attention/attending*—I need to take my time and concentrate. What's the best way to do this problem?
- *Strategy-related*—I need to remember to use my strategy.
- *Self-evaluation*—I need to check and see how I am doing. Does this answer make sense? This is not right; I need to fix it.
- *Coping*—I can do this if I keep at it. I know I can do it. Take a deep breath and relax.
- *Self-reinforcement*—I did it! Great job! I worked hard and got it right!

In *self-reinforcement*, students self-evaluate and then judge whether or not they have earned a reward. Self-administered consequences can be overt (such as a tangible outcome) or covert (such as positive self-talk). Often, initially, rewards are provided by an adult to motivate the student to engage in the intervention. Teachers can use a reinforcement menu, ask the student what they would like as a reward, or develop a contract. The goal, though, is to stretch and fade external reinforcers, so eventually the student reinforces him- or herself.

Some students may not require self-reinforcement. Many self-management interventions are effective without this component. Therefore, add self-reinforcement only if self-monitoring and self-instruction do not produce the desired outcome. Further, some students find making self-statements (e.g., I am a good piano player; I can complete this study guide by myself) childish and therefore will not consider this component.

WHY SHOULD WE TEACH SELF-REGULATION?

Experts have noted reasons why students should learn self-regulation strategies. Some of those include the following:

1. They are evidence-based interventions. Researchers have documented positive results when students with various disabilities were taught self-regulatory strategies. For a meta-analysis of

studies regarding self-regulatory strategies for students with attention issues, see Reid, Trout, and Schartz (2005). Similarly, Lee, Simpson, and Shogren (2007) conducted a meta-analysis of research associated with self-management for students with autism.

2. Students with disabilities often do not use self-regulatory strategies, which is one reason why they struggle in school.

3. Self-regulatory strategies are necessary for academic, social, and job success.

4. Self-regulatory strategies reduce students' reliance on extrinsic reinforcement and their codependence on others. Some students, such as those with autism spectrum disorders, do not respond well to teacher-directed behavioral approaches involving the external manipulation of antecedents and consequences (Myles & Simpson, 2003). Self-management interventions minimize power struggles associated with teacher-developed and managed systems (Myles & Simpson, 2003).

5. When students use self-regulatory strategies, teachers have more time to teach rather than attend to behavior issues or dispense chips or tokens. The initial time teaching self-regulatory skills, then, seems well worth the effort.

INFORMAL ASSESSMENTS

Teachers can develop and use several informal assessments to gather data on students' self-regulatory behaviors. Results from observations, interviews, inventories, role-plays, and permanent products are helpful when designing self-regulatory interventions. Figure 15.3 describes these methods.

Observations

The most common observational techniques include (a) frequency or event recording—used to count the number of times a particular behavior occurs, (b) duration recording—used to measure how long a behavior lasts, (c) interval recording—used to measure the occurrence or nonoccurrence of a behavior within specified time intervals, and (d) time sampling—used to record the occurrence of a behavior at the end of an interval.

Figure 15.3 Informal Assessments for Measuring Self-Regulatory Behaviors

Method	Description	James's Results
Observation— Frequency or Event Recording	Counting the number of times the behavior occurs	James brings all of his materials to his classes on average three of five days.
Observation— Duration	Measuring the amount of time a behavior lasts	On average, James takes 15 minutes to complete the daily science, math, and English warm-ups, which are intended to take 5 minutes.
Observation— Interval	Measuring the occurrence or nonoccurrence of a behavior within short specified time intervals (e.g., 5 to 30 seconds)	James is on task 60% of the time during independent math seat work.
Observation— Time Sampling	Measuring the occurrence or nonoccurrence of a behavior immediately at the end of a specified interval (e.g., at the end of each 5-minute interval)	At the end of every 3-minute interval, teachers observed James and discovered that he was on task 40% of the time during daily science warm–ups.
Interviews	Individualized dialogue to assess students' views of their self-regulation skills	James indicated that he uses a planner, completes hardest homework assignments first, wants to graduate from high school, gets up out of his chair to deal with distractions, and is unaware of his use of any self-talk or self-reinforcement.
Inventories	Written questionnaire to assess students' perceptions of their self-regulation skills	James indicated that he does not use his neatest writing, proofread, stop and redo steps, use positive self-talk, or reward himself.
Role-Plays	Simulation in which students are asked to show and tell how to do a specific task and say aloud what they are thinking as they complete the task	When given math problems, sentences to edit, and study guide questions to complete, James showed how to complete each task and stated logical steps toward their completion. He skipped harder problems, never used positive self-talk, and did not double-check any answers.
Permanent Products	Analysis of recent work samples to note completion and accuracy rate	James submits 90% of homework/ seatwork but his average score on written work is only 65% correct. His written work is messy, words and letters are crowded, and some numbers are difficult to discern.

Interviews

Interviews are a dynamic and flexible tool that can be individualized to gather information from a student. Because we cannot infer what students are thinking as they complete a task, we have to ask. Some interview questions related to self-regulatory skills include these:

1. Explain how you know what assignments are due.

2. If you have several homework assignments to complete on the same night, which would you do first? Last? Explain your reasoning.

3. How do you estimate how long assignments might take you to complete?

4. Provide an example of when you worked on a hard assignment. What made it hard? How did you continue working on it?

5. How do you handle distractions when you study?

6. What do you tell yourself when the work is hard?

7. Share one of your academic goals.

8. What is your plan for meeting that goal?

9. How will you reward yourself when you reach that goal?

10. What can teachers do to help you learn better?

Inventories

Inventories are typically written self-assessments that capture the students' sense of their present level of performance in a particular area. Results provide a framework for dialoguing with students regarding which specific skills to target. Figure 15.4 provides inventory questions to informally assess self-regulation.

Role-Plays

Teachers can use role-plays to gather data on a student's self-regulatory skills. Because role-plays are often used as part of the instructional sequence when teaching self-regulatory strategies, they could also be considered as pre- and posttest measures. To use a role-play as a pre- (or post-) test, develop several scenarios for the student to portray. The goal is to learn how the student approaches various tasks. Select skills of varying levels of difficulty (e.g., algebra problem, spelling words), ask students to show and tell you how they complete those skills, and indicate that the goal is to complete [a certain number] in [a certain time frame] with very

Figure 15.4 Self-Regulation Questionnaire

Directions: Read each question and place a check mark in the box that indicates how frequently you complete each task or activity.

When I am doing homework or school work, do I . . .	All of the Time	Most of the Time	Sometimes	Seldom/ Never
Set reasonable goals for completion?				
Make a prioritized list of things I need to do?				
Use a timer or watch, so I can manage my time well?				
Study in an environment that is best for me to learn?				
Check off items as I complete them?				
Double-check answers?				
Proofread all my written work?				
Reread information when I do not understand something?				
Use my neatest printing/writing?				
Say to myself that I can do the work?				
Think through steps of the assignment?				
Remember to use learning strategies that I have been taught?				
Stop and redo steps when I am confused?				
Reward myself when I have completed a hard task?				

few errors. Tell students to include anything that they tell themselves while they are doing the task. During role-plays, observe for student use of self-monitoring, self-instruction, and/or self-reinforcement.

Permanent Products

Academic permanent products include items such as recently completed worksheets, tests and quizzes, homework assignments, and writing assignments. Teachers can determine if the work was completed, if it was completed correctly, and what types of errors the student made. Knowing the amount of time the student was given to complete the task is helpful if the student's goal is to increase production rate.

Teachers can also count behavioral products such as the number of scuff marks the student made or the number of spit wads thrown. Tape recorders or video recorders can be used to assess permanent products.

JAMES'S INDIVIDUALIZED EDUCATION PROGRAM

Mrs. Harris shared information she gathered with James and his IEP team. She wanted to target self-regulation as an intervention. To document these efforts, she urged the IEP team to consider adding self-regulation as part of James's overall study skills plan. His self-regulation goal and objectives are shown in Figure 15.5.

Figure 15.5 James's IEP

Individualized Education Program

Name: James   Grade: 10   Skill Area: Study Skills/Self-regulation

Present Level of Performance: According to informal assessments, James submits 90% of homework/seatwork but only with 65% accuracy, even with adjustments. His hand-written work is messy and difficult to read. James brings necessary materials to class three of five days on average, takes 15 minutes to complete five math, science, or English warm-ups; and is on-task on average 50% of the time in his general education classes. He skips hard problems, reports that he does not use self-talk or self-reinforcement, and admits to "thinking about other things" rather than completing a particular task. His teachers are concerned with the poor quality of his work and his frequent off-task behavior.

Annual Goal: James will bring all necessary materials to each class, display on-task behavior, and produce accurate and neat written documents 80% of the time.

Objective 1: By the end of the first quarter, James will independently bring all necessary materials to each class on 8 out of 10 occasions as measured by daily checklists maintained by himself and his teachers.

Objective 2: By the end of the each quarter, James will increase his percentage of on-task behavior in his inclusion classes by at least 8% as measured by teacher observations.

Objective 3: By the end of each quarter, James will increase his accuracy on homework assignments, in-class independent work, and warm ups in his inclusion classes by at least 4% as measured by permanent products.

Objective 4: By the end of the year, James will submit written work that is well organized and neat on four of five occasions as judged by his inclusion teachers using a teacher-made rubric.

SUMMARY

Strategy instruction is enhanced through self-regulatory behaviors. Self-regulation refers to the student's ability to manage and organize thoughts and translate them into efficient behaviors associated with self-monitoring, self-instruction, and self-reinforcement. Teachers can gather informal data from observations, interviews, inventories, role-plays, and permanent products to informally assess a student's self-regulatory skills. Developing goals and objectives in self-regulation signals their importance to the student and IEP team members.

CHAPTER APPLICATION ACTIVITIES

Apply your knowledge from the chapter by discussing or completing the following application questions or activities. Suggested answers are provided below.

1. Some students are motivated, at least initially, when some external reinforcer is involved. Reinforcement menus provide choices for students as they pick, from the menu, what they are willing to work for. What are some items you would include on a reinforcement menu to increase a student's motivation to work with you on an intervention?

2. Role-plays can be used to assess some components of self-regulation. Assume you have taught Nora the PQRST strategy from Chapter 14 and you want to determine how she uses self-talk during the P (preview) step. What might you say to Nora to establish this role-play scenario?

3. Interviews and inventories can and should be individualized for the student. What are some questions you would ask Brett, a student who gives up easily and does not persevere in difficult tasks?

Suggested Responses

Responses will vary, but here are some suggested ideas:

1. You might first ask students what they are willing to work for. Some possibilities include food (ask for support from local vendors), free time, the opportunity to drop one homework assignment or one bad assignment grade, et cetera.

2. Nora, we have learned the PQRST strategy for using our textbooks. The first step of that strategy is the P, or preview, step. Using

Chapter 6 from your physical science text, I want you to show me what you would do to preview this chapter. Be sure to tell me what you are doing and thinking.

3. Some of the questions in the interview and inventories in the chapter would be interesting to ask Brett. Some others would be the following: Think of a time when you accomplished something that was difficult. How did that make you feel? What were the steps you took in accomplishing that task? What did you tell yourself when the task became difficult?

SUPPLEMENTAL RESOURCES FOR CHAPTER 15

Lee, S., Palmer, S., & Wehmeyer, M. (2009). Goal setting and self-monitoring for students with disabilities. *Intervention in School and Clinic, 44*(3), 139–145.

McDougall, D. (1998). Research on self-management techniques used by students with disabilities in general education settings. *Remedial and Special Education, 19*, 310–320.

National Research Center on the Gifted and Talented. (n.d.). *Self-regulation.* Retrieved November 20, 2013, from http://www.gifted.uconn.edu/siegle/SelfRegulation/printversion.pdf

Palmer, S., Wehmeyer, M., Gibson, K., & Agran, M. (2004). Promoting access to the general curriculum by teaching self-determination skills. *Exceptional Children, 70*, 427–439.

Wilkinson, L. (2008). Self-management for children with high-functioning autism spectrum disorders. *Intervention in School and Clinic, 43*(3), 150–157.

Self-Regulation: Methods and Strategies

16

Self-regulation strategies should be an integral part of the strategy instruction process.

(Reid & Lienemann, 2006, p. 110)

CHAPTER OVERVIEW

James's IEP team members agreed to teach James self-regulatory strategies, especially in self-monitoring. They were hopeful that James would learn to assume more responsibility for his work and behavior. Knowing his grades were in jeopardy, James was interested in learning ways to become a better student and worker. As noted in James's IEP, Mrs. Harris decided to focus on helping James (a) remember to bring all necessary materials to class, (b) increase his time attending, (c) increase the accuracy of his work, and (d) improve the neatness of his work.

This chapter describes how Mrs. Harris helped James meet his self-regulation goals. The chapter includes examples of various tools teachers can use when teaching self-regulation and steps teachers should consider when developing and implementing a self-regulation system. The chapter also includes a think-aloud for teaching self-regulation.

FEATURED METHODS AND STRATEGIES

Chapter Strategies	Corresponding Common Core State Standards
SPIN Two-what WAM	Follow precisely a complex multistep procedure when carrying out experiments, taking measurements, or performing technical tasks, attending to special cases or exceptions.
CARD NEAT	Develop and strengthen writing as needed by planning, revising, editing, rewriting.

Source for standards: Common Core State Standards Initiative, 2012

INSTRUCTIONAL APPROACHES AND MATERIALS

Teachers can use a variety of approaches and materials when teaching self-regulatory behaviors. Here are some ideas from Joseph and Konrad (2009):

- Use a MotivAider, an electronic device (similar to a pager) that vibrates at predetermined intervals to prompt students to monitor their behavior. This can be purchased at www.habitchange.com.
- Consider self-management software programs such as those produced by KidTools and KidSkills. These programs include examples of contracts, learning strategies, and self-monitoring plans and can be downloaded from kidtools.missouri.edu.
- Use the KidTools software programs to help students with self-regulation, strategic learning, and self-determination behaviors. The software consists of two levels of computerized template tools to help children with self-management, problem-solving, and making plans and contracts (Miller, Fitzgerald, Koury, Mitchem, & Hollingsead, 2007).
- Use (a) stopwatches to determine how long it takes students to begin or complete an assignment, (b) kitchen timers to help students work for longer periods of time, and (c) tape recorders to develop prerecorded tones for self-monitoring of attention.
- Develop a self-determination contract. Martin, Mithaug, Cox, Peterson, Van Dycke, and Cash (2003) developed contracts for students that included four sections: (a) a plan section where students indicated when they would begin their assignments, wrote their academic tasks, wrote the number of problems or pages they would complete, indicated their level of anticipated accuracy, and noted how many points they would earn; (b) a work section where they

noted information similar to that in the planning section upon work completion; (c) an evaluate section where students self-evaluated whether they began and ended on time and accurately completed their work, and (d) an adjust section where they wrote future goals based on their performance that day.

- Use checklists, graphs, charts, cue cards, and rubrics to clarify expectations, scaffold instruction, provide reminders to students, and document results.
- Encourage students to use self-talk and self-questioning that encourage good work habits.
- Encourage self-assessment by having students reflect upon their progress, check their work with a rubric, provide a rationale for strategies they used, set goals, or maintain a reflective journal regarding progress toward meeting goals.
- Have students use the copy-cover-compare strategy as appropriate for practicing spelling words, reviewing math facts, or learning definitions of vocabulary terms. Students copy a model, cover the model and what they copied, reproduce from memory, and check their work versus the model.
- Use video modeling, in which students learn a behavior by watching a video demonstration and then imitating the behavior of the model.

Structured Instructional Steps

Regardless of the student's age or grade or the targeted skill, experts have determined effective instructional sequences to use when teaching self-regulation strategies. For example, Reid and Lienemann (2006) noted these four basic steps:

1. Select a target behavior that is specific, observable, and appropriate to the setting and task.

2. Collect baseline data.

3. Obtain cooperation from the student.

4. Provide instruction.

Wilkinson (2008) expanded these four general steps into ten specific steps: (a) Identify the target behavior; (b) determine how often students will monitor their behavior; (c) meet with the student to explain self-management, identify goals, and establish rewards upon reaching goals; (d) prepare the self-recording sheet; (e) model the self-monitoring system, have the student practice, and provide feedback to the student; (f) implement the plan; (g) meet with the student to determine whether goals were obtained; (h) provide rewards when earned; (i) involve family members by sending completed self-recording forms home for signatures and possible home-based reinforcement; (j) fade the intervention by increasing the length of time intervals between self-monitoring cues.

The SPIN Strategy

King-Sears and Bonfils (1999) developed the mnemonic SPIN for teachers. SPIN represents these steps:

S—Select the behavior for self-management.

  Identify and define the target behavior.

  Identify the criteria for mastery.

  Measure students' current level of performance.

P—Prepare materials and lesson plans for self-management.

  Select the type of management system.

  Develop the system.

I—Instruct students about the system using three main instructional steps with a total of ten substeps among them.

  1. Introduce the target behavior. (Identify and demonstrate examples and nonexamples of the target behavior; discuss the importance of the target behavior; have students practice the target behavior.)
  2. Introduce the self-management program. (Describe the self-management program and its benefits; model, using a think-aloud, how to use the self-management recording device while performing the target behavior.)
  3. Provide practice opportunities and assess student mastery. (Incorporate the target behavior and the use of the recording device within a guided practice role-play; assess student performance during the role-play; discuss the actual situation in which the self-management will be used; provide independent practice in the actual setting; assess student mastery within the actual setting.)

N—Note short-term and long-term effects on student's performance.

  Assess short-term performance of the target behavior.

  Assess long-term maintenance of the system.

  Encourage/provide generalization.

BRINGING MATERIALS TO CLASS

James's IEP targeted bringing materials to class, increasing on-task behavior, improving accuracy of assignments, and improving neatness of assignments. This section summarizes how Mrs. Harris introduced a self-monitoring intervention for each of these. Mrs. Harris began by helping James remember to bring necessary materials to each class, because she thought this goal would be the least complicated, easiest to teach, and easiest for James to understand, document, and generalize to the remaining interventions.

Mrs. Harris used a modified version of the SPIN steps to teach James to monitor his behavior with respect to bringing materials to class. Here's a summary of what occurred in each step:

S—*Select the behavior for self-management.* James's present level of performance data indicated that he brought necessary materials to class on three of five occasions. Teachers were becoming impatient with this behavior. His IEP objective is to bring necessary materials to classes on 8 of 10 occasions.

P—*Prepare materials and lesson plans for self-management.* Mrs. Harris developed a self-monitoring checklist on a card that James will take to each class every day. On his card, James will note what materials are needed for each class and which ones he actually brought to class. For accountability, each teacher will initial the card after each class. Each day in the resource room, James and Mrs. Harris will discuss his progress and together calculate progress toward his IEP objective. The bottom of the card includes a place for James to self-assess. The requirement for teacher initials will be eliminated after three consecutive weeks of meeting the objective. Mrs. Harris did not include an external reinforcement but instead offered verbal feedback. James's card is shown in Figure 16.1.

I—*Instruct students about the system.* Mrs. Harris discussed self-monitoring by making an analogy to driving because James would be driving soon. She emphasized that before drivers enter the driver's seat, they need to make sure (or monitor) that they have their driver's license and insurance card and that the car has enough gas. These are like materials students need when they enter a classroom. Mrs. Harris and James reviewed the benefits of being prepared for every class, and Mrs. Harris introduced the self-monitoring card and explained its use. Mrs. Harris reminded James of the importance of being responsible to bring all materials to every class and the consequences of forgetting them. The two discussed materials typically needed for each class and ways for James to keep materials available. Mrs. Harris demonstrated examples and nonexamples of bringing all materials to class. Because this was the first introduction to

Figure 16.1 Abbreviated Form of James's Materials Card

Remember the two-what strategy as you complete your card.

Class	What was I supposed to bring to class today? (circle all that apply)	What did I bring to class today? (circle all that apply)	Teacher's initials
Algebra 1	Textbook, Pencil, Paper, Homework, Calculator Other: _____	Textbook, Pencil, Paper, Homework, Calculator Other: _____	
German 1	Textbook, Pencil, Paper, Homework, German-English Dictionary Other: _____	Textbook, Pencil, Paper, Homework, German-English Dictionary Other: _____	
P. E.	P. E. Clothes Other: _____	P. E. Clothes Other: _____	
List other classes here			

How did I do? Check the statement that applies.

	I brought all my needed materials to my classes today. I did a great job!
	I brought most of my needed materials to my classes. I did a good job.
	I brought some of my needed materials to my classes. I need to work on this.

self-monitoring, Mrs. Harris used a think-aloud as she modeled use of the card. She emphasized the two questions James should be asking himself, both starting with the word *what*. Therefore, she and James called this the two-what strategy. Her modeling sounded like this:

OK—I am using this card to help me to bring materials to class. How do I use this card? Well, I am in math class, so I complete just this row pertaining to math. The first question I ask myself is, What was I supposed to bring to class today? For math class today, we need our math book, today's math homework assignment, a pencil, and a calculator. I know that because yesterday Mr. Ryan assigned homework, and he told us it was due today. A rule in this class is to always bring the book, a pencil, and a calculator. We don't need anything else, so in Column 1 titled What was I *supposed* to bring to class today, I will circle *book, homework, pencil,* and *calculator.* Ok—I finished that step. Great! What's next?

For the second step, I ask myself: What *did* I bring to class today? I look at each item I circled in Column 1 and ask myself if I brought that item to class. Did I bring my book? Yes—I have it right here. What about my homework assignment? Yes—I worked on it last night and placed it in this folder, which I have right here. Super! How about a pencil? Yes—I have several here in my backpack. Last, what about a calculator? Yes—I have that, too, in my backpack. So—I will circle all of those items in the What did I bring to class column. Now that I have all my materials with me, I am ready to begin class.

[Mrs. Harris skips to modeling the end of class.] Mr. Ryan just dismissed us, and before I leave for German class, I'll catch his attention to initial my card. Mr. Ryan—See, I brought everything I needed today for class. Could you please initial my card for me? Thanks. I'll place the card here in this pocket and take it to my next class.

After modeling, Mrs. Harris provided practice opportunities and assessed James's ability to use the card. Specifically, she shared various scenarios that each involved a specific class, required materials for that class, and materials James brought to class. For each scenario, she asked James to say the two *what* questions aloud and to ask the teacher to initial the form. After several practice sessions, the team agreed to begin the intervention.

N—*Note short-term and long-term effects on student's performance.* James was motivated to improve his grades and reduce his dependence on friends. He reached his objective and no longer needed to secure each teacher's signature.

INCREASING ON-TASK BEHAVIOR

After James experienced sustained success with bringing materials to class, Mrs. Harris introduced the next intervention—monitoring attention in class. She chose this skill next because she thought it would yield a high dividend in all of James's classes.

Again, Mrs. Harris introduced this skill using a driving analogy. She emphasized that drivers need to monitor many things—such as their speed, the traffic, road signs, road conditions, and their route. This process is similar to what students need to do in their classes. They need to attend to teachers, listen to what they say, and watch what they write or show on the board. When we get distracted, we miss important teacher instructions.

Mrs. Harris introduced the Am I Paying Attention card. She explained that James would be using a system similar to the one he used successfully to remember to bring materials to class, but this system would be used during teacher-led instruction, such as when the teacher is lecturing, leading a class discussion, going through a PowerPoint presentation, or demonstrating how to do something, like solving a math problem. Mrs. Harris explained that during teacher-led instruction, paying attention means (1) watching the teacher, (2) listening to the teacher, (3) being quiet, and (4) sitting in my seat. James would monitor whether or not he was exhibiting *all* of these behaviors at critical points during his classes. Mrs. Harris used the MotivAider with James. Whenever he felt the vibration, James would mark his card to indicate whether or not he was paying attention. Mrs. Harris modeled how to use the MotivAider with the Am I Paying Attention self-monitoring card. James's card is shown in Figure 16.2.

Figure 16.2 James's Paying Attention Card

Directions: Remember the WAM strategy

  W—*Wait for the vibration from the MotivAider.*

  A—*Ask yourself if you were paying attention.*

  M—*Mark your card by checking yes or no.*

During teacher-led instruction, paying attention means you were (1) watching the teacher, (2) listening to the teacher, (3) being quiet, and (4) sitting in your seat. If you were doing *all* of these, check yes. If you were not doing *all* of these, check no.

Time Segment	Yes	No
1.		
2.		
3.		
4.		
5.		
6.		
7.		
8.		
9.		
10.		

My percentage today was: _____

My goal is: _____

James and Mrs. Harris practiced using the card by role-playing situations in which they were—and were not—paying attention—and began to use it in the co-taught science class because (1) much of the science instruction is teacher-led, (2) the science teacher noticed James's inattention, and (3) Mrs. Harris co-teaches science and can provide on-the-spot support, as needed. Additional classes will be added (as needed) after James has experienced success in science.

COMPLETING WORK ACCURATELY: THE CARD STRATEGY

Next, Mrs. Harris provided instruction on improving James's accuracy of work. Mrs. Harris and James discussed the importance of doing accurate work. To encourage James to produce more accurate documents, Mrs. Harris presented the CARD strategy:

C—Check every answer twice.

A—Answer all problems or questions.

R—Return to difficult items.

D—Do ask for help when needed.

Mrs. Harris described and modeled these steps. She showed how to double-check answers to math problems, study guide questions, and lab reports. Mrs. Harris told James to answer all items on assignments and exams, even if he was unsure of the answer. He might receive partial credit, plus teachers could help him more if he showed his work. James could place a dot by difficult items and return to those. Finally, Mrs. Harris reminded him that if he could not complete a problem, he could ask a peer, the teacher, or his parents for help, or he could receive support in the resource room.

The team also discussed ways to improve accuracy on homework assignments such as scheduling homework time earlier in the evening to avoid feeling rushed; taking frequent, short breaks; and reinforcing oneself with a short, fun activity when finished. Mrs. Harris emphasized the importance of asking for help, and they brainstormed names of peers in various classes to contact for assistance.

Mrs. Harris and James practiced the CARD strategy with upcoming assignments from James's classes. James used positive self-talk as he practiced the strategy. For this intervention, James kept track of his use of the CARD strategy plus the accuracy of his assignments. When each graded assignment is returned, James will record his score in the last column, as shown in Figure 16.3.

Figure 16.3 James's Homework Assignment Accuracy Card

Week of _____

Directions: For each homework assignment you were assigned this week, indicate what steps of the CARD strategy you used and then record the grade you received on the assignment when your teacher returns it.

Class	Brief description of assignment	Did I use the C step by checking every answer twice?	Did I use the A step by answering every problem or question?	Did I use the R step by returning to difficult items?	Did I use the D step by deciding to ask for help, when needed?	My score on the assignment

Average score on assignments: _____

Based on my average score, I need to: _____

Mrs. Harris will check the form each Friday, and together James and Mrs. Harris will discuss James's use of the CARD strategy and his scores on assignments to determine adjustments to the intervention.

INCREASING NEATNESS OF WORK

James's last objective targeted increasing the neatness of his handwritten work. Mrs. Harris called James's attention to the appearance of his work. His teachers noted that his written work was difficult to read. Specifically,

James often wrote numbers and letters too close to each other, and numerals such as 1, 7, and 9 as well as 2, 3, 8, 5, and 6 were difficult to discriminate. Teachers may find these ideas helpful for working with students on neatness:

- Allow the student to print, use a word processor, or use cursive whenever possible.
- Provide study guides, guided notes, or other materials with sufficient space for student responses.
- Have students circle their final math answer to separate it from other numbers.
- Use graph paper with large squares for aligning numbers for math problems.
- Reduce the amount of student copying of material, such as math problems from the text.
- When students must first copy math problems, have them use a bracket or finger space after the number *of* the math problem to separate it from numbers *in* the problem, as in this example:

$$1. \ 65 \times 44$$

- Encourage use of a finger space between each problem.
- Have students use wide-lined paper (or laptops) for taking notes.
- If necessary, teach how to correctly form letters and numbers.
- Consider consultation with an occupational or physical therapist.

The NEAT Strategy

Mrs. Harris met with James and discussed these suggestions. Together, they analyzed samples of James's recent work; noted numbers, letters, or spacing issues; and discussed the importance of producing neat documents that others can easily read. Mrs. Harris developed the NEAT strategy to help James monitor his written work, especially his math papers:

N—Notice your spacing of letters, numbers, and math answers.

E—Enter your letters and numbers using correct form.

A—Ask yourself if your paper is easy for others to read.

T—Take your time to examine your paper before completion.

As Mrs. Harris explained and modeled the strategy, she showed James examples and non-examples of neat and messy papers. She used self-talk to model the correct way to form letters and numbers that they identified as being messy on James's papers. After guided practice, Mrs. Harris introduced James's self-monitoring cue card, shown in Figure 16.4. James would use the card as a reminder to use the NEAT strategy while doing math assignments.

Figure 16.4 Producing NEAT papers

Directions: For each math paper, use the NEAT strategy to produce a legible document. Check off each step as you complete it.

N—*Notice your spacing of letters, numbers, and math answers.*

E—*Enter your letters and numbers using correct form.*

A—*Ask yourself if your paper is easy for others to read.*

T—*Take your time to examine your paper before completion.*

Date	Item	Did I *notice* my spacing?	Did I *enter* numbers and letters using correct form?	Did I *ask* myself if the paper is easy for others to read?	Did I *take* my time to examine my paper?

I used all steps of the NEAT strategy during _____ of _____ assignments.

TIME SAVERS

Self-regulation interventions are typically individualized, so they take time. Having an array of self-monitoring forms available will save time later when attempting to develop one on the spot. Having a system in place in which the student's self-monitoring responses are electronically recorded saves teacher time in scoring and developing a visual, such as a graph. Finally, having a routine time of the day to check self-monitoring systems adds structure to the system and increases efficiency.

SUMMARY

Strategy instruction is enhanced with a self-regulation component. The goal of adding a self-regulation component to strategy instruction is for students to monitor their skills or behavior based on an exemplar that the teacher has carefully explained and modeled. Teachers can creatively develop individualized strategies and self-monitoring cards for students to use for independent practice. Enlisting students as active partners throughout the process promotes their cooperation, involvement, and ownership of the strategy.

CHAPTER APPLICATION ACTIVITIES

Apply your knowledge from the chapter by discussing or completing the following application questions or activities. Suggested answers are provided below.

1. Assume you taught Rochelle the two-what strategy for bringing materials to her classes. She met the criteria quickly, so you removed the need for her to fill out a daily card and gather teacher's signatures. A few weeks later, several general education teachers informed you that Rochelle was forgetting her materials again. What might you do?

2. The last step of the CARD strategy is to ask for help. Some students are reluctant to do this, or they do not know how. How might you describe this step for Kevin?

3. This chapter includes several forms for students to use to improve their self-regulation. Often, these forms are in paper copy. What are some substitutes for paper copies of these forms?

Suggested Responses

Responses will vary, but here are some suggested ideas:

1. You might have to reinstate the system with Rochelle. She has been successful, so you know that she has the skills to remember her materials. As you meet individually with Rochelle, you and Rochelle can decide what level of support she needs: from reinstating the entire system to providing minimal supports such as posted reminders in her locker, backpack, and/or elsewhere. Sometimes a peer accountability partner can also help.

2. Kevin, the last step of the CARD strategy is to ask for help. It's OK to ask someone to help you if you are stuck on something. You can ask your peers, parents, or a teacher for help. Using a polite tone of voice and making eye contact, you might want to first ask if they have a minute to help you. If they say no, say thanks anyway and find someone else to help you. If they say yes, thank them, ask your question, and patiently wait for their response. If you still do not understand, ask again but use different words. Always thank the person for helping you.

3. Rather than use paper copies, students can use electronic copies of these forms and send their responses back to their teacher or to a designated website. The student could later be involved in analyzing results using graph building software.

SUPPLEMENTAL RESOURCES FOR CHAPTER 16

Guerra, N. (2009). LIBRE stick figure tool: A graphic organizer to foster self-regulated social cognitive problem solving. *Intervention in School and Clinic, 44*(4), 229–233.

Kern, L., Ringdahl, J., Hilt, A., & Sterling-Turner, H. (2001). Linking self-management procedures to functional analysis results. *Behavior Disorders, 26,* 214–226.

Mitchem, K., & Young, K. (2001). Adapting self-management programs for classwide use: Acceptability, feasibility, and effectiveness. *Remedial and Special Education, 22*(2), 75–88.

Mitchem, K., Young, K., West, R., & Benyo, J. (2001). CW-PASM: A classroom peer-assisted, self-management program for general education classrooms. *Education & Treatment of Children, 24*(2), 111–140.

Ness, B., & Middleton, M. (2012). A framework for implementing individualized self-regulated learning strategies in the classroom. *Intervention in School and Clinic, 47*(5), 267–275.

Rock, M. (2005). Use of strategic self-monitoring to enhance academic engagement, productivity, and accuracy of students with and without disabilities. *Journal of Positive Behavior Interventions, 7,* 13–17.

Self-Monitoring Curriculum and Teaching Resources

Bachel, B. (2001). *What do you really want? How to set a goal and go for it: A guide for teens.* Minneapolis, MN: Free Spirit.

Henley, M. (2003). *Teaching self-control: A curriculum for responsible behavior.* Champaign, IL: Research Press.

Knapczyk, D. (2004). *Teaching self-discipline for self-reliance and academic success.* Champaign, IL: Research Press.

Lane, K. L., Menzies, H., Bruhn, A., & Crnobori, M. (2010). *Managing challenging behaviors in schools: Research-based strategies that work.* New York, NY: Guilford Press.

Strichart, S., Mangrum, C., & Iannuzzi, P. (2001). *Teaching learning strategies and study skills to students with learning disabilities, ADD, or special needs for middle and high school.* Boston, MA: Allyn & Bacon.

Wehmeyer, M., & Field, S. (2007). *Self-determination: Instructional and assessment strategies.* Thousand Oaks, CA: Corwin.

Mathematics: Informal Assessments

17

An essential element for teachers of students with disabilities in math is the practice of collecting ongoing data on student progress.

(Sayeski & Paulsen, 2010)

MEET EBONY

Ebony is an 11th grader who has been receiving special education services since fifth grade. Throughout the years, she has made steady growth in most academic areas. However, she still struggles with reading comprehension and math. With recently increased academic requirements needed for her graduation, Ebony receives the majority of her instruction in general education classrooms. She is frequently frustrated with the quick pace and language demands of her classes, but she has a strong work ethic and good study skills.

To meet district graduation requirements, Ebony needs to complete three years of general education mathematics. Even with accommodations such as extra time, shortened assignments, and reading support, she continues to struggle in math. Ebony performs well on daily math assignments, but despite the best intentions of Mr. Ginther, her math teacher, and Ms. Ewing, her special education teacher, her math unit test scores and district and state exam scores indicate minimal growth.

> ### CHAPTER OVERVIEW
>
> This chapter focuses on informal mathematics assessments. The chapter provides a rationale for using frequent informal math assessments, illustrates examples of various types of informal assessments, and includes Ebony's math IEP based on her assessment results.

RECENT INTEREST IN MATHEMATICS

Ebony is like many students with mild disabilities nationwide who are expected to meet rigorous math standards and who receive the majority of their math instruction in general education classes. Because they take state and district math tests, secondary students with mild disabilities are being held accountable for mastering advanced skills in algebra, geometry, problem solving, and statistics.

These critical skills support the belief that mathematics is a core academic competency. Mastering basic mathematics skills is critical for successful functioning in society (Reid & Lienemann, 2006). Specifically, students with disabilities require problem-solving skills to navigate the demands of the 21st century, even though the prevailing mathematical instructional practice has focused almost exclusively on computational skills for students with learning disabilities (Gallagher-Landi, 2001).

The recent shift in mathematics reform, rooted in standards from the National Council of Teachers of Mathematics (NCTM), emphasizes mathematics in real-life contexts, higher level math skills, and open-ended problem solving. In contrast to traditional instructional methods such as emphasizing a single algorithm for solving a problem, practice with mathematics symbols, and fluency in math facts, teachers are now encouraged to allow students to problem-solve in groups while using calculators, manipulatives, and student-generated algorithms (Sayeski & Paulsen, 2010). This shift in thinking about what and how we teach mathematics as well as making a rigorous curriculum accessible to students with disabilities presents unique student and teacher challenges.

STUDENT AND TEACHER CHALLENGES

Students experience difficulty in mathematics for many reasons, and while often identified in elementary school, these challenges persist in middle and high school. Attention, memory, language, and metacognition skills affect overall mathematics skills. For example, students with attention issues may not identify relevant information or recall critical steps used in algorithms or problem-solving strategies. Students with memory issues may experience difficulty retaining basic facts, recalling procedural steps, and performing well on review lessons, especially tasks involving mixed problems and multistep word problems (Impecoven-Lind & Foegen, 2010). Language skills are necessary for understanding symbols, differentiating math vocabulary, solving word problems, organizing multiple steps, and recalling math facts. Finally, students use metacognitive skills to identify, monitor, and coordinate multistep problems.

In addition to these processing challenges, students may have insufficient mathematics preskills or knowledge, which impacts math performance. For example, students apply knowledge and skills with whole numbers, fraction operations and concepts, and basic geometry and measurement skills when completing algebra problems. Students with mild disabilities often lack conceptual knowledge of fractions, which leads to further difficulties with estimation and proportion. Similarly, students may have misconceptions related to the relationship between area and perimeter, which impacts performance in algebra and geometry (Impecoven-Lind & Foegen, 2010).

These student characteristics pose challenges for teachers, also. When developing a curriculum for students with disabilities, secondary mathematics and special education teachers often ask themselves questions such as these: Should we . . .

- Emphasize an applied math curriculum or the standard high school math curriculum?
- Use traditional instructional techniques, approaches advocated by NCTM, or a combination?
- Require that students master prerequisite skills before introducing advanced skills?
- Focus on automaticity of math facts or allow calculators?
- Reduce student dependence on accommodations?
- Co-teach general education math classes?
- Focus on preparing students for state and district high-stakes tests?
- Offer specialized general math classes for students with disabilities?

Analyzing student data provides guidance as teachers consider these and other questions.

INFORMAL MATHEMATICS ASSESSMENTS

Due to the importance of student performance on state or district math assessments and the importance of correcting misconceptions and errors before students internalize them, teachers should use data from various informal math assessments to inform their instruction. Collecting ongoing data helps teachers determine if students are making adequate progress and if teachers need to reteach concepts or skills or provide more student practice. Numerous informal assessment tools are available for general and special education math teachers, some of which we describe here. In addition to these, teachers can use student journals, group assessments, observations, long-range projects, and student conferences. Together, Mr. Ginther and Ms. Ewing will use data from these assessments to design a program for Ebony, so she can advance in her math skills.

Interest Surveys

Weber (1999) noted that an interest inventory can be part of a student's math portfolio. She emphasized that inventories provide a vehicle for collaborating, dialoguing, and setting goals with students. Weber suggested that teachers ask students to describe what they enjoy and do not enjoy about math, contributions they would like to make in math, changes they would like to suggest for the math class, what they would like to do more in math, and frustrations they feel about math. Students can write their responses or share them verbally if they are comfortable doing so. Knowing how the student feels about mathematics helps teachers plan lessons and activities while remaining sensitive to individual needs and preferences.

Pretests

At the beginning of a grading period or instructional unit, teachers can develop, administer, and score pretests to determine student skills and instructional priorities for individuals as well as groups of students. Some curriculum and texts include pretests or placement tests, which save teachers time in terms of test construction and curriculum placement.

When developing a pretest, be sure to strategically sift the curriculum and develop problems and tasks representative of the curriculum and curriculum emphasis. For example, if Mr. Ginther's upcoming unit on fractions includes skills regarding recognizing fractional parts as well as adding, subtracting, multiplying, and dividing fractions—all receiving the same instructional emphasis, then his pretest could contain equal numbers of problems assessing each of these skills. The pretest should also parallel the instructional sequence and present easier items first. If assessing a single skill, the test should contain at least 10 items. If assessing a span of skills, each skill included should have at least three test items (Deshler, Ellis, & Lenz, 1996).

If teachers plan to teach students a specific strategy, they can develop and administer a two-part pretest using the format presented in previous chapters. The first part asks students to list the steps of the strategy, and the second part provides tasks or problems in which students must apply the strategy. Figure 17.1 provides an example of a pretest for the CAP algebra strategy, which includes these steps: Combine like terms, Ask yourself how you can isolate the variable, and Put the values in the variable to check the problem.

Teachers can differentiate instruction based on pretest scores by allowing students who have mastered certain skills to complete enrichment activities while others receive instruction on needed skills. Administering a pretest, which also later serves as a posttest, documents student growth over time and can be used as part of IEP data.

Inventories

Teachers can administer informal math inventories to individuals or a whole class. An informal math inventory typically assesses numerous skills, often sampling all the skills covered at a particular grade level. An elementary math inventory, for example, might include items assessing counting, one-to-one correspondence, place value, addition, subtraction, time, money, and so forth, while a secondary inventory could include items assessing probability, statistics, advanced word problems, algebra, geometry, et cetera. Students respond to as many of the items as they can. Information gathered through inventories highlights skills the student possesses and those yet to be developed.

Figure 17.1 Pretest for CAP Strategy

Name _____

Directions: Do your best to complete this pretest on the CAP algebra strategy.

Part 1: Steps

What do the letters C, A, and P stand for in the CAP algebra strategy?

C—

A—

P—

Part 2: Use the CAP Strategy to solve these problems:

1) $5p - 14 = 8p + 4$
2) $5n + 34 = -2(1 - 7n)$
3) $2(4x - 3) - 8 = 4 + 2x$

Curriculum-Based Assessments

Curriculum-based assessments are tools that help teachers analyze if students have mastered skills or material taken directly from the local curriculum. In other words, teachers directly test what they teach by developing problems or questions from the actual books and materials students use in class. They collect these data as frequently as feasible and make instructional decisions based on student performance. For example, Ms. Ewing frequently reviews student work using *error analysis* to determine patterns. She determines if errors are due to a defective algorithm, computation error, use of the wrong operation, issues with place value, poor writing skills, reversals, reading issues, or random response (Deshler, Ellis, & Lenz, 1996). Also, if a student obtains low scores on math assignments for two or three days in succession, she makes a curricular adjustment by reteaching the skill needed to complete the assignments.

In math, teachers use numerous tools to directly assess student skills such as teacher- or publisher-developed quizzes or tests based on daily instruction or the present unit; homework assignments, classroom activities, and daily problems tied to core standards; or worksheets assessing a specific outcome. They can also use various types of student response systems such as dry erase boards, response cards, or clickers or personal response systems to engage students in daily review work throughout class. Admit slips, warm-ups, sponges, quick writes, and bell ringers are additional 2- to 5-minute activities that capture a critical skill.

Although teachers do not need to collect and grade every activity, collecting and analyzing ongoing student performance measures paints a picture of each student. The goal of reviewing data is to catch student errors before they escalate and reteach to reduce student confusion and misunderstanding.

Curriculum-Based Measurements

Curriculum-based measurements (CBMs) are quick probes assessing fluency with a specific skill. Typically, students (and/or the teacher) chart performance on equal-interval graph paper and compare the student's performance to an aim line—a line drawn from the student's baseline performance to the goal, often determined by local norms.

A frequently used math CBM probe involves allowing students a short period of time (i.e., 1–3 minutes) to complete a math fact sheet that includes 50 or 100 math facts or problems. However, teachers can develop CBMs for any math skill requiring fluency, such as recognizing shapes or angles, matching formulas to their purpose, or memorizing steps of a strategy.

Oral Diagnostic Interviews

Teachers use the oral diagnostic interview to gain an understanding of the student's approach to solving a particular type of problem. Sometimes, even after completing error analysis, teachers wonder why students continue to err. The interview is conducted individually and includes these steps:

1. The teacher notices that the student is making errors on a particular type of problem.

2. The teacher develops a few additional problems just like the one(s) the student missed.

3. The teacher works individually with the student and says something like, "I am interested in learning what you say to yourself while you do this problem. Say aloud what you are thinking when you do this problem," or "Teach me how to do this type of problem."

4. The teacher listens and watches as the student shares his or her approach.

5. The teacher uses this information to reteach the skill.

Mathematical Problem-Solving Assessment (MPSA)

The MPSA is a two-part structured interview designed for middle school students to assess affective factors and cognitive and metacognitive processes and strategies associated with problem solving. The short form includes 3 word problems, 5 Likert-type items, and 35 open-ended questions. The assessment takes about 25 minutes to administer and score. Montague (1996) provided more information and examples of student results.

Authentic Tasks

Paralleling the NCTM's recommendations that math should involve higher-level thinking and meaningful problem-solving skills, teachers can assess students' ability to apply math skills to authentic real-world application tasks. These investigations allow teachers to observe both product and process. In other words, teachers note if students arrived at a correct solution but also—and perhaps just as important—how they arrived at their solution by observing students as they work, noting processes they use to solve the task, and examining final results. Students might be asked to write responses to open-ended questions such as, How did you arrive at your solution? What other procedures did you consider? How could you test your solution? Performance tasks must be motivating and sufficiently challenging for students, so they remain engaged. Often, these are completed in small groups or with partners.

Portfolios

Students showcase their mathematical skills and progress in their portfolio, a purposeful collection of work. Students with math-related IEP goals can share their math artifacts during their student-led IEP conference. Rather than including only homework assignments and tests, students can include artifacts that demonstrate growth over time, provide evidence of problem solving, and show connections to their life outside of school.

EBONY'S INDIVIDUALIZED EDUCATION PROGRAM

Based on Ebony's assessments results, Mr. Ginther and Ms. Ewing decided to target algebra, geometry, and problem-solving skills for purposeful intervention. Ebony's IEP is shown in Figure 17.2.

Figure 17.2 Ebony's IEP

Individualized Education Program

Name: Ebony   Grade: 11   Skill Area: Mathematics

Present Level of Performance: Ebony indicates that she enjoys math, likes working in groups, enjoys showing solutions on the Smart Board, and likes graphing but is frustrated by the fast pace of and confusing vocabulary used in her math class. She has mastered all her math facts and completes daily assignments with 80% accuracy and quizzes and tests with 60% accuracy. On pretests and inventories, Ebony solved algebra problems (e.g., linear equations) with 40% accuracy, geometry problems (e.g., surface area) with 35% accuracy, and word problems (e.g., two step problems involving more than one function) with 60% accuracy. Ebony scores 80% or above on assignments when she can apply a rule to a problem.

Annual Goal: Ebony will solve teacher-selected grade-level algebra, geometry, and word problems with 75% accuracy.

Objective 1: By the end of the first quarter, Ebony will evaluate expressions, solve linear equations, factor polynomials, and graph solutions on a coordinate plane with 75% accuracy.

Objective 2: By the end of the second quarter, Ebony will calculate volume, surface area, circumference, and perimeter of given shapes; name angle measurements and side measurements of various geometric shapes; and name corresponding and congruent parts of similar figures with 75% accuracy.

Objective 3: By the end of the third quarter, Ebony will solve word problems involving purchases including taxes and tips (decimals and percentages) and units of time, distance, and rates of speed with 75% accuracy.

SUMMARY

Students with mild disabilities are increasingly receiving more of their math instruction in general education classrooms where they receive rigorous instruction from highly qualified teachers. These students often struggle with complex math concepts and skills due to processing issues, inadequate preskills, or inaccurate conceptual understanding. Therefore, to avoid having students continue to make the same error, teachers need to be proactive and frequently assess students in different ways. Daily assessments can include journals, 1- to 3-minute timed tests, warm-ups, closure activities, or homework assignments. Students can complete assessments with partners, in groups, individually, or as part of an authentic problem-solving project or portfolio.

CHAPTER APPLICATION ACTIVITIES

Apply your knowledge from the chapter by discussing or completing the following application questions or activities. Suggested answers are provided below.

1. How might you use the results of math interest surveys?

2. Administering math pretests takes class instructional time, and it also takes time for teachers to correct them. What are some time-saving tips for either of these tasks?

3. Abe wants to include every homework assignment, every quiz, and all of his class notes into his math portfolio. How could you help him be more strategic in his portfolio entries?

Suggested Responses

Responses will vary, but here are some suggested ideas:

1. Teachers can discuss the results of the math interest surveys with the class. They can capitalize on what students like, address frustrations, consider changes students suggested, and respect contributions students would like to make. Special education teachers can discuss these items with students individually or in small groups.

2. Pretests could be given as homework (if students would do them and if they would not look up answers). Students could do the pretests during their study hall and return them that day, or pretests

could be posted online, and students could take them online. To save time scoring, teachers could use Scantron sheets, have students self-correct their work, or have an automated online system correct and maintain scores.

3. Remind Abe that he can keep all of those items if he wants to, but the portfolio is a purposeful collection of his work. Suggest he keep in his portfolio a few homework assignments that show his thinking process, a few quizzes that show improvement, and a few class notes that show how he summarized and processed new information or linked new information to known skills.

SUPPLEMENTAL RESOURCES FOR CHAPTER 17

Bigge, J., & Stump, C. (1999). *Curriculum, assessment, and instruction for students with disabilities.* Belmont, CA: Wadsworth.

Layton, C., & Lock, R. (2008). *Assessing students with special needs to produce quality outcomes.* Upper Saddle River, NJ: Pearson/Merrill.

Middle school math. http://jc-schools.net/tutorials/tools/math-ms.html

Spector, L. (2012). *The math page: Skill in algebra.* Retrieved from http://www.themathpage.com/alg/equations.htm#four

Mathematics: Methods and Strategies

18

Because it is often highly procedural and rule based, mathematics is a natural area for strategy instruction.

(Reid & Lienemann, 2006, p. 189)

CHAPTER OVERVIEW

Ebony's team agreed that her IEP should emphasize algebra, geometry, and problem-solving skills, as identified by assessment data and deemed important for state and district tests. Ms. Ewing will provide consultative support to Mr. Ginther, as needed, for developing supports for Ebony such as cue cards and graphic organizers. Ms. Ewing will also preteach math vocabulary words using visuals and hands-on activities, when possible. Ebony will maintain a math portfolio with artifacts documenting growth in her IEP skill areas. Team members were hopeful that Ebony's skills would improve given her teacher's commitment to using evidence-based practices.

This chapter provides an array of math strategies for secondary students with mild disabilities. Because the literature provides few examples of strategies for algebra and geometry, teachers like Mr. Ginther and Ms. Ewing will have to develop their own or modify those from their textbook. A temptation may be to teach students only steps of the strategy, but this alone does not encourage conceptual understanding. Many older students still need hands-on activities and manipulatives to fully understand math concepts.

FEATURED METHODS AND STRATEGIES

Chapter Strategy	Corresponding Common Core State Standard
SET CAP	Create equations that describe numbers or relationships.
Factor, set, solve, check	Solve equations and inequalities in one variable.
RAP-Graph	Represent and solve equations and inequalities graphically.
3R	Express geometric properties with equalities.
What-Four	Prove geometric theorems.
STAR	Reason quantitatively and use units to solve problems.

Source for standards: Common Core State Standards Initiative, 2012

STRATEGIES AND MATH

A critical component of math instruction for students with disabilities is strategy instruction (Deshler, Ellis, & Lenz, 1996). Math lends itself well to strategies and procedures, which can be comforting to students like Ebony. Especially when given a cue card that includes the steps and a completed example, many students can be successful following steps and applying a strategy.

Secondary students have used several well-known math strategies for years, such as these:

- PEMDAS for executing the rules of order (*Please excuse my dear Aunt Sally* for parentheses, exponents, multiplication, division, addition, subtraction) and
- FOIL for remembering the sequence of multiplying binomials. *First*—multiply the first variable in each binomial; *Outside*—multiply outside variables (the ones on the edges); *Inside*—multiply inside variables; *Last*—multiply the last variable in each binomial.

STRATEGIES FOR ALGEBRA

Choike (2000) summarized that algebra is the *process* of organizing the *arithmetic* needed to find answers to questions involving unknown quantities. Possibly because algebra involves so many different skills, and until recently, students with disabilities have not been expected to learn algebra, researchers have not focused on developing algebra strategies (Reid & Lienemann, 2006). However, because students typically solve algebra problems using predictable procedures or rules, teachers can use task analysis and teach students a series of steps as an efficient strategy.

This section presents algebra strategies found in the literature and textbooks as well as strategies Mr. Ginther developed by conducting a task analysis of skill steps.

Note of Caution: At the onset, we emphasize two reminders or words of caution. First, often students can devise more than one method to arrive at a solution for an algebra problem, so encourage them to develop and explain multiple methods to solve a problem. Second, just teaching a series of steps—or a rule—does not exemplify effective strategy teaching. Students can memorize steps and use them but attach no meaning to their use. Consequently, include the reason for each step and demonstrate when possible through visuals or hands-on manipulatives, such as algebra tiles, pictures, or diagrams to promote conceptual understanding.

The SET Strategy

To help Ebony evaluate expressions, Mr. Ginther developed the SET strategy, which includes these steps:

Problem: $2x^3 - x^2 + y$ when $x = 3$ and $y = -2$

> S—*Substitute each letter with its value:* $2(3^3) - (3^2) + -2$
>
> E—*Execute the operation:* $2(27) - 9 + -2 = 54 - 11 = 43$
>
> T—*Try the problem once more to double-check*

Before teaching SET, Mr. Ginther reviewed preskills such as exponents and operations with integers. After he modeled SET, students worked in pairs using the strategy to determine if they reached the same answer. Pairs later developed problems for other pairs to solve. After success with evaluating basic expressions, students would soon be ready for solving basic algebra problems.

The CAP Strategy

One strategy from the literature for solving basic algebra problems is CAP (Mercer, Jordan, & Miller, 1996). The steps include the following:

> C—*Combine like terms.*
>   Combine terms on each side of the equation that have the same variable.
>
>   Combine terms on each side of the equation that do not have a variable.
>
>   Combine terms by doing the same computations indicated by the signs.

A—*Ask yourself, How can I isolate the variable?*
Remove nonvariable numbers by changing to 0 (perform the opposite computation).

Remove a variable number by changing it to 1 (perform the opposite computation).

P—*Put the values of the variable in the initial equation, and check to see if the equation is balanced.*

Mr. Ginther modeled the CAP strategy using think-alouds with many different examples, operations, and variables. He modeled examples that used every substep as well as problems that did not use every substep, so students saw the full range of examples. He also emphasized that when combining like terms in an expression, only terms raised to the same power may be combined (e.g., in $2x + 5x^2 + 3x$, only the $2x$ and $3x$ can be combined).

These reminders were important because initially Ebony wanted to use every sub-step with every problem and add every x, regardless of the exponent. To support Ebony's use of the CAP strategy, Mr. Ginther developed a cue card like the one shown in Figure 18.1.

The Factor, Set, Solve, Check Strategy

A more advanced skill involves solving problems that require factoring. Haenisch (2004) presented this four-step process (factor, set, solve, check) for solving quadratic equations that involve factoring. The steps include the following:

Problem: $x^2 + 3x + 2 = 0$

F—*Factor the equation:* $x^2 + 3x + 2 = 0 = (x + 2)(x + 1) = 0$

S—*Set each factor equal to 0:* $x + 2 = 0$ or $x + 1 = 0$

S—*Solve each factor for x:* $x + 2 = 0$, therefore $x = -2$; or $x + 1 = 0$, therefore $x = -1$

C—*Check*

Let $x = -2$; then $(-2)^2 + 3(-2) + 2 = 4 - 6 + 2 = 0$, true

Let $x = -1$; then $(-1)^2 + 3(-1) + 2 = 1 - 3 + 2 = 0$, true

The solutions are -2 and -1.

The RAP-Graph Strategy

Finally, for graphing solutions on a coordinate plane, one of Ebony's IEP objectives, Mr. Ginther developed the RAP-graph strategy. He had to

Figure 18.1 CAP Cue Card

Step	Example Problem: 2x + 4 + x + 7 + x + 18 + x + 4	Check when completed or write N/A if the step does not apply.
C—*Combine like terms.* On each side that has the same variable On each side that does not have a variable By doing the same computations indicated by the signs	3x + 4 + 7 = 2x + 18+ 4 3x + 11 = 2x + 22	_____ _____ _____
A—*Ask yourself, How can I isolate the variable?* Remove nonvariable numbers by changing to 0 (perform the opposite computation). Remove a variable number by changing it to 1 (perform the opposite computation).	3x = 2x + 11 x = 11	_____ _____
P—*Put the values* of the variable in the initial equation and check if the equation is balanced	2(11) + 4 + 11 + 7 = 44 11 + 18 + 11 + 4 = 44	_____

elaborate only minimally on textbook steps that taught students to plug in a number for x, plug in four more numbers for x, and graph the data. He provided more detail and modeled more examples than were in the text using this elaborated strategy.

R—*Read the problem* $y = 2x + 1$

A—*Ask yourself,* What number can I plug in for x to solve for y?
　　Example: I will plug in 0 for x.
　　If $x = 0$, then $y = 0 + 1$, or when $x = 0$, $y = 1$

P—*Plug in four more numbers for x to solve for y*
　　Example: I will plug in 3 for x.
　　If $x = 3$, then $y = 6 + 1$, or when $x = 3$, $y = 7$
　　(Do this with three more numbers.)

Graph your coordinates using the value pairs you found for x and y.

These basic strategies represent foundational skills in an early algebra class. Because few algebra strategies exist, teachers often need to develop their own or modify those found in their textbook.

STRATEGIES FOR GEOMETRY

Geometry is the study of shapes and configurations. Students understand and classify spaces in various mathematical contexts as they study points, lines, angles, surfaces, and solids. Like algebra strategies, geometry strategies have not been well researched for students with mild disabilities (Reid & Lienemann, 2006), so teachers need to develop their own strategies based on the most efficient way of approaching a task.

Supports

The study of geometry uses a vocabulary that may be overwhelming to students with language or math issues. Tools discussed in previous chapters such as note-taking systems provide needed support for students like Ebony. For example, Ebony's class used note-taking systems to remember and study geometry terms and concepts. Examples of these are shown in Figure 18.2.

Figure 18.2 Three-Column Note-Taking Format

Triangles		
Triangles are shapes that have three sides and three angles. The three angles always add up to 180°		
<u>Type</u>	<u>Description</u>	<u>Picture</u>
Equilateral	Three equal sides Three equal angles (always 60°)	
Isosceles	Two equal sides Two equal angles	
Scalene	No equal sides No equal angles (all different)	
Acute	All angles less than 90°	
Right	Has one 90° angle	
Obtuse	Has one angle greater than 90°	
Note: Sometimes a triangle will have two names such as a right isosceles triangle.		

Mnemonics are helpful in math for remembering formulas, vocabulary, or concepts. After learning about mnemonics in science and social studies, Ebony's class developed these geometry mnemonics:

At 90 degrees

One angle is tight

We will remember

It is right

Each angle is the same

At 60 degrees

That's how to remember

An equilateral is me

Perimeter is the sum of the lengths of all sides

Area refers to units needed to cover the inside

Many students enjoy developing rhymes, jingles, sayings, poems, or mnemonics for remembering material. These often add interest and novelty to the class while stimulating creativity.

Manipulatives for Geometry

After developing conceptual understanding using objects such as algebra tiles (square or triangle manipulatives) or geoboards (plastic squares with raised pegs or nails half driven in, around which are wrapped rubber bands), teachers can introduce formulas. Virtual algebra tiles (http://illuminations.nctm.org/ActivityDetail.aspx?ID=216) and geoboards (www.mathplayground.com/geoboard.html) are also available online.

Using the Smart Board, Mr. Ginther modeled (with an overhead and geoboard) various shapes and their respective areas. He showed, explained, and allowed students to confirm the interrelatedness of the area of common shapes. For example, if students cut a parallelogram along its height, they would quickly realize by fitting together the two pieces that the area of a parallelogram is the same as the area of a rectangle. Similarly, they can see that a right triangle can be considered half a rectangle. These associations help students understand area and can be illustrated using the geoboard (Scavo, 1997). Now, formulas have more meaning (the area of a parallelogram and rectangle are both b x h; the area of a triangle is ½ b x h), but if students forget the reasoning associated with formulas, they can experiment with their geoboard.

The 3R Strategy

When students are ready to use only formulas, they can use a basic strategy such as the 3R strategy that Mr. Ginther presented:

R—*Read and understand the question* (e.g., What is the area of the triangle that is shown?)

R—*Remember the formula* (e.g., What is the formula for calculating the area of a triangle?)

R—*Recheck your work* (Do the formula and my answer make sense?)

Mr. Ginther modeled the strategy like this:

> Now that we have used our geoboards for "seeing" the area of a triangle, we can use the formula ½ b (or base) x h (or height). Let's use the 3R strategy as we use this formula.
>
> So, what is the first step? The first step is R for *read and understand the question*. Our example shows a triangle and asks, What is the area of this triangle? OK—I have read the question, and I think about what it is asking. I see the diagram of a triangle with the sides labeled, and I recall practicing how to compute area on the geoboards. Area was the space inside the triangle. I understand what the question is asking.
>
> Alright, what is step 2? The second R is for *remember the formula*. Well, I could check my cue card, textbook, or notes or remember from our class activities. I remember the formula of the area of a parallelogram or rectangle is b x h, and when we made a triangle on the geoboard, the triangle was half of those shapes, so the area of a triangle is ½ b x h. I will check my cue card just to be sure [checks]. Yes, that is the right formula. OK—so base is the length across the bottom, and height is how tall the triangle is. Good. Both of those are labeled in the diagram for me. The base is 8, and the height is 6. So, what do I do? I know that 8 × 6 = 48, but that is not the area of a triangle. I have to take half of that because the triangle takes up half as much space or area as a parallelogram or rectangle. When we take half of something, we divide it in two. Let me see . . . 48 divided by 2 is 24. [Mr. Ginther models making this computation.]
>
> Am I done? No, I need to do step 3—the third R is for *recheck my work*. Does this make sense? If a triangle had a base of 8 and a height of 6, could the area be 24? I know I am using the right

formula because I have it in my notes and it makes sense, and I will double check my math with the calculator. Yes, 6 × 8 = 48, and 48 divided by 2 = 24, so I am confident that this answer is correct. I solved the problem and am ready for the next one.

The What-Four Strategy

Ebony's IEP team also identified angle measurement as an objective. In other words, Ebony needs to determine the measures of angles when given a specific geometric shape and one or more of the angle measures of that shape.

Ebony needed to review how to use a protractor to measure angles to ensure she was reading the correct numbers on the protractor. Once again, using the geoboard helped her see how various shapes and their angles were related—for example, she now knew that triangles have three sides and their angles add up to 180°. Using this prior knowledge, Mr. Ginther's class experimented with geoboards to learn that a four-sided quadrilateral is composed of two triangles, so the sum of the interior angles is 360°. Similarly, a five-sided pentagon is composed of three triangles with the sum of the interior angles measuring 540°.

Now, Mr. Ginther could present Ebony with problems in which the shape and two angles were known, and she needed to determine the missing angle. He presented the what-four strategy:

W—*What is the given information?* (e.g., look at the picture of the quadrilateral. Three of the interior angle measures are given.)

W—*What is the question asking?* (e.g., what is the measure of the fourth angle?)

W—*What do I know?* (The interior angles of a quadrilateral measure 360°.)

W—*What is the missing value?* (Solve for the missing value.)

Ebony was also expected to name corresponding parts of similar figures. Ebony discovered that the what-four strategy also worked for naming congruent angles and sides and determining missing values.

W—*What is the given information?* (e.g., quadrilateral EDCF ≅ quadrilateral OLMN)

W—*What is the question asking?* (e.g., find the value of b)

W—*What do I know?* (DC ≅ LM; angle D ≅ L; angle M ≅ C; LM is 8)

W—*What is the missing value?* 2b = 8; b = 4

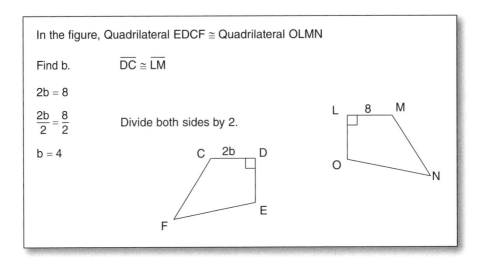

Mr. Ginther and Ms. Ewing frequently collaborated, so they would use the same language and similar examples with Ebony. Mr. Ginther learned that secondary students enjoy and benefit from hands-on and visualization techniques. He was able to show concepts before students memorized formulas and design strategies that students could apply to more than one skill.

STRATEGIES FOR PROBLEM SOLVING

Problem solving is a complex skill involving analytic reasoning and critical thinking skills. Problem solving has two stages: problem representation and problem execution. Unlike algebra and geometry, problem solving is a topic for which researchers *have* developed strategies for students with mild disabilities.

Teachers should select or develop medium-level strategies. Very detailed strategies, including those teaching students to always associate keywords (e.g., gave away) with a particular operation (e.g., subtraction) are ineffective as they do not generalize to complex word problems. Conversely, basic strategies such as read–decide what to do–solve–check are too general and not very helpful for students who are unsure how to approach a problem. Medium-level strategies provide structure and flexibility, so students can apply them to many problems.

The STAR Strategy

The STAR strategy (Maccini & Hughes, 2000) is an empirically validated mnemonic strategy that uses manipulatives. Teachers also develop cue cards to help students remember, organize, and check off important steps and substeps. The STAR strategy has these steps:

S—Search the word problem.

Read the problem carefully and ask questions like What do I know? and What do I want to know?

Write down facts.

T—Translate the problem.

Translate the word problem into an equation.

Translate the equation into a picture or use counters.

A—Answer the problem.

Calculate the answer.

R—Review the solution.

Reread the problem.

Ask yourself if the answer makes sense.

Check your answer.

Ebony's class was successful with STAR because they had already used the what-four strategy, which taught them to think about what they already knew and use that prior knowledge. Drawing a picture or using manipulatives (the T or *translate* step) was especially helpful for Ebony in "seeing" the problem.

Montague (2003) developed a seven-step problem-solving strategy that also emphasizes visualization. The steps of this strategy are (1) read the problem, (2) paraphrase the problem, (3) draw the problem, (4) create a plan, (5) predict or estimate the answer, (6) compute, and (7) check the answer. In addition, each of these seven main steps includes three substeps: *say, ask,* and *check.* For example in Step 1 (read the problem), students *say* to themselves, I will read (or reread) the problem; I will *ask,* Have I read and understood the problem? and I will *check:* Yes, I understand it. First, teachers teach the seven steps, and then they add the three substeps.

Students with language and math issues, like Ebony, benefit from incorporating visuals or pictures in their problem solving-strategies *and* hearing teachers think through a series of steps leading to a logical outcome.

TIME SAVERS

Math instruction often includes teacher demonstration of a new process or skill. Using more explicit instruction with a think-aloud may be new to some math teachers, and adding this component to instruction will take additional time. To provide more instructional flexibility and save time, math teachers can allow students to work in pairs or small groups during guided practice, use self-correcting materials during independent practice, correct and grade only selected assignments that were assigned for independent practice or homework, use Scantron sheets for some assessments, and allow students to grade some of their own work.

SUMMARY

Mathematics is a natural outlet for strategy instruction. As teachers develop math strategies, they can use known strategies, modify those from the textbook, create their own, or use a combination of these approaches. Medium-level strategies provide enough information and steps for students for the greatest utility. Few empirically researched math strategies exist in algebra and geometry, but researchers have developed effective problem-solving strategies such as STAR. Problem-solving strategies emphasize reading and understanding the problem, visualizing the action to be taken, developing a number sentence, calculating, and double-checking to ensure the answer makes sense.

CHAPTER APPLICATION ACTIVITIES

Apply your knowledge from the chapter by discussing or completing the following application questions or activities. Suggested answers are provided below.

1. This chapter introduced the SET strategy. Mr. Ginther needed to teach (or accommodate for) some preskills before he taught this strategy. What specific preskills would he need to address?

2. The 3R strategy is a general strategy that students can use in various contexts. What are some other math contexts or other subjects in which students could use this strategy?

3. In the STAR strategy, the first of two substeps in the T or *translate the problem* step is for students to translate the word problem into an equation. What are some questions teachers could pose for students to promote conceptual understanding as students think about translating the problem into an equation?

Suggested Responses

Responses will vary, but here are some suggested ideas:

1. Among others, Mr. Ginther may need to preteach or review the sequence of completing problems like these, what to do with parentheses, how to identify an exponent, and the rules of adding, subtracting, dividing, and multiplying integers.

2. Students could use the 3R strategy in math whenever any formula is part of the problem—even a word problem. They could also use this in science when working with chemistry formulas. Students could even use this strategy in music theory and literature when analyzing a specific genre.

3. Teachers could pose questions such as, What operation do you think we should use? Why do you think so? When do we use that operation? In this problem, do we need more than one step or operation? Why do you think so? Have we had similar problems like this—and if so, what did we do? Can we draw this out, act it out, or use any of our manipulatives to show what it would look like before we translate the problem into an equation?

SUPPLEMENTAL RESOURCES FOR CHAPTER 18

Maccini, P., & Gagnon, J. (n.d.). *Math graphic organizers for students with disabilities.* Washington, DC: The Access Center. Retrieved from http://www.k8access center.org/training_resources/mathgraphicorganizers.asp

Maccini, P., & Gagnon, J. (2000). Best practices for teaching mathematics to secondary students with special needs: Implications from teacher perceptions and a review of the literature. *Focus on Exceptional Children, 32*(5), 1–22.

Maccini, P., Mulcahy, C., & Wilson, M. (2007). A follow-up of mathematics interventions for secondary students with learning disabilities. *Learning Disabilities Research & Practice, 22*(1), 58–74.

Montague, M. (2007). Self-regulation and mathematics instruction. *Learning Disabilities Research & Practice, 22*(1), 75–83.

Sayeski, K., & Paulsen, K. (2010). Mathematics reform curricula and special education: Identifying intersections and implications for practice. *Intervention in School and Clinic, 46*(1), 13–21.

Mathematics Curriculum and Teaching Resources

Borenson and Associates. (2009). *Hands-on equations.* Allentown, PA: Author. Retrieved from http://www.borenson.com

Brutlag, D. (2009). *Active algebra: Strategies and lessons for successfully teaching linear relationships, Grades 7–10.* Sausalito, CA: Math Solutions.

Cummins, J., Malloy, C., McClain, K., Mojica, K., Price, J., & Zike, D. (2008). *Algebra concepts and applications.* Columbus, OH: Glencoe/McGraw-Hill.

Essentials for algebra, grades 7–12. Columbus, OH: SRA/McGraw-Hill.

Montague, M. (2003). *Solve it! A practical approach to teaching mathematical problem solving skills.* Reston, VA: Exceptional Innovations. Retrieved from http://www.exinn.net

Montague, M., & Jitendra, A. (2006). *Teaching mathematics to middle school students with learning difficulties.* New York, NY: Guilford Press.

Woodward, J., & Stroh, M. (2005). *Understanding algebraic expressions.* Longmont, CO: Sopris West.

Science: Informal **19** Assessments

Science is a challenge for students who face difficulties acquiring and retaining knowledge and demonstrating their competence in assessments.

(Brigham, Scruggs, & Mastropieri, 2011)

MEET RAFAEL

Rafael arrived in the United States a few years ago when his parents emigrated from Central America. At home English is rarely spoken, and he did not learn English in school prior to moving to the United States. He could read but was approximately two years below grade level in Spanish, his first language. Consequently, he learned to read in English fairly quickly, transferring his Level 1 (entering) reading skills to English. After three years in the United States, he has strong basic interpersonal communication skills (BICS) with English. Like many English language learners, he still struggles with cognitive academic language proficiency (CALP), or vocabulary in specialized areas such as science, history, and math, which affects his comprehension even though he decodes English text with accuracy and fluency. He was also tested for and qualified for special services as a student with a learning disability. Rafael is interested in science but sometimes cannot communicate his thinking in English.

CHAPTER OVERVIEW

This chapter presents an overview of science for students with disabilities by first sharing ways science is taught and then noting reasons why science is difficult for these students. The chapter also includes various ways teachers can informally assess student skills related to science and presents accommodations particularly useful in science.

SCIENCE FOR STUDENTS WITH DISABILITIES

Recent reports have indicated that up to "70% of U.S. students are unable to connect science to real life situations and integrate science content across disciplines" (Therrien, Taylor, Hosp, Kaldenberg, & Gorsh, 2011, p. 188). Not surprisingly, students with mild disabilities have difficulty in science classes and score significantly lower than typically achieving peers on standardized science tests. At the same time, secondary students with mild disabilities are included in rigorous science classes. Access to and instruction in general education science curriculum helps prepare them for high-stakes testing, fulfill high school graduation and college entrance requirements, and expand postsecondary options. However, some instructional approaches in science pose challenges for students with disabilities.

Science typically follows a "spiral curriculum" with topics repeating across grades but with increasing depth and sophistication. As instruction progresses, students are expected to increase and deepen their understanding of science concepts and revise previously developed naïve notions.

Inquiry-Based Approaches

Science is a dynamic field that includes making observations, generating hypotheses, and systematically testing these hypotheses. Because learning from textbooks may not communicate the true nature of science, many science courses involve inquiry-based problem solving or experiments to teach processes and content.

Inquiry-based experiments allow students to take the scientist role by completing hands-on activities that illustrate scientific phenomena. During these activities, students use the scientific method to explore relationships among phenomena by

- Following sequential steps,
- Making detailed observations,
- Connecting observations to prior knowledge or lecture or text information,
- Drawing conclusions, and
- Evaluating previous understandings

Students with mild disabilities may have limited background knowledge or experience with inquiry, which constrains their ability to construct or complete inquiry tasks or draw correct conclusions from experimental observations. Therefore, they need additional structure to complete inquiry activities and develop correct conclusions.

Although various supports and accommodations promote learning for students with disabilities, general educators may not have time or resources to scaffold inquiry activities. Therrien et al. (2011) reported that students with mild disabilities benefit most with inquiry-based activities when the teacher:

- Explains the "big idea" or overarching concept of inquiry.
- Guides students completing hands-on activities.
- Provides formative feedback during activities.
- Reinforces positive behavior and allows for high rates of student engagement.
- Reinforces concepts through additional review and practice.
- Uses supplemental instructional supports such as mnemonics, graphic organizers, or interaction with peers.

Textbook Approaches

Traditional textbook and lecture instruction also pose challenges for students with disabilities because of the reliance on reading and writing. Students are expected to read science textbooks independently to construct new understandings, revise misconceptions, and complete activities and assignments, yet they often lack the reading and writing skills needed to complete these tasks. Reading to learn critical course content presents challenges because students with mild disabilities often read several years below grade level and therefore have difficulty independently reading grade-level science texts. Further, some science texts do not provide sufficient reading supports such as graphic organizers, vocabulary instruction, explicit connections among and between concepts, and extensive review—all of which are helpful for students with mild disabilities.

Students must also apply math skills to solve science problems and construct and solve equations based on information. These complex activities also present substantial challenges for students who struggle with language, memory, problem-solving, or reasoning skills.

Challenges With Informational Text

By the time students enter middle or high school, teachers assume that they read to learn critical course concepts. As noted in chapters 13 and 14, this type of text presents several challenges for students with disabilities.

Unfamiliar content, organization, density, and coherence may decrease students' reading rate, which in turn affects comprehension. Rasinski et al. (2005) estimated that high school students at the 50th percentile for fluency read approximately 174 words correct per minute (wcpm). He suggested that secondary students who read at a rate of 100 wcpm are at substantial risk for poor comprehension and academic failure. Therefore, if students' decoding and reading rates for science passages fall below 94% and 100 wcpm respectively, teachers should consider text adaptations and accommodations.

Dyck and Pemberton (2002) suggested six types of text adaptations based on readers' strengths and needs and the characteristics of the text:

- Bypass reading
- Reduce amount of reading
- Support reading with supplemental information and instruction
- Organize reading with graphic organizers
- Guide reading with previews, anticipation guides, or structured notes

Assistive technology may be used in each of these adaptations to support students' learning. Use of any or all of these adaptations depends on assessment data. Remember that just *listening* to a text (instead of reading silently) may not help students if they have limited or no background knowledge, because they might not be able to predict or identify a purpose for reading and construct new knowledge or revise past understandings.

INFORMAL ASSESSMENTS

In science, teachers need information regarding students' conceptual knowledge *and* the skills they have to complete reading and math tasks similar to those included in course assignments and assessments. Informal assessments described in previous chapters provide teachers with information regarding students' reading and math skills.

Reading Assessments

Often, students' reading rate, accuracy, and comprehension decrease when they switch from narrative to informational text (Leslie & Caldwell, 2008). To address students' performance with informational text, many informal reading inventories (IRIs) include science or social studies passages that provide information regarding students' fluency and comprehension in these areas.

Teachers may select textbook sections to use as informal assessment passages. Select free-standing passages, that is, passages in which the reader can gain the passages' meaning without reference to previous paragraphs, illustrations, or other text features. Then conduct a running record and comprehension measure. Students whose scores fall below 100–120 wcpm for reading rate, 95% for reading accuracy, or 80% for comprehension may be at risk for academic failure with primarily text-based instruction.

Index of Science Reading Awareness

To assess whether students know how to and actually use support features of science text, Yore, Craig, and Maguire (1998) developed the Index of Science Reading Awareness (ISRA) as an inventory specific to metacognitive problem-solving and science reading. Three sections measure students' conceptual knowledge of science, awareness of science text features, and ability to use these features to problem-solve during reading. Yore et al. (1998) reported that students took about 60 minutes to complete all sections. Results provide a baseline regarding students' conceptual knowledge and help teachers decide how much instruction students need regarding textbook use.

Pretests

Another approach to assessing background knowledge is the chapter or unit pretest. Pretests vary in length and can take many forms such as forced-choice items, open-ended questions, matching or cloze assessment (fill in the blank) items with or without a word bank, or completion of a graphic organizer or concept map.

Unit or chapter pretests and study guides provide information about students' background knowledge in a structured format. Pretests may be included with textbooks series, constructed from textbook unit tests, or created by the teacher to reflect critical content. These tools benefit students most when they share the same format as the final assessment.

Know, Want to Know, Learned (KWL) Charts

KWL charts (Ogle, 1989) are perhaps the most familiar form of assessment for background knowledge. To use these to assess science conceptual knowledge, introduce the topic and major concepts and ask students to complete the K (what I *know*) and W (what I *want to learn,* or sometimes this is also called what I *think I will learn*) portions of the chart. This is sometimes done as a whole class; however individual completion provides teachers with clues about strengths and weaknesses in individual students' background knowledge.

PReP

Teachers can use the Pre-Reading Plan (PReP; Langer, 1981) as an assessment before beginning a chapter or unit of instruction. To use PReP, first *prepare* students by stating the key concept from the unit and the big idea (e.g., all living things are composed of chemical substances including water, carbohydrates, proteins, and fats) or overarching purpose of the unit (to describe chemical processes and substances common among and essential to living things). This can include key pictures or a hands-on demonstration that stimulates class discussion and activates students' background knowledge and interest. Within the discussion, have students brainstorm about the concept and write their words, ideas, and associations on the board or overhead.

Next, have students *reflect* on their ideas: "What made you think . . . [the phrase given by each student in the discussion]" (Bos & Vaughn, 2006, p. 193). This helps students think deeply about what they know and how they came to that understanding. Students listen to one another's associations and can challenge one another with additional examples and nonexamples.

Finally, ask students to *reform* their ideas or tell whether they have any new ideas about the key concept. That is, did the discussion cause students to remember more than they initially knew about the concept or revise their previous ideas?

Although younger students may need to complete all PReP steps orally with teacher support, secondary students can write the two final steps independently. For example, as part of the third step, *Reform*, students could create a graphic organizer or concept map to show relationships among concepts. After students have completed these steps, evaluate their background knowledge using the following scale (Langer, 1981):

- *Much knowledge:* defines concepts and gives examples; makes links between or among key concepts; makes analogies; differentiates among main ideas or "superordinate concepts" and supporting concepts or examples
- *Some knowledge:* mainly gives examples, characteristics, or obvious features of the concept; some differentiation between or among main ideas and supporting concepts or examples
- *Little knowledge:* provides little elaboration and few examples; does not differentiate between main ideas and supporting details; restates teacher example or demonstration without new information; makes no new connections from background

Students with little knowledge likely need substantial concept instruction prior to reading for information. Science teachers may also need to provide instruction related to reading, writing, and math within their content area to address IEP goals.

ASSESSMENT ACCOMMODATIONS

Assessment is a method of collecting decision-making data about instructional methods and materials; however, a disability may interfere with a student's performance on an assessment, thereby invalidating results. Therefore, students with disabilities receive assessment accommodations, so they may more accurately demonstrate their ability. Accommodations include ways the assessment is formatted and physical conditions in which the assessment is completed. "The purpose of these accommodations is to minimize the impact of test-taker attributes that are not relevant to the construct that is the primary focus of the assessment" (Ricketts, Brice, & Coombes, 2010, p. 266). Thurlow, Rogers, and Christenson (2010) reported on various science assessment accommodations and their effectiveness. Figure 19.1 includes common accommodations with examples.

Science assessments are usually presented as a written test. Students read items and either select the correct response or write a response. Native language test translation is important for students with disabilities who are also English language learners.

Presentation and response formats are ways in which the test is shown to students and ways they answer questions. Timing and scheduling conditions particularly impact students with attention issues or students lacking math or reading fluency. Setting accommodations include changing who administers the test and the test group size. Some students take the test individually with the special educator or in a small group. Often, if the special educator proctors the test and provides accommodations, the student takes the test in the special education setting. Although this arrangement supports presentation accommodations and controls distractions, students are removed from the environment in which they learned the content, which may contain visual cues and memory associations that support their performance. When possible, therefore, teachers should test in the same setting in which learning took place. If students must complete assessments in a new environment, allow them to work in that setting prior to testing to help them acclimatize. Carefully consider test accommodations required by the students' IEPs and how those can be best implemented.

Figure 19.1 Assessment Accommodations

Testing Feature	Typical Conditions	Purpose of Accommodation	Example Accommodations
Presentation Format	Typed questions or prompts; open-ended or forced-choice answers	Reduce reading load Eliminate distracters Support vocabulary knowledge Assist in problem solving and identifying key information	Read questions aloud Audiotape questions Highlight key terms in questions Provide thesaurus; paraphrase questions or forced-choice responses; translate into first language; provide additional examples Write or highlight in test booklet; read and/or clarify directions
Response Format	Forced-choice answers are marked on the test or Scantron Student handwrites open-ended, short answers, or essay responses	Eliminate tracking errors Eliminate issues with writing organization, fluency, and conventions	Monitor students' marking or "bubbles" on Scantron or mark responses for student; allow use of computer to type answers Allow oral response through use of scribe, computer (speech-to-text software), or audiotaped responses; support written response with computer (typed) or adaptive writing tools; allow spellcheckers
Equipment and Materials	Print tests with small font Test with open-ended written responses or large number of problems to solve	Reduce reading fatigue; increase clarity of print Eliminate issues with memorization of basic facts, so student can demonstrate conceptual knowledge	Color overlays; text magnification; change room lighting Allow keyboards, math tables and number lines, calculators, manipulatives, thesaurus, and dictionaries
Timing and Scheduling	Lengthy testing period Large number of test items to complete, usually at	Support sustained attention and engagement Allow increased processing time	Allow breaks within the testing period; divide testing period into shorter segments; spread testing across

Testing Feature	Typical Conditions	Purpose of Accommodation	Example Accommodations
	a rate of 1 item per minute or more Majority of students in school tested immediately in the morning	Create optimal testing conditions	the school day or across a larger number of days Extended time to complete test Identify optimal testing time; test at a different time of day than others
Setting	Majority of students tested in large group Students complete test at various times and quietly shift to another activity Majority of students tested in homeroom or science classroom	Allow for individualized support Reduce visual and auditory distractions	Complete test in small group or individual setting Test in small group or individual setting; move students to quiet environment; create testing carrels for student to eliminate visual distractions

RAFAEL'S INDIVIDUALIZED EDUCATION PROGRAM

Ms. Nyack and Mr. Brewster administered Sections I and II of the ISRA to students with disabilities to assess whether these students understood the importance of various features of the science text and how to use these features. Additionally, Mr. Brewster completed IRIs with all students with disabilities using sections of the chemistry textbook.

Rafael's IEP contained results of his most recent IRI. His science-related IEP is shown in Figure 19.2.

Figure 19.2 Rafael's IEP

Individualized Education Program

Name: Rafael   Grade: 11   Skill Area: Science

Present Level of Performance: On IRIs, Rafael orally read 10th-grade passages at a rate of 178 wcpm with 94% accuracy and answered comprehension questions with 50% accuracy for both explicit and implicit questions without referring back to the passage. He decoded two textbook chemistry passages with 95% accuracy at a rate of 150 wcpm and answered comprehension questions with 25% accuracy, both with and without referring

(Continued)

Figure 19.2 (Continued)

> back to the passages. His answers relied on background knowledge rather than on the information in the text. On the ISRA, Rafael did not use text features to support comprehension.
>
> **Annual Goal:** Rafael will state the meaning of science vocabulary terms and outline science text with at least 80% accuracy.
>
> **Objective 1:** By the end of the fourth quarter, given a 750-word section from the tenth-grade science text and 10 new English vocabulary terms, Rafael will use context to define the word and verbally state or write a synonym or antonym for 8 of the 10 terms.
>
> **Objective 2:** By the end of the fourth quarter, given a 750-word section from the tenth-grade science text, Rafael will write an outline of the section with 80% accuracy, based on a teacher-developed rubric.

SUMMARY

Students with mild disabilities need the opportunity to participate in rigorous science courses to learn content presented in standardized tests. However, these courses often pose challenges for students with disabilities because they may not have the reading, writing, or mathematics skills needed to communicate ideas, formulate questions, test hypotheses, solve scientific problems, and evaluate results of experiments.

Some teachers use inquiry-based learning in science to facilitate construction of conceptual knowledge. Students with mild disabilities often need guided rather than open-ended inquiry to complete experimental steps correctly, observe relevant phenomena during hands-on activities, and draw correct conclusions. Teachers should provide instructional supports and adaptations of science texts, particularly if students have poor decoding skills (< 95% accuracy) or poor reading rates (below 100 wcpm) or if they answer comprehension questions with less than 80% accuracy.

CHAPTER APPLICATION ACTIVITIES

Apply your knowledge from the chapter by discussing or completing the following application questions or activities. Suggested answers are provided below.

1. What features of textbooks do students need to use to support comprehension during science reading?

2. Mr. Brewster was planning a unit of study on flight using hands-on activities, demonstrations, and a variety of reading materials. Suggest three ways he can assess his students' background knowledge.

3. Mr. Brewster wanted to revise the test for Raphael, an English language learner, but he did not have the time or resources to translate the entire test or Raphael's answer if Raphael wrote or responded in his first language. What are some accommodations that Mr. Brewster could make for Raphael?

Suggested Responses

1. Students need to use chapter and unit objectives, chapter divisions such as headings and subheadings, and text cues such as highlighted words and embedded references to illustrations, graphs, tables, diagrams, and definitions within the text.

2. Mr. Brewster could prepare and use a pretest using vocabulary from the chapter or the chapter summary; prepare and use an informal reading inventory, cloze, or maze using one of the sections of the textbook or passage on flight; develop and complete a PReP lesson with students to identify those with much, some, or little knowledge; or have students develop or complete a teacher-made graphic organizer using unit vocabulary (could include KWL).

3. Mr. Brewster could provide Raphael with visual supports such as diagrams or pictures of key concepts. He could translate just key terms and ask Raphael to match them to visual representations, use these terms to label a diagram, or match each term to its English equivalent. He could allow Raphael to write his initial paragraph in his first language and then either work with a peer or the teacher to translate his writing into English. The oral discussion during translation could allow Raphael to elaborate with the support of a native English speaker.

SUPPLEMENTAL RESOURCES FOR CHAPTER 19

Banerjee, A. (2001). Teaching science using guided inquiry as the central theme: A professional development model for high school science teachers. *Science Educator, 19*(2), 1–9.

Discovery Education Science. http://www.discoveryeducation.com/administrators/curricular-resources/science/

Forensic Science Technician. (2012). *100 best websites for science teachers.* Retrieved from http://www.forensicsciencetechnician.org/100-best-websites-for-science-teachers/

Herr, N. (2007). *Academic language and content literacy: Science.* Retrieved from http://www.csun.edu/science/ref/language/index.html

Jefferson Lab. (n.d.). *Reading comprehension passages.* http://education.jlab.org/reading/index.html (for cloze assessments on science topics)

Keeley, P. (2008). *Science formative assessment.* Thousand Oaks, CA: Corwin.

Museum of Science. (1997). *The atoms family.* Retrieved from http://www.miamisci.org/af/sln/

Scruggs, T., & Mastropieri, M. (2007). Science learning in special education: The case for constructed versus instructed learning. *Exceptional Children, 15,* 57–74.

Watson, S., & Houtz, L. (2002). Teaching science: Meeting the academic needs of culturally and linguistically diverse students. *Intervention in School and Clinic, 37,* 267–278.

Science: Methods **20** and Strategies

If we are to improve instruction for students with disabilities and probably for all students, science teachers must be willing to accommodate instruction and adjust the learning environment . . . teaching fewer concepts with richer insights, to facilitate greater student understanding, and to present opportunities for students to apply what they learned to real-life situations.

(Stefanich, 1998, p. 2)

CHAPTER OVERVIEW

This chapter presents methods and strategies that Ms. Nyack and Mr. Brewster decided to use in their science class. They recognized that many strategies would benefit all students in their chemistry class, not just Rafael. They knew that students with mild disabilities learn best when they actively participate in instructional activities that add to their background knowledge and support learning; tie abstract information to explicit, concrete information such as hands-on activities; understand connections among concepts and the overarching organization of information; anchor new information in their background knowledge and experiences; and differentiate main ideas from supporting details and trivial information (Bulgren & Schumaker, 2001).

The teachers also recognized that supports that organize and help students understand information are critical to learning in science; therefore, they developed a unit organizer to introduce the next unit, considered ways to establish background knowledge, taught how to use context clues, planned instruction with graphic organizers, introduced an outlining strategy, and ensured students received accommodations or modifications as noted on their IEPs or 504 plans.

FEATURED METHODS AND STRATEGIES

Chapter Strategies	Corresponding Common Core State Standards
Context Clues Power Notes Graphic Organizers	Determine the central ideas or information of a primary or secondary source; provide an accurate summary that makes clear the relationships among key details and ideas.
	Determine the meaning of words and phrases as they are used in a text.
	Analyze how the text structures information or ideas into categories or hierarchies, demonstrating understanding of the information or ideas.

Source for standards: Common Core State Standards Initiative, 2012

UNIT ORGANIZER

Ms. Nyack and Mr. Brewster developed a unit organizer that made "big ideas" explicit and showed how the new unit fit with previous topics. They used it during the first lesson to orient students to the new topic. This organizer helped them and their students establish goals for learning and connect lessons explicitly to big ideas for both the unit and the course as a whole.

ESTABLISHING BACKGROUND KNOWLEDGE

Although some students with disabilities have adequate science background knowledge or experiences to support new learning, many do not. After teachers present activities to build background knowledge, some students draw incorrect conclusions leading to misconceptions or reinforcement of naïve notions. Other students understand concepts but have language and vocabulary limitations that impede their ability to revise or deepen their knowledge. By activating background knowledge, teachers can build on students' strengths by determining what foundation already exists.

Ms. Nyack and Mr. Brewster activated students' background knowledge in several ways. For example, for one of their lessons, they used the PReP strategy (Langer, 1981; see Chapter 19). The teachers

- Showed a textbook graph comparing percentages of water in living things and a 45-second YouTube clip from a *Star Trek* episode in which an alien calls the crew "ugly bags of mostly water."

- Wrote the big idea *all living things exist in a water solution* on the white board.
- Helped students brainstorm what they believed this meant.
- Thought aloud about how the brainstormed information fit together.
- Invited students to assist in creating a preliminary concept map (graphic organizer).
- Asked students to reflect and comment on connections and related meanings. (What made you think . . . ? or Why do you want to put those together . . . ?)

Following this preparation, students completed the assigned reading in small groups and revised the initial concept map created by the whole class.

For Rafael and other students needing English vocabulary support, the teachers anticipated some connections students might make and created vocabulary cards. Each card contained the science term in English, a simple picture of the term and its meaning, and if appropriate, the term in the students' first language. Groups used these cards after reading to create their revised concept map. In other cases the teachers had students sort the cards under two or three headings (chosen by the teachers) before reading to reflect the organization of the information. After students arranged the cards, they began their reading and rearranged cards to reflect changes in their understanding. This method provided language support and assessed background knowledge.

Ms. Nyack and Mr. Brewster realized that some students need concrete examples such as hands-on activities and analogies to establish background knowledge. To introduce the difficult concepts of carbon bonding and the structure of carbon-based molecules, they used the analogy of Lego building. First, students "explored" using these rules:

- Yellow bricks with four total slots/bumps connect with any other brick.
- Black bricks (one slot/bump) connect on bump side only.
- White bricks (two slots/bumps) connect on slot side only.
- Yellow bricks need four connections, white need two, black one.
- Make as large a structure as you can.

After several minutes, the teachers defined the analogy: yellow bricks were carbon atoms, white were oxygen, and black were hydrogen. They later introduced the structures of carbohydrates, lipids, and amino acids and used the analogy to demonstrate "breaking the bonds" when explaining energy release during metabolism. To prevent misconceptions, the teachers described limits of the analogy. For example, molecules do not have the rigid shape or size of plastic Legos, and instead of slots/bumps, atoms share electrons to form covalent bonds.

Finally, the teachers used hands-on experiences to activate background knowledge. For example, the teachers used a simple experiment with acids and bases to remind students of work in a previous study of pH and extend this knowledge to the effects of acids and bases on enzymes. Students tested the pH of milk, vinegar, and a baking soda solution—an activity from a prior unit. They then added vinegar to milk to reach an acidic pH, observed the effects of changing pH on the milk (curdles), and drew what they believed happened in the milk. Visible changes to proteins in milk established necessary background knowledge.

USING CONTEXT CLUES

The teachers also wanted to make sure that Rafael and other students made best use of the text. They knew several ways to use context but wanted to make these explicit for students. Consequently, they developed and taught a strategy to help them understand vocabulary from context.

Check, Ring, Study, Substitute Strategy

Their strategy was the *check, ring, study, and substitute* strategy, which reminded students to

Check for synonyms and definitions next to or near the unknown word.

Ring around the word by rereading several sentences before and reading on for several sentences for clarification.

Study illustrations and tables for clues regarding the meaning of the unknown word.

Substitute a synonym for the unknown word and say whether it makes sense.

The teachers taught the first three steps with vocabulary and passages that supported their use. After students learned each step and successfully implemented it with a matched passage, the teachers added the next step. Students learned to use context clues in the same order each time. If they still could not understand the word using context, they flagged the word with a sticky note and either read on or asked for assistance. The teachers asked students what they had tried, supported student use of context if appropriate, or provided students with a synonym.

GRAPHIC ORGANIZERS

Graphic organizers (GOs) prepare students for information they will learn before, during, and after instruction. Concepts are written in shapes, columns, or sections with line labels or connectors (e.g., words or phrases on or near the line) indicating relationships between concepts. GOs are most useful when aligned with the structure of the concepts or text. For example, organizers representing chemical reactions forming salts (cause–effect) would differ from those presenting characteristics of acids and bases (description–enumeration or compare–contrast). GOs can be used as a study guide, note-taking plan, or outlining strategy.

Before and During Instruction

If implemented before instruction, GOs activate students' background knowledge, set a purpose for learning, and provide the big idea. Before and during instruction, they visually represent the overall structure or organization of concepts and their relationships.

To consider ways to use GOs, both teachers examined textbook chapters, lecture notes, and activities to identify potential areas of difficulty for students and determined the appropriate GO. As shown in Figure 20.1, they made cue cards to help students identify signal words providing clues to the text structure, match specific text structures with appropriate GOs, and remember to find the main idea.

Students used these cards as they followed along in the lesson, taking notes in their science journals. GOs and text structure, however, required explicit systematic instruction, so students understood the usefulness of the procedure.

The 3Cs Strategy

To support memorization of the procedure, the teachers developed and taught students the *3Cs:*

C—*Carefully examine the text for signal words.*

C—*Choose the graphic organizer that fits.*

C—*Construct the graphic organizer using big ideas, details, and connectors.*

Figure 20.1 Various Graphic Organizers

To identify whether the text structure is **Compare–Contrast,** carefully examine text for signals;	Then choose and construct one of these graphic organizers.
Venn diagrams Tables comparing characteristics or features These words or phrases: *similar to, same as, like, just as . . .* *unlike, by contrast, but . . .* *differs, the difference between . . .*	Item 1 and 2 same Item 1— different Item 2— different
Ask Myself	
More than one person, place or *thing* discussed? Two or more things compared? Purpose for comparison? How are these the same? How are they different?	Same Different

To identify whether the text structure is **Main Idea, Definition, List (no order),** or **Argument–Persuasion,** carefully examine text for signals;	Then choose and construct one of these graphic organizers.
Bold or italicized word followed by definition Illustrations Definition sentence, principle These words or phrases: *there are (number) types of . . .* *can be classified as . . .* *groups, types, kinds. . . .* *the most important. . . .*	Detail 1 Detail 2 Main Idea Detail 4 Detail 3
Ask Myself	
Is passage describing Who What When Where How Why Is passage mainly using descriptive terms (*looks, feels, smells, tastes, sounds like*) or describing action?	Timeline Argument Support

(Continued)

Figure 20.1 (Continued)

To identify whether the text structure is **Sequence, Procedure, Order,** or **Classification,** carefully examine text for signals;	Then choose and construct one of these graphic organizers:
Numbers Letters These words or phrases: *the (number) steps in this process include . . .* *first, second, third . . .* *first, next, then . . .* *finally, in conclusion* *beginning, middle, end*	☐ 1 ☐ 2 ☐ 3 ☐ 4
Ask Myself	Process Title → Step 1 → Step 2 → Step 3
Does passage describe . . . How to complete a process (e.g., recipe, experiment, etc.) Relationship between groups of things (apples, oranges = fruit)	Stage 1, Stage 2, Stage 3 Group 1 | Group 2

To identify whether the text structure is **Cause–Effect** or **Problem Solution**, carefully examine text for signals;	Then choose and construct one of these graphic organizers:
Arrows, flowcharts... These words or phrases: *if ... then ...* *before ... after ...* *when. . . .* *this affects X by ...* *as a result of ...* *consequently, thus, hence, therefore, following ...* *action-reaction* *stimulus-response* *cause-effect*	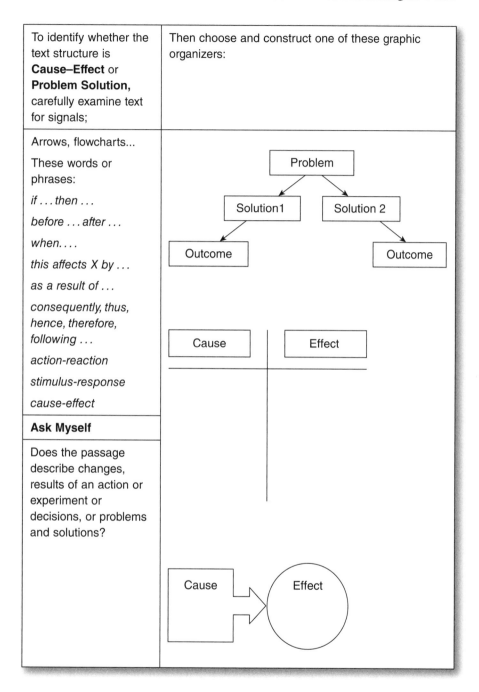
Ask Myself	
Does the passage describe changes, results of an action or experiment or decisions, or problems and solutions?	

To teach the use of GOs, the teachers planned 10-minute minilessons, one on each text structure: cause–effect, description–enumeration, sequence–procedure, compare–contrast, problem–solution, and argument–persuasion consisting of brief text written at the sixth- to eighth-grade level for easy decoding.

Modeling the 3Cs Strategy

Mr. Brewster introduced the 3Cs strategy using a think-aloud that went like this:

> I am going to use the 3Cs strategy as I read the science passage and develop a graphic organizer that best fits. So, what is my first step? As I read, first I *carefully* examine the text for signal words. My cue cards have different signal words as examples, so I will keep them handy. I will also use highlighter tape to mark signal words as I read: "All living things are formed from one important element: carbon. When carbon combines with hydrogen and oxygen atoms, three types of molecules essential for living things are formed: sugars, amino acids, and lipids, or fats. These carbon compounds provide living things with energy but also are part of the structures of cells. Sugars are the first type of carbon molecule that all living things need and use."
>
> I notice the words *types of* and then a list of carbon compounds, so based on my cue card, I predict this is a main idea paragraph with supporting details. OK—now I am ready for the second step: *Choose* the graphic organizer that fits. If I look on the cue card that lists "main idea" as one of the text types, I see that I can use a time line, T-chart, or web for my graphic organizer. The paragraph does not indicate dates or order for a timeline, and I could use different headings for a T-chart, but I think I'll use a web. I will draw the central figure for the main idea and several smaller circles for details.
>
> The last step in the 3Cs strategy is to *construct* the graphic organizer. First I need to find the big idea or what the paragraph is mostly about. I will read the passage again with that in mind [orally reads passage again]. After rereading, I know that the paragraph indicates what living things have in common and specifically three carbon compounds that all living things have in common. I know this is the main idea because it tells who or what the passage is mostly about. Hmm, this is kind of long to add to the GO. I can restate that as "carbon compounds necessary for life."
>
> Next I need to find the details. I will skim for the signal words like *next, then,* and *first* [teacher points to text while skimming]. Here is the word *first.* I will read around the word to make sure it is a supporting detail: "Sugars are the first carbon molecules that all living things have in common. Sugars such as glucose and

fructose are used by all living things for energy. Chains of sugars make carbohydrates." Yes, this is one detail about the main idea—sugars are one type of carbon compound. I'll write "sugar" as a detail in a small circle and add the connector "include" because sugars are one kind of carbon molecule. Are there more words that tell about sugars that I should remember? Yes, glucose and fructose. I will add a smaller circle for these under "sugar" in the GO and add the connecting words "which include." I need to add "carbohydrates" as a smaller circle, too, and I'll write the connector "in chains called." Now I notice, in the text, the word *second*. I need to read around again, but I predict that this will be about the second kind of molecule, amino acids.

Does this GO still seem like a good match for the passage? If it doesn't match well with what I need to add, I will consider a different GO. I think the web is working well for the information.

Mr. Brewster continued with the GO and when he was finished, he thought aloud by restating what he learned using the GO to take notes:

The main idea is the way carbon, hydrogen, and oxygen atoms make molecules important for living things. First, I read about sugars made from carbon, hydrogen, and oxygen. Sugar is used by living things for energy, and long chains of sugars make carbohydrates. Two kinds of sugars are glucose and fructose. . . .

After Mr. Brewster modeled the process, the class practiced with different paragraph structures and graphic organizers. As Ms. Nyack modeled constructing a GO on the board, students created their own on white boards. To close, the class discussed how well the organizer fit the text structure, why a different GO was used for each passage, and whether a different visual might be better.

After Ms. Nyack and Mr. Brewster introduced each text structure, student partners completed the 3Cs strategy with short passages during minilessons. Teachers gradually increased passage lengths and complexity. For example, in one lesson they illustrated situations with text with more than one structure, and these complex passages challenged students to create hybrid organizers.

Similarly, the teachers used GOs during guided inquiry and mathematical calculations. They created flowcharts for hands-on activities containing yes–no questions and if–then statements to prompt students' observations and help them determine the next activity step. For mathematical calculations, Ms. Nyack and Mr. Brewster created a GO that structured multiple steps. They explicitly modeled use of these GOs, provided students with multiple opportunities to practice using them across several lessons, and made GOs available as an accommodation during assessments.

After Instruction

Graphic organizers can be used after instruction to structure students' writing, provide support when studying for tests, or assess student learning. After instruction, students used their GOs to write a short report on what they learned to check their lesson understanding. Similarly, GOs can be used for assessment. Ms. Nyack provided students with a GO completed during instruction as part of the end-of-unit test. She provided connectors, but students had to place vocabulary words (from a word bank) into the GO to reflect the relationships among them.

GOs are a flexible tool to support student learning before and during instruction and assess knowledge after instruction. Additionally, they can be transformed into traditional outlines, which is one strategy for helping students understand complex conceptual knowledge and cope with various text structures.

OUTLINING

Outlines can be used before, during, or after reading. Before instruction or reading, teachers can preview the text and prepare outline headings using the chapter section titles as superordinate terms (e.g., I, II, III, etc.) and main ideas within sections as subordinate terms (e.g., A, B, C, etc.). The outline reflects the organization of the information in a hierarchical format and prepares students to identify important concepts and vocabulary terms.

After reading, teachers can use outlines during instruction to direct students' attention to important information and guide note taking. Teachers can provide students with the basic framework for the outline including blank spaces for super- and subordinate headings. Teachers then guide completion of the outline as part of a review session.

Power Notes

Power notes are a nontraditional approach for teaching outlining. According to the International Reading Association (2011), power notes are a structured outlining technique to help students differentiate between main ideas and details. Main ideas and details are each assigned a number. Main ideas are Power 1 ideas, and details and examples are either Power 2, 3, or 4 ideas. Power notes visually display main ideas and supportive details in outline form and are helpful for categorizing information.

Using power notes as a textbook note-taking approach, Gore (2004) suggested that, after teacher modeling, students work in pairs to identify the chapter title (Power 1), bold subheadings within the chapter (Power 2), and key information from subheadings (Power 3). Gore noted that this format helps students take notes and helps them later write about the content they have studied. Power notes use this format: Power 1 = main idea; Power 2 = detail or supportive information for Power 1 above; Power 3 = detail or supportive information for Power 2 above (and so forth). Ideas or words with the same power numbers have a similar relationship to the power above them. Here's an example from the science unit:

1. Carbon compounds provide energy for living things
   2. Sugars and carbohydrates
      3. Glucose, fructose (sugars) in chains form carbohydrates
      3. Glucose is main source of energy for living things
   2. Amino acids and proteins
      3. Amino acids in chains form proteins
      3. Proteins have several functions in the body
   2. Lipids or fats
      3. Long chains of carbon atoms with hydrogen and oxygen
      3. Store more energy than carbohydrates or proteins

Santa, Havens, & Valdes (2004) noted that students can use power notes as an organizational tool for reading, writing, and studying. Students can also use Inspiration software (www.inspiration.com) to convert power maps to power notes.

Connecting Outlines to Graphic Organizers

If students are familiar with and can already construct graphic organizers during reading, teachers can use this skill to scaffold independence with outlining. To do this, teachers explicitly connect graphic organizers and outlines by telling students that both reflect the structure of information and help them to organize and remember important details.

Ms. Nyack and Mr. Brewster's class drew a GO on the white board while reading a passage. The GO had several shapes at each level that would be represented in the outline. Next, Mr. Brewster modeled how to label the GO shapes with outline levels (major shapes = I, II, III, etc.; first subordinate shapes = A, B, C, etc.). Finally, Ms. Nyack rewrote the GO in outline form, directly transcribing GO information into an outline. After modeling, students engaged in guided and independent practice.

Outlines After Instruction

Finally, teachers can use outlines after instruction to review the chapter or assess students' understanding of concepts. Teachers can model transforming notes into outline format, which may benefit students as they review. The outline would incorporate concepts from several lessons, making connections among lessons more explicit. If students completed outlines as part of note taking during reading, they can also use these to construct speeches, write summaries and reports, or create PowerPoint presentations. Additionally, the outline may be an assessment tool. For example, students can complete partially completed outlines. Depending on students' skill level, teachers can determine the outline complexity, whether or not to include a word bank, and how many anchor concepts to add to the outline. Before assessing students using this format, however, teachers should model and guide them in practicing the task.

ACCOMMODATIONS AND MODIFICATIONS

Because science instruction often relies heavily on print-based resources, teachers should carefully consider accommodations and modifications for students who struggle with reading. Chapter 19 includes several text adaptations to use when students have fluency or comprehension issues (Dyck & Pemberton, 2002).

Graphic organizers and outlining fit within these text adaptations by supporting reading rather than eliminating reading from instruction. Also, teachers should examine accommodations students will use during testing (see Chapter 19) and include these during instruction. Otherwise, students may be unfamiliar with the accommodation and not benefit from its use. For example, having the text read orally during lessons and tests may help students if they have good listening comprehension, are familiar with the readers' inflection, and will request their readers to reread when needed.

If students cannot meet lesson expectations with accommodations, teachers should consider modifications, which range from reducing the amount of information students are responsible for learning to selecting a learning standard from a lower grade level to selecting a completely different learning standard. In the first case, modifications to content students will learn can be indicated on a planning pyramid (Schumm, Vaughn, & Leavell, 1994). Selecting a different learning standard or a standard from an earlier grade reduces the conceptual complexity and rigor of the general education curriculum and therefore should be used only when appropriate, based on students' IEPs.

TIME SAVERS

Maintaining a system (grade book, Excel spreadsheet, etc.) that prominently lists student accommodations or modifications saves teachers from frequently searching for the list every time they provide an assignment or test. Establishing a routine for such accommodations (e.g., on test days, students with testing accommodations go to the resource room) also saves time and is appreciated by students. Using structure within the science classroom saves time and provides predictability, so students know how to prepare for certain days. Teachers can enlist the support of others (volunteers, older students, etc.) to locate and develop exemplar graphic organizers and maintain a bank of these that illustrate critical science concepts.

SUMMARY

Methods that support understanding and organization of information have a profound positive impact on learning for students with disabilities. These include activating background knowledge, using context clues, and explicitly teaching the use of graphic organizers and outlining. Students with mild disabilities may need accommodations (and in fewer instances, modifications) for text-based instruction; these should be discussed by IEP team members.

CHAPTER APPLICATION ACTIVITIES

Apply your knowledge from the chapter by discussing or completing the following application questions or activities. Suggested answers are provided below.

1. Think about a unit of study in science that you have previously taught or will teach in the future. What are three activities you could add to build accurate background knowledge for students?

2. List steps you would use to select and introduce the graphic organizer to students using one of the types of text structure.

3. Describe ways you could use an outline or a graphic organizer to scaffold students' learning before, during, and after reading.

Suggested Responses

1. Anchor new information in background experiences with analogies; use hands-on activities and demonstrations; show video clips; use a unit organizer to show the relationship of the new unit to past learning; use other graphic organizers and KWL to activate background knowledge; model a think-aloud about what I know; complete word sorts with vocabulary words and pictures; or preview the chapter by completing a "walk" through the chapter.

2. To teach students how to use a graphic organizer, (a) plan the purpose and type by examining the text and either drawing your own or selecting a graphic organizer that best fits; (b) decide whether to use the graphic organizer before, during, or after reading and how much information you will supply in advance to students; (c) explain to students the purpose of the graphic organizer; (d) model using the graphic organizer; and (e) provide guided and independent practice.

3. Graphic organizers and outlines show students the organization of the information in a section of text or lesson. Teachers can scaffold reading and learning by adjusting the complexity of the outline or graphic organizer (i.e., the number of levels and supporting details) and the amount of information they supply. That is, partially completing the outline or graphic organizer provides scaffolded support. Using an outline or graphic organizer matched to text information can assist students (a) before reading to set a purpose for reading, anticipate connections within the material, and preview text headings and key vocabulary; (b) during reading to organize information in support of memory, prompt note taking, identify main ideas and key vocabulary, check relationships between concepts, and monitor comprehension; and (c) after reading to review and evaluate comprehension, structure written summaries, and support studying for assessments.

SUPPLEMENTAL RESOURCES FOR CHAPTER 20

Babelfish.yahoo.com (translation service)

Dexter, D., Park, Y., & Hughes, C. (2011). A meta-analytic review of graphic organizers and science instruction for adolescents with learning disabilities: Implications for the intermediate and secondary science classroom. *Learning Disabilities Research & Practice, 26* (4), 204–213. (Note: This issue focuses on science instruction for students with disabilities.)

EverythingESL.net. http://www.everythingesl.net/inservices/graphic_organizers .php

Graphic organizers. (2011). Retrieved from http://freeology.com/graphicorgs/page/2/

Radcliffe, R., Caverly, D., Pearson, C., & Emmons, M. (2004). Improving textbook reading in a middle school science classroom. *Reading Improvement, 41*(3), 145–156.

TEACHING Exceptional Children, 44(6). (2012, July/August). This issue includes several articles on science instruction for students with disabilities.

Watson, S., & Houtz, L. (2002). Teaching science: Meeting the academic needs of culturally and linguistically diverse students. *Intervention in School and Clinic, 37*, 267–278.

Science Curriculum and Teaching Resources

American Guidance Systems science series. Circle Pines, MN: American Guidance Systems.

Iscience modules. (2012). Columbus, OH: SRA.

National Association of Biology Teachers. (2012). *Resource links.* Retrieved from http://www.nabt.org/websites/institution/index.php?p=38

National Science Teachers Association. http://www.nsta.org/highschool/?lid=hp

Pacemaker biology. Upper Saddle River, NJ: Globe Fearon/Pearson.

Pacemaker general science. Upper Saddle River, NJ: Globe Fearon/Pearson.

Power basics series (earth/space science, chemistry, biology, physics). Portland, ME: Walch Education.

Science worx. http://www.scienceworx.org/about-science-worx.php

SRA science laboratory (life, earth, physical). (2009). Columbus, OH: SRA.

The chem blog archive. http://www.thechemblog.com/?page_id=725

Appendices

Appendix A

Prefixes, Suffixes, Roots,
and Combining Forms

MOST COMMON PREFIXES

Prefix	Meaning	Example
in	not	incorrect
un	not, opposite of	unhappy
dis	not, opposite of	distrust
mis	wrongly	misspell
fore	before	forefather
re	again	rethink
de	down, away from	deplane
pre	before	pretest
en, em	cause to be	enable
non	not	nonskid

Prefix	Meaning	Example
in, im	in or into	input
over	too much	overeat
sub	under	subway
inter	between	interstate
trans	across	transatlantic
super	above	superhero
semi	half	semicircle
anti	against	antiwar
mid	middle	midday
under	too little	underpaid

All other prefixes (about 100) together account for only 3% of the total number of words containing prefixes.

MOST COMMON SUFFIXES

Suffix	Meaning	Example
s, es	plural	cats, boxes
ed	past tense verbs	jumped
ing	verb, present participle	running

Suffix	Meaning	Example
ly	characteristic of	sadly
er, or	person connected with	jogger, actor
ion, tion, ation, ition	act or process	action

Suffix	Meaning	Example
ible, able	can be done	fixable
al, ial	having characteristics of	formal
y	characterized by	messy
ness	state of, condition of	kindness
ity, ty	state of	activity
ment	action or process	enjoyment

Suffix	Meaning	Example
ic	having characteristics of	strategic
ous, eous, ious	possessing qualities of	joyous
en	made of	golden
er	comparative	smaller
ive, ative, itive	adjective form of noun	active
ful	full of	helpful
less	without	headless
est	comparative	smallest

All other suffixes (about 160) together account for only 7% of the total number of words containing suffixes.

Sources:

Blevins, W. (2001). *Teaching phonics and word study in the intermediate grades.* New York, NY: Scholastic Professional Books.

Henry, M. (2003). *Unlocking literacy: Effective decoding and spelling instruction.* Baltimore, MD: Paul H. Brookes.

Yoshimoto, R. (1997). Phonemes, phonetics, and phonograms; Advanced language structures for students with learning disabilities. *TEACHING Exceptional Children, 29*(3), 43–47.

MOST COMMON LATIN ROOTS

Root	Meaning	Example
port	carry	transport
rupt	to tear apart	disrupt
scrib, script	to write	transcribe
tract	pull	distract
cept, ceive	take, catch	accept
spect	see, watch, observe	inspect
ject	throw	reject
struct	build	construct
dict	tell, speak	diction
mis, mit	send	transmission

Root	Meaning	Example
flect, flex	to bend	inflect
cred	believe	credible
duc, duct	lead	conduct
pend	hang, weigh	suspend
pel	drive, push	expel
fac, fect	make, do	factory
vers, vert	to turn, change	convert
form	to shape	reform
aud, audi	to hear, listen	audible
vid, vis	see	visible

COMMON GREEK COMBINING FORMS

Greek word parts are referred to as *combining forms* because several Greek word parts combine to form a word. Some examples are *telegraph, geology,* and *photography*. Many of these words are specialized words used in science and mathematics.

Combining form	Meaning	Example
micro	small	microscopic
scope	see	telescope
photo	light	photocopy
graph	written down	graphic
tele	far off, distant	telegraph
phon	sound	phonograph
geo	earth	geography

Combining form	Meaning	Example
meter	measure	diameter
ology	study of	biology
auto	self	autograph
bio	life	biography
chrono	time	chronometer
biblio	book	bibliography
hydro	water	hydrant

Sources:

Henry, M. (2003). *Unlocking literacy: Effective decoding and spelling instruction*. Baltimore, MD: Paul H. Brookes.

Henry, M. (2010). *Words: Integrating decoding and spelling instruction based on word origin and word structure*. Austin, TX: Pro-Ed.

Kieffer, M., & Lesaux, N. (2007). Breaking down words to build meaning: Morphology, vocabulary, and reading comprehension in the urban classroom. *The Reading Teacher, 61*(2), 134–144.

Moats, L. (2003). *Speech to print workbook: Language exercises for teachers*. Baltimore, MD: Paul H. Brookes.

Appendix B

Test-Taking Tips

FOR OBJECTIVE-TYPE QUESTIONS

Skim the whole test to get an idea of length and sections.

Read each question carefully and slowly and note special words such as *not, except, all but*, et cetera.

Answer known questions first.

Mark questions for which you are unsure of the answer with a bullet or dot and return to those later.

Eliminate answers that are identical, silly, or unrelated to the question.

Carefully read all options. Put a check mark by each option after you read it.

Immediately write on the test any formulas or mnemonics that serve as prompts.

After reading the question, anticipate the answer and look for that answer in the choices.

If one answer choice in a multiple choice question is "all of the above," and more than one choice is correct, pick "all of the above."

Change an answer only if you are sure.

If you do not know the answer, pick (B) or (C), as those tend to be used most frequently as correct answers or pick the longest and most detailed response.

Generally, if a true/false question uses absolute terms (*all, always, every, only, none, never*), the answer is "false."

Generally, if a true/false question uses terms such as *sometimes, mostly, many, often, usually,* or *generally,* the answer is "true."

All parts of the true/false item must be true for the answer "true" to be correct.

If you are unsure of a true/false answer, answer "true," as "true" tends to be used more frequently as the correct answer.

Check the test for clues to help you answer challenging questions.

FOR SUBJECTIVE-TYPE QUESTIONS

Read the question or prompt slowly and several times.

Underline key terms in the question or prompt.

Pay attention to the "writing word" in the prompt. Are you being asked to *describe, compare, compare and contrast, contrast, analyze, define, illustrate, explain,* or *defend?* Each of these has a different meaning.

Note special considerations in the prompt such as the number of items to be explained and if the prompt wants you to use information from the text, class notes, et cetera.

Spend a few minutes thinking about and planning your response by making an outline, graphic organizer, or bulleted list.

Write the first topic sentence as a direct reply to the prompt by using some words in the prompt.

Spend most of your writing time on the body of your essay, which includes details and facts. Spend considerably less time writing the introduction and conclusion.

If you cannot think of a response specific to the prompt, write something on the topic that you remember. Reading through the test might help you remember some concepts for your response. You might still get partial credit.

Proofread for spelling, punctuation, and grammar.

Appendix C

Tips for Developing Effective Study Guides

Develop a study guide that matches unit objectives such as the following:

(a) two-column study guides that have factual questions listed in the left column and their corresponding answers in the right column

(b) flip flop study guides (two-column guides with definitions or examples in the right column and their corresponding key concepts or terms in the left column)

(c) compare-and-contrast study guides for analyzing similarities and differences between items or groups

(d) summative study guides for indicating vocabulary terms, short-answer questions, and review questions likely to appear on the exam

(e) textbook activity study guides for noting main ideas and details and for providing a place for students to indicate if they understand or do not understand the material

(f) interactive study guides that allow students to collaboratively complete the study guide and discuss responses with a partner

(g) sequential or cause and effect study guides that provide items in a graphic organizer with some cells empty that students complete as they read

Write questions in the same order that the corresponding concepts are presented in the chapter.

To differentiate study guides, include page numbers where answers can be found for students who need this.

If students are writing on their guide, leave adequate space for answers.

Include clear and specific directions.

Reduce the number of items by including only the most critical content or use the same study guide for all students but mark questions that are most important.

Simplify the language of the question without sacrificing the objective. Reduce unnecessary wordiness.

Minimize writing demands by including more true/false, matching, or fill-in-the-blank questions rather than short-answer or essay items, especially for students who struggle with written expression.

When including vocabulary items, provide the definition and have students provide the word; this reduces unnecessary copying of definitions.

Use only one or two different formats.

When writing true/false items, make sure each question assesses only one concept, is clearly true or false, is not copied word-for-word from the text, avoids tricky words, and does not include the word *not* just to make an obviously true statement false.

When writing fill-in-the-blank questions, include one blank per question, place the blank at the end of the sentence, provide blanks of the same length, ensure that the blank is an important concept, and include enough detail in the sentence so only one response is correct. (For example, "Our president is _____" is too vague. "The last name of the current U.S. president is _____" is much more clear.)

When writing matching questions or sections, include no more than 10 items per section, use only homogeneous items, write the longer phrases in the left column, and include lines for students to write the letter of their choice rather than having students connect lines from one column to the other.

When writing short-answer or essay questions, provide context for the question, indicate a general length, note the learning objectives, and include the point value.

References

American Academy of Child and Adolescent Psychiatry. (2008). *Facts for families: Teen suicide.* Retrieved from http://aacap.org/page.ww?name=Teen+Suicide &section=Facts+for+Families

Bear, G., Kortering, L., & Braziel, P. (2006). School completers and non-completers with learning disabilities: Similarities in academic achievement and perceptions of self and teachers. *Remedial and Special Education, 27,* 293–300.

Berk, L. (2003). *Child development.* Boston, MA: Allyn & Bacon.

Berry, G., Hall, D., & Gildroy, P. (2004). Teaching learning strategies. In B. K. Lenz, D. D. Deshler, & B. R. Kissam (Eds.), *Teaching content to all: Evidence-based inclusive practices in middle and secondary schools* (pp. 258–278). Boston, MA: Allyn & Bacon.

Biemiller, A. (2001). Teaching vocabulary: Early, direct, and sequential. *The American Educator, 25*(1), 24–28.

Blachowicz, C. (2004). *Reading fluency reader* (Level H). New York, NY: Jamestown Education/Glencoe.

Bos, C., & Vaughn, S. (2006). *Strategies for teaching students with learning and behavior problems* (6th ed.). Boston, MA: Allyn & Bacon.

Boyle, J., & Scanlon, D. (2010). *Methods and strategies for teaching students with mild disabilities.* Belmont, CA: Wadsworth.

Brigham, F., Scruggs, T., & Mastropieri, M. (2011). Science education and students with learning disabilities. *Learning Disabilities Research & Practice, 26*(4), 223–232.

Bulgren, J. A., Deshler, D., & Schumaker, J. (1993). *The concept mastery routine.* Lawrence, KS: Edge Enterprises.

Bulgren, J., & Schumaker, J. (2001). *Instructional practices designed to promote success for students with disabilities in inclusive secondary content classrooms: A review of the literature* (research report). Lawrence: University of Kansas Center for Research on Learning.

Bursuck, W., & Damer, M. (2007). *Reading instruction for students who are at risk or have disabilities.* Boston, MA: Pearson.

Cancio, E., West, R., & Young, K. (2004). Improving mathematics homework completion and accuracy of students with EBD through self-management and parent participation. *Journal of Emotional and Behavioral Disorders, 12*(1), 9–22.

Chalk, J. C., Hagan-Burke, S., & Burke, M. (2005). The effects of self–regulated strategy development on the writing process of high school students with learning disabilities. *Learning Disability Quarterly, 28,* 75–87.

Choike, J. (2000). Teaching strategies for "Algebra for All." *Mathematics Teacher, 93*(7), 556–560.

Clark, F., Deshler, D., Schumaker, J., Allen, G., & Warner, M. (1984). Visual imagery and self-questioning: Strategies to improve comprehension of written materials. *Journal of Learning Disabilities, 17*(3), 145–149.

Common core state standards initiative. (2012). Retrieved from http://www .corestandards.org/assets/CCSSI_ELA%20Standards.pdf

Conderman, G., & Bresnahan, V. (2010). Study guides to the rescue. *Intervention in School and Clinic, 45*(3), 169–176.

Conderman, G., & Elf, N. (2007). What's in this book? Engaging students through a textbook exploration activity. *Reading & Writing Quarterly, 23*(1), 111–116.

Conderman, G., Hartman, P., & Johnston-Rodriguez, S. (2009). Mnemonics to the rescue: Strategies for memory and recall. *LD Forum,* 6–8.

Conderman, G., & Hedin, L. (2011). Cue-cards: A self-regulatory strategy for students with learning disabilities. *Intervention in School and Clinic, 46*(3), 165–173.

Conderman, G., & Katsiyannis, A. (2002). Instructional issues and practices in secondary special education. *Remedial and Special Education, 23*(3), 169–179.

Conderman, G., & Pedersen, T. (2007). Twenty ways to avoid the tutoring trap. *Intervention in School and Clinic, 42*(4), 234–238.

Conderman, G., & Pedersen, T. (2010). Preparing students with mild disabilities for taking state and district tests. *Intervention in School and Clinic, 45*(4), 232–240.

Deshler, D., Ellis, E., & Lenz, K. (1996). *Teaching adolescents with learning disabilities: Strategies and methods.* Denver, CO: Love.

Deshler, D., & Schumaker, J. (2005). *Teaching adolescents with disabilities: Accessing the general education curriculum.* Thousand Oaks, CA: Corwin.

Dyck, N., & Pemberton, J. (2002). A model for making decisions about text adaptations. *Intervention in School and Clinic, 38,* 28–35.

Ellis, E. (2011). *Makes sense strategies.* Retrieved from http://www.graphic organizers.com/edwin–ellis–ph–d.html

Englert, C. S., Tarrant, K. L., Mariage, T., & Oxer, T. (1994). Lessons talk as the work of reading groups: The effectiveness of two interventions. *Journal of Learning Disabilities, 27,* 171–175.

Fountas, I., & Pinnell, G. (2011). *Benchmark assessment system* (2nd ed.). Chicago, IL: Heinemann.

Friend, M., & Bursuck, W. (2012). *Including students with special needs: A practical guide for classroom teachers.* Boston, MA: Pearson.

Gallagher-Landi, M. (2001). Helping students with learning disabilities make sense of word problems. *Intervention in School and Clinic, 37*(1), 13–18, 30.

Gartland, D. (2007). Reading instruction. In P. J. Schloss, M. A. Schloss, & C. N. Schloss (Eds.), *Instructional methods for secondary students with learning and behavior problems* (4th ed.) (pp. 233–254). Boston, MA: Pearson.

Gore, M. (2004). *Successful inclusion strategies for secondary and middle school teachers: Keys to help struggling learners access the curriculum.* Thousand Oaks, CA: Corwin.

Graham, S., & Harris, K. (2003). Students with learning disabilities and the process of writing: A meta-analysis of SRSD studies. In H. L. Swanson, K. R. Harris, & S. Graham (Eds.), *Handbook of learning disabilities* (pp. 323–344). New York, NY: Guilford Press.

Graham, S., Harris, K., & MacArthur, C. (2006). Explicitly teaching struggling writers: Strategies for mastering the writing process. *Intervention in School and Clinic, 41,* (5) 290–294.

Graham, S., Harris, K. R., & Mason, L. (2005). Improving the writing performance, knowledge, and self-efficacy of struggling young writers: The effects of self-regulated strategy development. *Contemporary Educational Psychology, 30,* 207–241.

Gunning, T. (2010). *Assessing and correcting reading and writing difficulties.* Boston, MA: Allyn & Bacon.

Haenisch, S. (2004). *Algebra.* Circle Pines, MN: American Guidance Service.

Harris, M., Schumaker, J., & Deshler, D. (2008). *The word mapping strategy.* Lawrence, KS: Edge Enterprises.

Hoover, J., & Patton, J. (2007). *Teaching study skills to students with learning problems. A teacher's guide for meeting diverse needs* (2nd ed.). Austin, TX: Pro-Ed.

Hughes, C., Schumaker, J., & Deshler, D. (2005). *The essay test taking strategy.* Lawrence: University of Kansas.

Hughes, C., Schumaker, J., Deshler, D., & Mercer, C. (1988). *The test-taking strategy.* Lawrence, KS: EXCELLenterprises.

Impecoven–Lind, L., & Foegen, A. (2010). Teaching algebra to students with learning disabilities. *Intervention in School and Clinic, 46*(1), 31–37.

Jacobson, L., & Reid, R. (2010). Improving the persuasive essay writing of high school students with ADHD. *Exceptional Children, 76*(2), 157–174.

Jitendra, A., Hoppes, M., & Yin, P. (2000). Enhancing main idea comprehension for students with learning problems: The role of a summarization strategy and self-monitoring instruction. *The Journal of Special Education, 34,* 127–139.

Joseph, L., & Konrad, M. (2009). Have students self-manage their academic performance. *Intervention in School and Clinic, 44*(4), 246–249.

King-Sears, M., & Bonfils, K. (1999). Self–management instruction for middle school students with LD and ED. *Intervention in School and Clinic, 35*(2), 96–107.

King-Sears, M., & Duke, J. (2010). Bring your textbook: Using secondary texts to assess reading demands and skills required for students with high-incidence disabilities. *Intervention in School and Clinic, 45*(5), 284–293.

Klingner, J., & Vaughn, S. (2002). *Using collaborative strategic reading.* Retrieved from http://www.readingrockets.org/

Knight–McKenna, M. (2008). Syllable types: A strategy for reading multisyllabic words. *TEACHING Exceptional Children, 40*(3), 18–24.

Langer, J. (1981). From theory to practice: A prereading plan. *Journal of Reading, 25*(2), 152–156.

Lee, S., Simpson, R., & Shogren, K. (2007). Effects and implications of self–management for students with autism: A meta-analysis. *Focus on Autism and Other Developmental Disabilities, 22,* 2–13.

Lenz, B., Deshler, D., & Kissam, B. (2004). *Teaching content to all: Evidence-based inclusive practices in middle and secondary schools.* Boston, MA: Pearson.

Lenz, K., Schumaker, J., Deshler, D., & Beals, V. (1984). *Learning strategies curriculum: The word identification strategy.* Lawrence: University of Kansas.

Leslie, L., & Caldwell, J. (2008). *Qualitative reading inventory–4.* New York, NY: Longman.

Maag, J. (2004). *Behavior management: From theoretical implications to practical applications.* Belmont, CA: Wadsworth.

Maccini, P., & Hughes, C. (2000). Effects of a problem solving strategy on the introductory algebra performance of secondary students with learning disabilities. *Learning Disabilities Research & Practice, 15,* 1021.

Martin, J., Mithaug, D., Cox, P., Peterson, L., Van Dycke, J., & Cash, M. (2003). Increasing self-determination: Teaching students to plan, work, evaluate, and adjust. *Exceptional Children, 69*(4), 431–447.

Mason, L. (2004). Explicit self-regulated strategy development versus reciprocal questioning: Effects on expository reading comprehension among struggling readers. *Journal of Educational Psychology, 96,* 283–296.

Mastropieri, M., & Scruggs, T. (2010). *The inclusive classroom: Strategies for effective differentiated instruction.* Upper Saddle River, NJ: Merrill.

Mather, N., Wendling, B., & Roberts, R. (2009). *Writing assessment and instruction for students with learning disabilities.* San Francisco: Jossey-Bass.

McKenzie, R. G. (2009). A national survey of preservice preparation for collaboration. *Teacher Education and Special Education, 32*(4), 379–393.

Mercer, C., Jordan, L., & Miller, S. (1996). Constructivistic math instruction for diverse learners. *Learning Disabilities Research and Practice, 11,* 147–156.

Mercer, C., & Pullen, P. (2008). *Students with learning disabilities* (7th ed.). Upper Saddle River, NJ: Pearson.

Miller, K., Fitzgerald, G., Koury, K., Mitchem, K., & Hollingsead, C. (2007). Kid tools: Self-management, problem-solving, organizational, and planning software for children and teachers. *Intervention in School and Clinic, 43*(1), 12–19.

Montague, M. (1996). Assessing mathematical problem solving. *Learning Disabilities Research & Practice, 11*(4), 238–248.

Montague, M. (2003). *Solve It! A mathematical problem-solving instructional program.* Reston, VA: Exceptional Innovations.

Morningstar, M., Kim, K., & Clark, G. (2008). Evaluating a transition personnel preparation program: Identifying transition competencies of practitioners. *Teacher Education and Special Education, 31*(1), 47–58.

Myles, B., & Simpson, R. (2003). *Asperger syndrome: A guide for educators and parents* (2nd ed.). Austin, TX: Pro-Ed.

Nagel, D., Schumaker, J., & Deshler, D. (1986). *The first-letter mnemonic strategy.* Lawrence, KS: Edge Enterprises.

National Reading Panel. (2000). *Teaching children to read: An evidence-based assessment of the scientific research literature on reading and its implications for reading instruction.* Bethesda, MD: National Institutes of Health.

Ogle, D. M. (1986). K-W-L: A teaching model that develops active reading of expository text. *The Reading Teacher, 39,* 564–570.

Ogle, D. M. (1989). The know, want to know, learn strategy. In K. D. Muth (Ed.), *Children's comprehension of text* (pp. 205–223). Newark, DE: International Reading Association.

Palincsar, A., & Brown, A. (1984). Reciprocal teaching of comprehension-fostering and comprehension-monitoring activities. *Cognition and Instruction, 1,* 117–175.

Peterson, C., Caverly, D., Nicholson, S., O'Neal, S., & Cusenbary, S. (2000). *Building reading proficiency at the secondary level: A guide to resources.* Austin, TX: Southwest Educational Development Laboratory.

Power notes. (2011). International Reading Association. Retrieved from http://www.readwritethink.org/professional–development/strategy–guides/power–notes–30759.html

Pressley, M., & Afflerbach, P. (1995). *Verbal protocols of reading: The nature of constructively responsive reading.* Hillsdale, NJ: Erlbaum.

Raphael, T., & Au, K. (2005). QAR: Enhancing comprehension and test taking across grades and content areas. *The Reading Teacher, 59,* 206–221.

Rasinski, T. V., Padak, N. D., McKeon, C. A., Wilfong, L. G., Friedauer, J. A., & Heim, P. (2005). Is reading fluency a key for successful high school reading? *Journal of Adolescent and Adult Literacy, 49*(1), 22–27.

Rasinski, T., Padak, N., Newton, R., & Newton, E. (2008). *Greek and Latin roots: Keys to building vocabulary.* Huntington Beach, CA: Shell Education. Retrieved from http://www.turuz.info/Sozluk/0330-Qreek-Latin%20Roots-Key%20to%20building%20Vocabulary.pdf

Reid, R., & Lienemann, T. (2006). *Strategy instruction for students with learning disabilities.* New York, NY: Guilford Press.

Reid, R., Trout, A., & Schartz, M. (2005). Self-regulation interventions for children with attention deficit/hyperactivity disorder. *Exceptional Children, 71*(4), 361–377.

Ricketts, C., Brice, J., & Coombes, L. (2010). Are multiple choice tests fair to medical students with specific learning disabilities? *Advances in Health Science Education: Theory and Practice, 15*(2), 265–275.

Rooney, K. (2010). *Strategies for learning: Empowering students for success, grades 9–12.* Thousand Oaks, CA: Corwin.

Sabornie, E., & deBettencourt, L. (2009). *Teaching students with mild and high-incidence disabilities at the secondary level.* Upper Saddle River, NJ: Pearson.

Saenz, L., & Fuchs, L. (2002). Examining the reading difficulty of secondary students with learning disabilities: Expository versus narrative text. *Remedial and Special Education, 23*(1), 31–42.

Salend, S. (2008). *Creating inclusive classrooms: Effective and reflective practices.* Upper Saddle River, NJ: Pearson.

Sammons, R., & Davey, B. (1993/94). Assessing students' skills in using textbooks: The textbook awareness and performance profile (TAPP). *Journal of Reading, 37*(4), 280–286. Retrieved from http://www.jstor.org/stable/40017435?seq=1

Santa, C., Havens, L., & Valdes, B. (2004). *Project CRISS.* Dubuque, IA: Kendall/Hunt.

Sayeski, K., & Paulsen, K. (2010). Mathematics reform curricula and special education: Identifying intersections and implications for practice. *Intervention in School and Clinic, 46*(1), 13–21.

Scavo, T. (1997). *Geoboards in the classroom.* Retrieved from http://mathforum.org/trscavo/geoboards/intro3.html

Schumaker, J. (2003). *Learning strategies curriculum: Fundamentals in the theme writing strategy.* Lawrence, KS: Edge Enterprises.

Schumaker, J., Denton, P., & Deshler, D. (1984). *The paraphrasing strategy.* Lawrence: University of Kansas.

Schumaker, J., Nolan, S., & Deshler, D. (1985). *Learning strategies curriculum: The error monitoring strategy.* Lawrence: The University of Kansas.

Schumaker, J., & Sheldon, J. (1985). *Learning strategies curriculum: The sentence writing strategy.* Lawrence: The University of Kansas.

Schumm, J., Vaughn, S., & Leavell, A. (1994). Planning pyramid: A framework for planning for diverse student needs during content area instruction. *The Reading Teacher, 47,* 608–615.

Scott, B., & Vitale, M. (2003). Teaching the writing process to students with LD. *Intervention in School and Clinic, 38*(4), 220–224.

Scott, V., & Compton, L. (2007). A new trick for the trade: A strategy for keeping an agenda book for secondary students. *Intervention in School and Clinic 42*(5), 280–284.

Shanker, J., & Cockrum, W. (2009). *Locating and correcting reading difficulties* (9th ed.). Boston, MA: Allyn & Bacon.

Shinn, M., & Shinn, M. (2002). *Aimsweb training workbook: Administration and scoring of reading maze for use in general outcome measurement.* Eden Prairie, MN: Edformation.

Spinelli, C. (2011). *Linking assessment to instructional strategies.* Boston, MA: Pearson.

Stahl, K., & Bravo, M. (2010). Contemporary classroom vocabulary assessment for content areas. *The Reading Teacher, 63*(7), 566–578.

Stauffer, R. (1969). *Directing reading maturity as a cognitive process.* New York, NY: Harper & Row.

Stefanich, G. (1998, March). *Curriculum development in teaching science to students with disabilities.* Paper presented at CSUN Conference, Los Angeles, CA.

Swanson, H. L., & Sachs-Lee, C. (2000). A meta-analysis of single-subject design intervention research for students with LD. *Journal of Learning Disabilities, 33,* 114–136.

Therrien, W., Taylor, J., Hosp, J., Kaldenberg, E., & Gorsh, J. (2011). Science instruction for students with learning disabilities: A meta–analysis. *Learning Disabilities Research and Practice, 26*(4), 188–203.

Thurlow, M., Rogers, C., & Christenson, L. (2010). *Science assessments for students with disabilities in school year 2006–2007: What we know about participation, performance, and accommodations* (Synthesis Report 77). Minneapolis: University of Minnesota, National Center on Educational Outcomes.

Vaughn, S., & Bos, C. (2009). *Strategies for teaching students with learning and behavior problems.* Upper Saddle River, NJ: Pearson.

Vaughn, S., & Bos, C. (2012). *Strategies for teaching students with learning and behavior problems* (8th ed.). Boston, MA: Pearson.

Vaughn, S., Bos, C., & Schumm, J. (2003). *Teaching exceptional, diverse, and at-risk students in the general education classroom.* Boston, MA: Allyn & Bacon.

Weber, E. (1999). *Student assessment that works: A practical approach.* Boston, MA: Allyn & Bacon.

Wilkinson, L. (2008). Self-management for children with high-functioning autism spectrum disorders. *Intervention in School and Clinic, 43*(3), 150–157.

Wilson, C. (1963). An essential vocabulary. *The Reading Teacher, 17*(2), 94–96. Retrieved from http://www.jstor.org/stable/20197722

Yore, L. D., Craig, M., & Maguire, T. (1998). Index of Science Reading Awareness: An interactive-constructive model, test verification, and grades 4–8 results. *Journal of Research in Science Teaching, 35,* 27–51.

Zimmerman, B. J. (2001). Theories of self-regulated learning and academic achievement: An overview and analysis. In B. J. Zimmerman & D. H. Schunk, (Eds.), *Self-regulated learning and academic achievement: Theoretical perspectives* (pp. 1–65). Mahwah, NJ: Lawrence Erlbaum Associates.

Index

CORWIN

A SAGE Company

The Corwin logo—a raven striding across an open book—represents the union of courage and learning. Corwin is committed to improving education for all learners by publishing books and other professional development resources for those serving the field of PreK–12 education. By providing practical, hands-on materials, Corwin continues to carry out the promise of its motto: **"Helping Educators Do Their Work Better."**